Becoming
A Helper

Becoming A Helper

Marianne Schneider Corey
Private Practice

Gerald Corey
*California State University, Fullerton
Diplomate in Counseling Psychology,
American Board of Professional Psychology*

Brooks/Cole Publishing Company
Pacific Grove, California

Brooks/Cole Publishing Company
A Division of Wadsworth, Inc.

Printed in the United States of America

10 9 8 7 6 5 4 3

Library of Congress Cataloging-in-Publication Data

Corey, Marianne Schneider, [date]
    Becoming a helper / Marianne Schneider Corey, Gerald Corey.
        p. cm.
    Bibliography: p.
    Includes index.
    ISBN 0-534-09282-9
    1. Human services—Vocational guidance—United States. 2. Social
service—Vocational guidance—United States.   I. Corey, Gerald.
II. Title.
HV10.5.C67   1988   88-10897
361.3'2'02373—dc19   CIP

Sponsoring Editor: *Claire Verduin*
Editorial Assistants: *Linda Ruth Wright and Gay C. Bond*
Production Editor: *Fiorella Ljunggren*
Manuscript Editor: *William Waller*
Permissions Editor: *Carline Haga*
Interior Design: *Vernon T. Boes*
Cover Design: *Sharon L. Kinghan*
Cover Illustration: *Amy C. Storey*
Typesetting: *Bookends Typesetting, Ashland, Oregon*
Printing and Binding: *Malloy Lithographing, Inc., Ann Arbor, Michigan*

To our daughters, Cindy and Heidi,
who are on the path toward becoming helpers themselves

MARIANNE SCHNEIDER COREY is a licensed marriage and family therapist in Idyllwild, California, and is a National Certified Counselor. She received her master's degree in marriage, family, and child counseling from Chapman College. She is a Clinical Member of the American Association for Marriage and Family Therapy and holds memberships in the California Association of Marriage and Family Therapists, the American Association for Counseling and Development, the Association for Specialists in Group Work, and the Association for Religious and Value Issues in Counseling. She and her husband, Jerry, were cochairs of the Professional Standards and Ethics Committee of the Association for Specialists in Group Work in 1981–1982.

Marianne's professional interests are in counseling individuals and couples as well as in leading therapeutic groups and training groups for mental-health professionals. With her colleagues she has conducted professional workshops in the United States, Mexico, the Orient, and Europe. Each year she offers her time to California State University at Fullerton for training and supervising student leaders in a group-counseling class and for coleading weeklong residential growth groups. Marianne received an Award for Contributions to the Field of Professional Ethics from the Association for Religious and Value Issues in Counseling in 1986.

Marianne has co-authored several journal articles as well as the following books (published by Brooks/Cole Publishing Company):

- *Issues and Ethics in the Helping Professions*, Third Edition (1988)
- *Group Techniques*, Revised Edition (1988)
- *Groups: Process and Practice*, Third Edition (1987)
- *I Never Knew I Had a Choice*, Third Edition (1986)
- *Casebook of Ethical Guidelines for Group Leaders* (1982)

GERALD COREY, Professor and Coordinator of the Human Services Program at California State University at Fullerton and a licensed psychologist, received his doctorate in counseling psychology from the University of Southern California. He is a Diplomate in Counseling Psychology, American Board of Professional Psychology; is registered as a National Health Service Provider in Psychology; is a National Certified Counselor; and is a licensed marriage, family, and child counselor. He is a Fellow of the American Psychological Association (Counseling Psychology).

In addition to coordinating an undergraduate program in human services, Jerry teaches courses each semester in group counseling, theory and practice of counseling, and professional ethics. With his colleagues he has conducted workshops in the United States, Mexico, the Orient, and Europe, with a special focus on training in group counseling, and he often presents workshops and is a guest lecturer at various universities. Along with Marianne and other colleagues, Jerry offers week-long residential personal-growth groups and residential training and supervision workshops each summer in Idyllwild, California. Jerry was the recipient of an Award for Contributions in the Field of Professional Ethics from the Association for Religious and Value Issues in Counseling in 1986; the Association for Specialists in Group Work's 1984 Distinguished Service Award in the Field of Group Work; and the Distinguished Faculty Member Award in 1984 from the School of Human Development and Community Service of California State University at Fullerton.

The recent books he has authored or co-authored (all published by Brooks/Cole Publishing Company) include:

- *Issues and Ethics in the Helping Professions,* Third Edition (1988)
- *Group Techniques,* Revised Edition (1988)
- *Groups: Process and Practice,* Third Edition (1987)
- *Theory and Practice of Counseling and Psychotherapy,* Third Edition (and *Manual*) (1986)
- *Case Approach to Counseling and Psychotherapy,* Second Edition (1986)
- *I Never Knew I Had a Choice,* Third Edition (1986)
- *Theory and Practice of Group Counseling,* Second Edition (and *Manual*) (1985)
- *Casebook of Ethical Guidelines for Group Leaders* (1982)

Preface

Many books deal with the skills, theories, and techniques of helping. Yet few books mainly address the problems involved in becoming an effective helper or focus on the personal difficulties in working with others. In writing this book, we had in mind both students who are planning a career in the human services, counseling, psychology, social work, or related professions and helpers who have just begun their career. We intend this book to be used as a supplement to textbooks dealing with helping skills and with counseling theory and practice. It will be useful for introductory classes in human services and counseling as well as classes in practicum, fieldwork, and internship.

We focus on the struggles, anxieties, and uncertainties of helpers. In addition, we spend much time exploring the demands and strains of the helping professions and their effects on the provider. We begin with a discussion of the motivations for seeking a career in the helping professions. We encourage our readers to examine their personal motives and needs for helping, and we challenge them to be honest in assessing what they will get from their work. Since students are often conditioned to be passive learners, we challenge them to take an active stance in their educational program. Being active also applies to selecting field placements and internships as well as getting the most from supervision. On the basis of what students have told us, we develop some practical strategies for ensuring quality experiences in fieldwork and profiting from supervision.

We explore the belief systems of effective and ineffective helpers and discuss the positive and negative effects that a variety of beliefs and assumptions can have on one's practice. Values are an integral part of the client/helper relationship, and we devote considerable attention to an analysis of how they influence helping. Special consideration is given to the importance of understanding subtle cultural and life-style differences, and in the course of our discussion we develop the thesis that the job of helpers is not to impose values but to help clients define their own value system.

We provide an overview of the stages of the helping process, with a brief discussion of the skills and knowledge required to be a successful agent at each of these periods. The focus of this discussion is not on skill development but, rather, on the personal characteristics that enable helpers to be effective. Since helpers ask clients to examine their behavior in order to understand themselves more fully, we ask helpers to be equally committed to an awareness of their own life. Moreover, without a high level of self-awareness a helper will obstruct clients' progress, especially when these clients are struggling with issues that the helper has avoided facing.

Beginning and seasoned helpers face common problems in their work—problems that relate to dealing with resistance, transference and counter-transference, the life crises of clients, stresses at home and at work, and burnout. We have separate chapters on working with difficult clients, on stress management, and on recognizing the early signs of burnout and learning how to cope with it. Again, the focus is on the helper as a person.

Another problem of both beginning and experienced practitioners is forming a sense of ethical awareness and learning to resolve professional dilemmas. We raise a number of current ethical issues, along with case examples, as a way to sensitize readers to the intricacies of ethical decision making.

Although this book should be useful to any student planning to enter the helping professions, our backgrounds are in the field of counseling, and this orientation comes through in our approach. Therefore, those who want to work in the counseling aspects of the human services are likely to find this book especially meaningful. We have tried to write a personal book that will stimulate both thought and action on the part of the readers. At the end of each chapter we encourage them to commit to some specific action that will move them closer to their goals.

Acknowledgments

We are especially indebted to Lupe and Randy Alle-Corliss, who gave generously of their time to make this a better book. As they reviewed the manuscript, they greatly contributed to our discussion of the basic issues involved in working in a community agency. As licensed clinical social workers in agency settings and as college instructors, they were able to provide useful case examples and illustrations.

The following people reviewed the manuscript, offered helpful critiques, and encouraged us to think about ways in which to apply the contents of the book to diverse populations in the helping professions: Sally A. Fullerton of the University of Oregon; Jeffrey A. Kottler of the Center for Humanistic Studies; William Lynn McKinney of the University of Rhode Island; John Porter of McLennan Community College; Veronika Tracy of Bonita Unified School District; and Roger Worthington, a student reviewer.

We appreciate the input of Mary Moline of Loma Linda University on the chapter on fieldwork and supervision and on the section on AIDS. We also acknowledge Jerome Wright of California State University, Fullerton, for his assistance in reviewing the section on AIDS.

As is the case with all of our books, *Becoming a Helper* was produced as a result of a team effort, which included the combined talents of several people in the Brooks/Cole family. We continue to feel fortunate to be able to work with Claire Verduin, managing editor and psychology editor; with Fiorella Ljunggren, senior production coordinator; and with William Waller, the manuscript editor, who gave careful attention to the clarity, readability, and conciseness of the book. Finally, we wish to thank Joanna Quintrell for preparing the index for the book and Debbie DeBue for providing technical assistance and for typing the manuscript. We appreciate the efforts, dedication, and extra time given by these special people to ensure the quality of our books.

Marianne Schneider Corey
Gerald Corey

Contents

CHAPTER 3

The Helper in the Helping Process
38

CHAPTER 4

Values and the Helping Relationship
63

CHAPTER 5

Common Concerns Facing Beginning Helpers
89

CHAPTER 6

Self-Exploration and Personal Growth
113

CHAPTER 7

Managing Stress
131

CHAPTER 8

Dealing with Professional Burnout
158

C H A P T E R   9

Ethical Dilemmas
176

References and Reading List
204

Appendix A
Code of Ethics

Appendix B
Code of Ethics

Appendix C
Ethical Standards

Appendix D

Index
241

CHAPTER 1

Are the Helping Professions for You?

Focus of the Chapter

As you consider a career in one of the helping professions, you are probably wondering: "Are the helping professions for me? Do I know enough to help others? Will this career be satisfying in the long run? Will I be able to apply what I am learning in my education to my job?" We hope that this book will help you answer these and other questions about your career. The focus of the book is on *you* and on what you need personally and professionally to be the best helper possible. We also emphasize the realities you are certain to face when you enter the professional world. You will be best able to cope with the demands of the helping professions if you get an idea now of what lies ahead.

We begin in this chapter by inviting you to examine your diverse motives for becoming a helper. We challenge you to clarify what you get from helping others as well as what you are able to give others. Ideally, you will be able to meet your own needs and the needs of your clients through the helping process. We share our own experience as beginning helpers to demonstrate that learning to become a helper is a process, with its ups and downs. This chapter also introduces you to the attributes of the ideal helper. Although we do not think that there is one perfect pattern of characteristics that identifies effective helpers, we do present some attributes as a catalyst to encourage you to think about the characteristics you possess that could either help or hinder you in your work with others.

Examining Your Motives for Being a Helper

In choosing a career in the helping professions, you must examine your motivations. It is important that you be honest with yourself about your needs for entering this field. Your motives and needs can work both for and against you and your future clients. In fact, the same need or motive has the potential for becoming either a productive or a counterproductive force in your helping style.

Typical Needs of Helpers

Below are some motivations that have become apparent in our work with students and trainees in the helping professions.

The need to make an impact. Perhaps you are hoping that you will exert a significant influence on the lives of those whom you touch. Many helpers profess altruistic desires to make the world a better place. Yet it is all too rare that we hear students and trainees admit that they are entering a helping profession because they want to satisfy a diverse range of their own needs. They often want to know that they are important and that they have the power to help people help themselves. Although they may recognize that they won't be able to change the world in dramatic ways, they still want to make a dent in some corner of that world.

The need to return a favor. The desire to emulate a role model often plays a part in the decision to be a helper. Someone special may have entered the person's life in a very influential way. This role model may be a teacher or therapist. Many onetime clients in counseling, for example, decide to become counselors themselves. Or the influential person may be a grandmother, uncle, or parent.

Robert was a high school dropout. A coach took a special interest in him, pushing him to return to school and, eventually, to go on to college, where he attained a teaching credential. Robert's mission in life has been to help his own high school students reach for what often seems to be an impossible dream. In many ways his life has been devoted to repaying the gift given to him by a coach.

The need to care for others. You may have been a helper from a very early age. You were the one in your family who attended to the problems and concerns of other family members. Your peers and friends found it easy to come to you to unload their burdens. You heard that you were a "natural helper" and that you ought to make a profession of helping. Based on these life experiences and some of your early decisions, you sought out training to capitalize on your talent. One of the pitfalls of being a care giver to significant people in your life has been that your needs were not attended to and, thus, you never learned to ask for what you needed. While you were so busy making sure that others were taken care of, you forgot that you, too, needed someone to listen to you and understand your situation. You can easily become burned out, or emotionally exhausted, personally and professionally if you don't learn to ask for help when you need it. Even though it is foreign to you to ask others for help, it is essential that you learn to do so in order to continue to effectively give to those who want your help now.

One of the professionals who reviewed the manuscript of this book reported that out of 33 psychologists in the training program at his institute, half of them identified themselves as "rescuers" in alcoholic families. In his view they were recruited at birth and trained daily to stabilize the family. Many of our own students are adult children of alcoholics who adopted the role of peacemaker in their family. Although this pattern is not necessarily problematic, it is important that such helpers become aware of their dynamics and learn how they operate in both their personal life and their professional life.

If the pattern described above fits you, then you may profit from reevaluating your earlier decision to focus on taking care of others to the exclusion of taking care of yourself. If you burden yourself with the full responsibility of always being available for everyone who might need your help, you are likely to find that you will soon have little left to give. Furthermore, if you assume that whether your clients change depends primarily on what you do or don't do, you will be adding burdens to yourself. Clients need to take the responsibility themselves for deciding what choices and changes they will make.

The need for self-help.   You may want to go into the helping professions, at least in part, to work on personal issues. For example, you may have a good deal of difficulty in asking directly for what you want from others. You may often say yes when you really want to say no. You may often find yourself feeling timid when you need to stand up for your own rights. As a result, you may decide to lead an assertion training group. Again, this need can serve you well, especially if you have been willing to work on becoming more assertive in your own life. But this motive is likely to work against your efforts to help others become more assertive if you merely urge them to do for themselves what you are unwilling to do for yourself.

A college counselor we know designed a group for students who were struggling with perfectionism. Her purpose was to help the clients examine and modify irrational and self-limiting perfectionistic beliefs. These students often drove themselves to unreal aspirations and could never enjoy an achievement, because they felt it could have been even better. As you might guess, the young psychologist who designed and led this group was herself struggling with being perfect. In her own therapy she worked on her underlying beliefs and saw many of the ways that her perfectionism was affecting both her personal life and her professional life. She was aware of her own dynamics and was successfully challenging beliefs that restricted her joy. Thus she knew what her clients were concerned about and could teach them ways to combat their self-defeating thinking and change their behavior in the direction of being more accepting and appreciative of their achievements.

Sometimes therapists who work with alcoholic patients and members of their families were themselves the children of alcoholics. Helpers who specialize in abused children may have been victims of child abuse. Some women who were involved in abusive marriages eventually become counselors who specialize in working with battered women.

The main point is that the motivation for selecting a speciality can be the wellspring of creativity for you. It is not necessarily important that you be "adjusted"; rather, what is useful is to be aware of your own personal issues. As Rollo May has said, healers are most often able to heal others out of their own experience with psychological struggle. It is the wounded healer, not the adjusted helper, who can be authentically present for others searching to find themselves. If you have struggled successfully with a problem, you are able to identify and empathize with clients who come to you with similar concerns.

Of course, this motivation could also work against you and your clients. Take, for example, the case of a female counselor who works with women who are the victims of spousal abuse. The counselor may try to work out her own unfinished business and conflicts by giving plenty of advice and pushing these women in certain directions. Because of her unresolved personal problems, she may show hostility toward the abusing husband, especially if she becomes overinvolved with family dynamics.

The need to be needed. Very few helpers are immune to the need to be needed. The problem arises when they deny that they want to feel needed. It may be psychologically rewarding to you to have clients express that they are getting better because of your influence. These clients are likely to express their appreciation for the hope that you have given to them. You may value being able to take care of other people's wants, and you may get a great deal of satisfaction from doing this. To us, satisfying this need is perhaps one of the greatest rewards of being a helper. We hope that you will not be apologetic about having this need and will not deny that you like being needed and appreciated. If this need is consistently in the forefront, however, it can overshadow the needs of your clients. Some helpers foster dependency by encouraging their clients to call them often. Perhaps they need their clients more than their clients need them.

Wanting to feel appreciated for what you are doing for others can be perfectly all right. The danger exists when you *must* receive appreciation and recognition in order to feel worthwhile. If you depend exclusively on your clients to feel like a useful human being, your self-worth is on shaky ground. The reality is that many clients will not express appreciation for your efforts. Furthermore, agencies often do not give recognition or positive feedback. Instead, you may get feedback when your performance does not meet with the expected standards.

Some helpers love their work because they have so many opportunities to feel needed. In many ways their work becomes their life. The possible danger with relying completely on your work to satisfy your need to feel needed is that your purpose and meaning in life might vanish if you could no longer work.

The need for money. Some helpers have come to enjoy the financial rewards of being a helping professional. We usually suggest that if students have a need to make a great deal of money, they might reconsider going into one of the helping professions. In most cases beginning helpers are not likely to get rich. Many professionals feel that they are not adequately compensated financially for their contributions. You certainly do not need to feel guilty for wanting to earn a good living. Helping others does not have to be a strictly altruistic venture. You have a right to charge fees for your services, and this financial compensation does not in any way have to lessen the quality of your caring for others. If you were to donate most of your services and have to struggle to make ends meet, you might soon find yourself resenting all that you were giving to your clients. On the other hand, financial motives can work against the establishment of therapeutic relationships. If you make how much you are earning from each client contact your primary concern, you are likely to keep clients coming to you when it is no longer in their best interest.

The need for prestige and status.   You may have hopes of acquiring a certain level of prestige and status, if not a certain income level. Yet if you work in an agency, many of the consumers of the services you offer will be disadvantaged. You will be working with people on probation, those with various addictions, poor people, and people who are sent to you. Because of this clientele, you will frequently not be given the prestige and the status that you deserve. In fact, you are likely to receive society's disregard or lack of respect. In such a setting your need for professional recognition may be frustrated.

On the other hand, you may work in a setting where you can enjoy the status that goes along with being respected by clients and colleagues. If you have worked hard and become good at what you do, we certainly hope that you can allow yourself to accept the prestige that you have earned. You can be proud yet still be humble. If you become arrogant as a result of your status, however, you may be perceived as unapproachable, and thus your clients will be put off by your attitude. You become prone to accepting far more credit for your clients' changes than you deserve. Some clients will put you on a pedestal, and you may come to like this position too much. Remember, those on a pedestal have only one place to go—down.

The need to provide answers.   You may have a high need to direct the lives of your clients. You have a reserve of answers, and you are quick to supply clients with solutions for any problems they bring up. You have difficulty in living without certainty and without fixed answers to life's dilemmas. Thus, your professional mission is to straighten people out and put them on the right road. You feel good when you can influence others in the direction you want them to move. Although you may find satisfaction in influencing others, it is important to realize that your answers for your life situations may not be best for them. Your purpose is to provide direction and to assist clients in discovering their own course of action.

How Your Needs and Motivations Operate

Most of the needs and motives we have discussed can work either for or against the client's welfare. There is nothing wrong with most of these needs, nor do they have to get in the way of effective helping. When you are unaware of them, however, there is much more likelihood that they will determine the nature of your interventions. For example, if you are attempting to work through unconscious personal conflicts by focusing on the problems of others, there is more chance that you will use your clients to meet your needs.

We often say that in the ideal situation your own needs are met at the same time that you are meeting your clients' needs. Your chances for burnout are increased when you give of yourself but consistently get little in return. It is important that you feel a sense of fulfillment through your helping. Your needs become problematic when they assume priority or when you satisfy them at the client's expense.

Probably no single motive drives you; rather, needs and motivations are intertwined. They also can change over time. You may initially choose a helping profession because of a desire to see others challenge themselves and grow. After years of being in the profession, your motivation for remaining may be very different, such as a financial or psychological reward. You may stay in a profession because of the security it offers. Even though your original motive may no longer operate, your new needs may support your decision to remain in a position.

What Are Your Motives for Helping?

At this point we encourage you to reflect on your own motivations and needs for considering a career as a helper. Ask yourself the following questions and strive to answer them as honestly as you can at this time: "Have I given much thought to why I'm considering a helping career? How aware am I of my own needs and motivations? Have I tried to convince myself that I'm going into this profession solely to help others? Am I able to meet my needs and at the same time meet the needs of those I help? Do I feel guilty or apologetic for having needs? Do I think that the ideal is to be a selfless helper? Is my mission in life merely to take care of others and put myself second? Can I be genuinely interested in others and still interested in my own growth?" We hope you will at least begin to raise some of these questions and devote some time for reflection.

The answers will probably not be easy, and throughout your professional life you may need to continue asking "Why am I remaining in this profession? Why am I willing to work as hard as I do? What am I getting from making a career out of giving to those who want my help?"

Our Own Beginnings as Helpers

This is a personal book in two ways. It is personal in that we encourage you to find ways to apply the book to yourself. We consistently ask you to reflect on your motives, needs, values, beliefs, assumptions, and behavior. Second, the manner in which we have written the book is personal, and we share our own views and experiences whenever we think it is both appropriate and useful. As a concrete illustration of how personal motives and experiences can affect career choice, we discuss some of our own motivations for becoming helping professionals and remaining in the field.

Beginning a helping career is not always easy and can involve anxiety and uncertainty. Although at this point we feel more confident than when we were beginning our careers, we have not forgotten our own struggles. We, too, had to cope with many of the fears and self-doubts that we discussed in the previous pages. By sharing our own difficulties with you, we hope to encourage you not to give up too soon.

Jerry Corey's Early Experience

When I was in college, studying to become a teacher, I recall saying that I hoped to create a different type of learning climate for students than I was experiencing as a learner. I wanted to help others, and it was important for me to change the world. I recognize that the need to make a significant difference has been a theme throughout the 25 years I have been in the helping professions. As a child and as an adolescent I did not feel that my presence made that much difference. In many ways, during my early years, I felt that I did not fit anywhere and that I was unrecognized and useless. There was some pain attached to being ignored, and one of my early decisions was not to let myself be ignored. This took the form of making myself a nuisance, which of course resulted in negative attention. But I assumed that this type of recognition was better than being ignored! In college I experienced some success and found some positive routes to being recognized. Later, when I began my teaching career, I began to see that I could make a difference, at least within the confines of my classroom. In addition to helping students enjoy learning, I also got a great deal of personal satisfaction from knowing that I was a useful person, which was quite different from my perception of myself as a child.

At the beginning of my career as a counseling psychologist, however, I did not feel a great deal of confidence, and I often wondered whether I was suited for the field. I recall as being particularly difficult the times that I co-led a group with my supervisor. I felt very incompetent and inexperienced next to my co-leader, who was an experienced therapist. Much of the time I didn't know what to say or do. It seemed that there was very little place for me to intervene, since I believed that my co-leader was so effective. I had many doubts about my ability to say anything meaningful to the members. It just seemed that my supervisor was so insightful and so skillful that I would never attain such a level of professionalism. The effect of working with an experienced group leader was to heighten my own sense of insecurity and inadequacy.

Another thing that I found difficult was practicing individual counseling in a university center. When I began as a practicing counselor, I frequently asked myself what I could do for my clients. I remember progress being very slow, and it seemed that I needed an inordinate amount of immediate and positive feedback. When after several weeks a client was still talking about feeling anxious or depressed, I immediately felt my own incompetence as a helper. I frequently found myself thinking "How would my supervisor say this? What would he do?" I even caught myself copying his gestures, phrases, and mannerisms.

When I became a professor, it was easy for me to get a sense of whether students were with me or not. I received immediate feedback by checking their faces. I was not uncertain about what my students were learning, and I didn't have much anxiety about my effectiveness as a teacher.

When it came to my feelings about myself as a counselor, however, the matter was very different. I often had no idea of what, if anything, my clients were getting from our sessions. Indications of whether clients were getting better, staying the same, or getting worse were typically very subtle. What I didn't know at the time was that clients need to struggle as a part of finding their own answers. My expectation was that they should feel better quickly, for then I would know that I was surely a help to them. I also did not appreciate that clients often begin to feel worse as they give up their defenses and as they open themselves to their pain. When I saw clients expressing their fear and uncertainty about their future, it only brought out my own lack of certainty that I could be instrumental in helping them. I remember being very concerned with knowing the appropriate response and with doing something that would help them. Because I was concerned about saying "the wrong thing," I often listened a lot but didn't give too many of my own reactions in return.

Even though it is uncomfortable for me to admit this, I was more inclined to accept clients who were bright, verbal, attractive, and willing to talk about their problems than clients who seemed depressed or unmotivated to change. Those whom I considered "good and cooperative clients" I encouraged to come back. As long as they were talking and working, and preferably letting me know that they were getting somewhere with our sessions, I was quick to schedule other appointments. Those clients who seemed to make very few changes were the ones who increased my own anxiety. Rather than seeing their own part in their progress or lack of it, I typically blamed myself for not knowing enough and not being able to solve their problems. I had limited tolerance for uncertainty and for their struggle in finding their own direction. My self-doubts grew when they did not show up for following appointments. I was sure that this was a sign that they were dissatisfied with my work.

I particularly remember encouraging depressed clients to make an appointment with one of the other counselors on the staff. I learned in my own supervision that working with depressed clients was difficult for me because of my own reluctance to deal with my own fears of depression. If I allowed myself to really enter the world of these depressed clients, I might get in touch with some of my own fears of hopelessness. This experience taught me the important lesson that I could not take clients in any direction that I had not been willing to explore in my own life.

Even though I was teaching full time and counseling only part time, I went through a period of great self-doubt over whether to do any therapy work at all. I wondered if it would be better to stick to teaching and forget about any aspirations of counseling others. I doubted that I had what it took to be an effective counselor. This was particularly disconcerting in light of the fact that I had just completed a doctorate in counseling. I am glad now that I did not give up too quickly and that I persisted in working with others in spite of my fears and self-doubts.

One thing I became aware of is that I could not effectively imitate the therapeutic style of an esteemed supervisor or of other therapists whom I respected. Each had a style that fit his or her own personality. I learned to take selectively from different professionals what I could most comfortably incorporate into my own emerging style of counseling.

Marianne Corey's Early Experience

I was a helper long before I studied counseling in school. From childhood on I attended to the needs of my brothers and sisters. At age 8 I was made almost totally responsible for my newly born brother. I not only took care of him but also attended to other members of an extended family.

My family owned a restaurant in a German village. The restaurant, which was in our home, was the meeting place for many of the local men. These men came mostly to socialize rather than to eat and drink. For hours they would sit and talk, and I was taught that I had better listen attentively. Furthermore, I learned that I should not repeat the personal conversations and gossip to the other townspeople. At this early age I learned three very important skills: attentive listening, empathic understanding, and confidentiality. And at this time I had never even heard of Carl Rogers (a pioneer in the humanistic approach to counseling). It became apparent to me that a variety of people found it easy to talk to me and tell me about their personal problems.

In my growing-up years I felt liked and respected by most people. I remember feeling compassion, especially for those who had a difficult or unusual life situation. For example, I recall seeing a woman who had "gone crazy" standing naked by an upstairs window. She threw her clothes and furniture out of the window as onlookers baited her. I felt sad and thought that she must be very unhappy. I also had special feelings for two persons in my village who were considered "town drunks." I was curious about why they wanted to drink.

I have always been interested in looking beyond the facade that people present to others. I became convinced that people could be more than they appeared if they were willing to make an effort to change. My belief was atypical in my culture, which conveyed the message that "this is fate, and there is nothing you can do about it."

In my own life I overcame many obstacles and exceeded my dreams. As a result, I am often successful in challenging and encouraging my clients not to give up too soon when limits are imposed on them. Through my work I derive a great sense of satisfaction when I have been instrumental in the lives of individuals who are willing to take risks, to tolerate uncertainty, to dare to be different, and to live a fuller life because of their choices. When clients show appreciation for what I have done for them, I enjoy hearing it. However, I always let them know that their progress stems not only from my efforts but from their hard work as well.

In my life now I find it easy to give to my friends, family, and community as well as to clients. It seems natural to me to give both personally and professionally. It continues to be an ongoing struggle for me to find a good balance between giving to others and taking for myself. Although I am considered a good giver, I realize that I am a slow learner when it comes to making my needs known and asking for what I want.

It is interesting for me to compare my cultural conditioning and early role in my family with my development as a professional care giver. Although I seemed to "naturally" assume the role of caring for my brothers and sisters, I did not feel quite as natural when I began formal helping. In my first practical experiences as a part of my undergraduate program in behavioral sciences, I had my share of self-doubt.

In one of my earlier internships I was placed in a college counseling center. I remember how petrified I was when one day a student came in and asked for an appointment, and my supervisor asked me to attend to this client. The feedback that I received later from my supervisor on how confident I had appeared was very incongruent with what I had felt. Some of the thoughts that I remember running through my head as I was walking to my office with this client were "I'm not ready for this. What am I going to do? What if he doesn't talk? What if I don't know how to help him? I wish I could get out of this!" In my self-absorption I never once considered any of the client's feelings. For instance, how might he be approaching this session? What fears might he be having?

I was much more aware of myself than of my clients. I took far too much responsibility, put much pressure on myself to "do it right," and worried a lot about what harm I could do to them. I did not allow them to assume their rightful share of the responsibility for making changes. I often worked much harder than they did, and sometimes it seemed that I wanted more for some of my clients than they wanted for themselves. I think I had a tendency to exaggerate my capacity for causing harm because of my fears and insecurities as a helper. When I shared with my supervisor my concern about feeling so responsible for the outcomes of our sessions and about hurting my clients, she responded: "You are assuming more power than you have over your clients."

Another time I told a supervisor that I had doubts about being in my profession, that I was overwhelmed by all the pain I saw around me, and that I was concerned that I was not helping anybody. I remember being very emotional and feeling extremely discouraged. My supervisor's smile surprised me. "I would be very concerned about you as a helper," he said, "if you never asked yourself these kinds of questions and were not willing to confront yourself with these feelings." In retrospect, I think he was telling me that he was encouraged for me because I was acknowledging my struggles and was not pretending to be the all-competent counselor who was without fears.

As a beginning counselor I was acutely aware of my own anxieties. Now I am much more able to be present with my clients and able to enter their world. Although I am not anxiety-free now, I am not watching myself practicing therapy. Furthermore, although I take responsibility for the counseling process, I don't see myself as totally responsible for what goes on in a session, and I am usually not willing to work harder than my clients.

A Helping Career Is Not for Everyone

There is no disgrace in feeling that the helping professions may not be right for you. If you keep the question of whether you want to pursue a helping career open, you are bound to have periods of self-doubt. At times you may feel very excited about the prospects of your career choice, and at other times you may feel hopeless and discouraged. Give yourself room for some of these ambivalent feelings. Don't make the decision whether to pursue a helping career by yourself, based on your initial experiences. You will ultimately have to make this decision, but before you decide, consult with supervisors, colleagues, friends, and others who know you best.

The temptation to give up too soon is often greatest when you first have to apply what you have learned in your courses. A most difficult time will be when you step out of the lab and into the real world. The chances are that you will find that what worked in the lab will not work so well in real-life helping situations. In the lab you may have worked with fellow students who role-played clients who were cooperative. Now you are facing some clients who, no matter how hard you try, are not responding to you. Realize that it will take time and experience to learn how to apply your knowledge of theories and techniques to actual situations. At first your attempts at helping may seem artificial and rehearsed. You will probably be more aware of this artificiality than your clients. Again, allow yourself the time to gain a greater sense of ease in applying what you have learned and in functioning in your role as a helper. To illustrate what we have been saying, we will relate how Marianne struggled with this decision.

Marianne's Resolution of Her Doubts

I remember a time when I wanted to abandon the idea of becoming a counselor and considered a profession of teaching German. I was very aware of comparing myself to professionals who had years of experience, and I expected myself to be as effective as they were. What I eventually realized was that my expectations were extremely unrealistic, because I was demanding that I immediately be as skilled as these very experienced people. I had been giving myself no room for learning and tolerating my rudimentary beginnings.

One of my professional activities now is working with beginning helpers. I find that they are often in the same predicament I was when I began working with others. These students seem focused on how much I know and how easy interventions seem to come to me. By contrast, they feel discouraged with their lack of knowledge and how much they have to struggle to find "the right thing to say." They usually breathe a sigh of relief when I tell them about some of my beginnings and admit that I do not see myself as an expert but as someone who has a certain amount of expertise in counseling. I want most to convey to them that learning never stops and that beginnings are difficult and, at times, discouraging.

Counterproductive Attitudes

In addressing the issue of deciding whether to pursue one of the helping professions, we have so far encouraged you to remain a helper at a time when you might feel like abandoning this role. We would now like to point out some characteristics or attitudes that we see as counterproductive if you want to make a career of helping others.

- You believe that you have no problems in your life and therefore are in a position to help others resolve their problems.
- You are convinced that your way is the right way and that if your clients were to accept your values, they would be happy.
- You have very strong religious convictions and think that it is your calling to guide others to adopt these.
- You have no religious affiliation, do not believe in religion, and consider everyone neurotic who has religious convictions.
- Your vision of helping is telling clients what they should do. For every question they raise, you are quick to provide a ready-made answer.
- You have little tolerance for clients' expressing their feelings, for you see this as indulgent and as a waste of time.
- You could be described as a person with low affect, with little range to your emotions.
- Your basic belief about humankind is that people are evil, not to be trusted, and in need of being straightened out.
- You have had a rough life, and since you "made it," so should everyone else.
- You are hostile, indirect, and sarcastic.
- What you challenge your clients to do is not congruent with what you are actually doing in your life.
- You have made a minimal effort to expose yourself to learning situations and have avoided feedback from fellow students, professors, and supervisors as much as possible.
- The goal of getting a degree or a license was foremost in your mind; the process of getting there was seen as a necessary, but unpleasant, means to an end.
- You chronically felt that those who were teaching and supervising you knew less than you did.
- You get a sense of excitement out of intimidating people and having them be afraid of you.
- You use your power *over* people rather than *for* people; you can feel powerful only when you have been instrumental in putting down others and seeing them as impotent.
- You cannot tolerate seeing people in pain; you want to quickly take their pain away and turn them to more pleasant thoughts.
- You are filled with pain, yet you are unwilling to acknowledge this suffering and seek help for it; you think that your pain is being taken care of by attending to the pain of your clients.
- You consistently make your needs more important than your clients' needs.
- You need your clients more than they need you, and therefore you foster their dependency on you.

- You are unable to enter a client's world, for you can perceive reality only through your own eyes.
- You are chronically depressed when you listen to the sagas of others; you often overidentify with them, and you tend to make their problems your problems.
- You see counseling as something that others need, yet you cannot imagine yourself seeking this kind of help for yourself.
- You have a very fragile ego that is easily bruised, and thus you are overly sensitive to any criticisms from others.
- You are highly defensive and have an aversion to being challenged.
- You have lived a very sheltered life and have a limited and rigid vision of the world.
- You are unable to accept those who have different values from you.

Unfortunately, the people who possess many of these characteristics are those who are least likely to acknowledge them and therefore do not screen themselves out. Thus, those who teach and train helpers must find effective means of screening out potentially harmful helpers. If you see some of these traits in yourself, do not label yourself as unfit for the helping professions. With awareness and a willingness to change, you can modify some of these limitations. If you become aware of your limited life experience, for example, you certainly don't have an incurable disease. You can expose yourself to broader experiences. If you discover that you believe that your values are right for everyone else, you can be open to finding out that others fundamentally different from you can live a productive life. You might challenge your notion that help is good for others but not for you by getting for yourself what you offer to others. What is absolutely essential is a high degree of honesty and an openness to being challenged.

Attributes of the Ideal Helper

Although it is useful to describe some of the characteristics of the ideal helper, even the most effective helpers do not meet all of these criteria. If you try to match the ideal picture we are about to paint, you will be needlessly setting yourself up for failure and frustration. But it is surely possible to become a more effective helper if you are aware of those areas that need strengthening. You can hone your existing skills and acquire new ones. You can integrate knowledge that will enhance your abilities as a helper. You can make personal changes that will allow you to be more present and powerful as you intervene in the life of your clients. With these possibilities in mind consider the following perspective of the ideal helper.

Ideally, as a helper, you are committed to an honest assessment of your own strengths and weaknesses. You realize that you probably cannot help any clients do in their life what you are unable or unwilling to do in your own life. You recognize that who you are as a person is the most important instrument you possess as a helper. You are open to learning, and you have a basic curiosity. You realize what you don't know, and you are willing to take steps to fill the gaps in your knowledge. You recognize that your education is never finished but is something that you are continually acquiring. You have the social skills needed to establish good contact with other people, and you can apply these skills in the helping relationship.

As a good helper you realize that it takes hard work to bring about change, and you are willing to stick with clients as they go through this difficult process. You are able to enter the world of your clients and see the world through their eyes, rather than imposing your own vision of reality on them. You offer support when it is needed and confront clients on their unused potential when this is required. You genuinely care for the people you help, and this caring is expressed by doing what is in their best interest. You are able to deal with a wide range of your clients' feelings, thoughts, and behaviors. You share your persistent reactions to your clients in appropriate and timely ways.

You are able to inspire clients to dream and to take the steps necessary to fulfill these dreams in reality. You realize that clients often limit themselves through a restricted imagination of possibilities for their future. You stimulate them in creating a vision for change, and you encourage them to translate their goals into action. It is often your faith that enables clients who have little hope to begin to believe that they have the potential for a better future.

You are willing to draw on a number of resources to enable clients to move toward their goals. You are flexible in applying strategies for change, and you are willing to adapt your techniques to the unique situation of each client. This is especially true if the client's ethnic or cultural background is different from yours. Although you respect such differences, you are able to challenge your clients to examine how well their cultural values are working for them. You show this respect by not encouraging clients to fit into a neat mold. Even though you struggle with your own problems, this struggle does not intrude on your helping of others. You do not burden clients with long tales about your own personal problems, but you are willing to draw on your life experiences to deepen clients' self-exploration.

You take care of yourself physically, psychologically, socially, mentally, and spiritually. You do in your own life what you ask of your clients. If you are confronted with problems, you deal with them. You have healthy patterns of eating, sleeping, and exercising. You are aware of your needs and motivations, and you make choices that are congruent with your life goals. You are capable of establishing meaningful relationships with at least a few significant people. You question life and engage in critical self-examination of your beliefs and values. Although you have a healthy sense of self-love and pride, you are not arrogant. You are often more attracted to the process of living than to any end product. Your philosophy of life is your own creation, not one that has been imposed on you.

As we mentioned, this is an incomplete list, and none of us fits the portrait of the ideal helper. Yet an unskilled helper can become a skilled one, and all of us can become more effective in reaching and touching the lives of the clients we encounter.

By Way of Review

Near the end of each chapter we list some of the chapter's highlights. These key points serve as a review of the messages we've attempted to get across. We encourage you to spend a few minutes after you finish each chapter to write down central issues and points that have the most meaning for you.

- A helping career is not for everyone. We hope you will keep open the question of whether a helping career is right for you.
- In deciding whether to pursue one of the helping professions, do not give up too soon. Be prepared for doubts and setbacks.
- Although the ideal helper probably does not exist in reality, there are a number of behaviors and attitudes that characterize effective helpers. Even though you might not reach the ideal, you can progress, especially with the willingness to question what you are doing.
- It is essential that helpers examine their motivations for going into the helping profession. Helpers meet their own needs through their work, and they must recognize these needs. It is possible for both client and helper to benefit from the helping relationship.
- Some of the needs for going into the helping professions include the need to be needed, the need for prestige and status, and the need to make a difference. These needs can work both for you and against you in becoming an effective helper.
- Realize that you must have a beginning to your career. Be patient, and allow yourself time to feel comfortable in the role of helper. You don't have to be the perfect person or the perfect helper.

What Will You Do Now?

After each chapter review we provide three concrete suggestions that you can put into action. These suggested activities grow out of the major points that we have developed in the chapter. We hope that you will do more than merely read these chapters and that you will find some way to develop an action program. If you commit yourself to doing even one of these activities for each chapter, we think you will become more actively involved in the process of reading and reflecting.

1. Consider the idea of keeping a journal during this semester. You can express your thoughts, feelings, and reactions about what you are learning in this course. You can record your reactions to difficult clients, your difficulties with supervisors, and your successes. It will be an excellent way of keeping track of your learning and a great source for getting discussions going in class.

2. Seek out a helper whom you know, and ask this person about his or her motivations for becoming a helper and for remaining in the profession. What does this person get out of helping clients?

3. Create your own activity or project (for this chapter or any of the chapters to follow). Find some ways to get involved by taking action. Think of ways in which you can apply what you read in each chapter to yourself. Decide on something specific, a step you can take now, that will help you get actively engaged in a positive endeavor. After reading this chapter, for example, you could decide to reflect on your own needs and motives for considering a career in the helping professions. Review some significant turning points in your life that might have contributed to your desire to become a helper.

Suggested Readings

Benjamin, A. (1987). *The helping interview: With case illustrations.* Boston: Houghton Mifflin. This short book gives a very clear and fundamental description of the helping process in action. The author deals with the key factors in helping, the stages in the helping process, the attitudes and behavior of effective helpers, and practical interviewing procedures.

Hutchins, D. E., & Cole, C. G. (1986). *Helping relationships and strategies.* Pacific Grove, CA: Brooks/Cole. This well-written text covers a wide range of strategies for helping. Some of its topics are the building blocks of the effective interview, major techniques in the problem-solving process, and individual strategies to promote change.

National Organization for Human Service Education. *Human Service Education.* Articles in this journal deal with programs in the human services, innovations in practice, job possibilities, and a range of topics of value to practitioners. This journal is published twice yearly by the National Organization for Human Service Education, Box 29, Kingston, RI 02881.

Getting the Most from Your Education and Training

Focus of the Chapter

The theme of this chapter is that you will get far more from your program of studies and your fieldwork activities if you assume an *active stance* in your education. So often we hear students passively complaining about their department, their professors, their supervisors, and everything and everybody but themselves. There are faults within any educational system, but it is more useful in the long run to look beyond them. Rather than concentrating on all that you cannot do, for whatever reasons, take responsibility for your education and get what you want from it.

Any system imposes limitations on you. The challenge is to learn how to work creatively within that system to attain your key goals without sacrificing your integrity by "selling out." We often hear both students in college and professionals in a human-services system argue that the "system" won't allow them to be themselves, that they feel stifled, and that they could be creative and productive "if it weren't for . . . " Below we list some of these common assertions. See how many of them sound familiar to you.

For students: "I would be a good learner if it weren't for . . .

- . . . the dull professors, who really don't care."
- . . . the fact that I have to work and go to school."
- . . . my wife [husband], who won't support my efforts in going to college."
- . . . my children, who take up so much of my time and interrupt my studies."
- . . . an educational system that kills any creativity."
- . . . so much reading and so many papers to write, leaving me no time to be concerned with what I'm learning."
- . . . the other unmotivated students in my classes."
- . . . the silly requirements and the grading game."
- . . . the unrealistic pressures placed on me by my professors."

For professional helpers: "I would be a productive, dynamic, and creative mental-health professional if it weren't for . . .

- . . . my burned-out colleagues, who infect me with their cynicism."
- . . . the director at my agency, who is an unfeeling dictator."
- . . . forces that don't allow me to run things my own way and prevent me from being myself."
- . . . my resistant clients."
- . . . the lack of funding of our community program."
- . . . all the paperwork, bureaucratic demands, and politics."
- . . . my large caseload."
- . . . my family, which makes demands on me when I get home."
- . . . supervisors who are unsupportive of my ideas."

These lists could easily be extended, but the point we want to make is that you could eternally create reasons outside of yourself to justify why you are not productive. As long as you focus on "them out there," you are powerless to change your situation until someone or something else changes.

Exercising a measure of freedom within external demands and restrictions entails accepting responsibility for doing what you can do, rather than focusing on what you can't do. Therefore, we will be encouraging you to assume a more powerful role in choosing an appropriate educational program, working in meaningful fieldwork placements, demanding adequate supervision, and continuing your learning after graduation.

Selecting an Educational Program

At this point you may not be certain whether you want to pursue a career in the helping professions. Or you may be undecided about whether to get a job immediately after graduation or enter a graduate program. Whether you are an undergraduate or a graduate student, you have probably gone through some anxiety in selecting the right program. Be open to new ideas. Selecting a particular educational program is a personal decision. There are no absolute guidelines or perfect choices, but you can make better decisions by discussing options with others who are involved in a variety of programs and professions.

We typically encourage students to investigate many programs and to keep their options open. It's a good idea to go to a variety of universities, to gather material about the various programs, and to talk with the professors and students. Talking with professionals about their work experiences can also broaden your perspectives. Find out from them the specific educational and practical background that they most value. In selecting a program, ask yourself questions such as "Will the program give me what I need to do the work I want to do? Does the orientation of the program fit with my values? Am I compatible with the program?"

If you are taking an introductory course on the helping professions as an elective and are undecided about pursuing a career in the field, you can take selected courses and fieldwork classes to explore your interest in continuing. Working as a volunteer in a community agency is another excellent way to test out your interests. Going to the career center for information, testing, and vocational counseling is often a helpful adjunct to the decision-making process.

We have met students who remained in a course of study even though they had discovered that they were not enthusiastic about the field. They were hesitant to change because doing so could be interpreted as a failure. Others are reluctant to change majors because they would face added requirements for graduation. It seems to us that such students are likely to fail in the long run if they don't pursue their real interests. If you find yourself in a program that you really don't like, consider getting out. What is important to evaluate is the overall direction of the program, rather than a specific course or requirement that you do not like.

Recently, one of our graduates told us that some of the classes she had felt were unrelated to her career interests later became valuable in landing a job. Specifically, when she was taking research-oriented and grant-writing courses, she couldn't understand why they were required. In hindsight, she found value in a part of her education that she at one time had thought was meaningless.

Deciding Which Professional Route to Take

Students often ask which professional specialty we think is best for them. You can take many routes as a helper in the human services. You might ask, "Should I become a social worker? a psychiatric technician? a marriage and family therapist? a mental-health counselor? a psychologist? a paraprofessional worker?" These professional specialties have different focuses, yet all have working with people in common.

We tell students that they will have to choose a specialty through a process of reading and thinking about the alternatives. Much depends on what you want to do, how much time you are willing to invest in a program, where you want to live, and what your other interests are. Realize that there is no "perfect profession" and that each profession has its advantages and its drawbacks. In Appendix D we list the addresses of major professional organizations, from which you can obtain information on the educational and training background needed for the various professions.

In thinking about a professional route, be open to the reactions you receive from faculty and staff members. In some situations you may hear that you are not suited for a particular profession. Such feedback is certainly hard to accept. Your first inclination may be to decide that the professor does not like you, yet the advice may be in your best interest. If you hear such a recommendation, ask for specific reasons for the judgment, and find out what alternatives the person can suggest to you.

Making Your Educational Program Personal and Meaningful

Learning to cope with the system. As mentioned before, there are real problems in working within any system. The reality of an educational system is grades, requirements, courses, and evaluation. Although students often balk at being evaluated and feel that grades are unfair, this system of evaluation does exist. Moreover, it is a mistake to assume that grading stops when you graduate from a university. There are reviews and evaluation practices on all levels in the professional world. In a business, for example, your supervisors rate you and determine whether you get a promotion or a raise. If you are a professional, your clients rate you by the business they bring to you or take away from you.

Sometimes students assume that there are worlds of difference between the roles they play in college and the roles they will assume as professionals. Many of the traits that you have as a student will no doubt carry over into your behavior as a worker. If you have great difficulty in showing up for classes regularly, for example, you are likely to carry this habit into your work setting. Getting a position in a community agency is a highly competitive task. If you hope to gain entry into the professional world, it is essential that you be prepared to cope with the realities of the marketplace. You are not being treated kindly if little is expected of you and if you are allowed to get by with minimal effort.

Students in human services sometimes expect that their professors will make fewer demands on them or give them better grades because of the informal relationships that are established in the classroom. Many instructors in human-services programs are friendly, care about the students, and interact with them in a personal way. Sometimes students have problems in knowing where to establish boundaries. They mistakenly assume that there should be no limits and that no demands should be placed on them because of this relatively close relationship. From our perspective a humanistic approach to education can be balanced with reasonable standards and expectations. Developing these academic standards is one basic way of preparing students to cope with the demands of the job market.

We asked some human-services practitioners to comment on the degree to which both their undergraduate and graduate programs had been meaningful to them in preparing them for their job. We also asked them to say how much power they had had to provide input or to make meaningful changes in their educational program. Some of these responses are given below:

• "Undergraduate studies prepared me well for counseling and proposal writing. I would have liked to have more course work in drug abuse and family studies rather than so much focus on the individual. Since I was a student representative to the program I was part of, I felt I had a lot of power to provide input. I felt that my ideas were considered and that I had a voice."

• "I would have liked to have more administration-type classes that dealt with how to best manage people. I often felt that I had the power to provide input, but I did not exercise this very often."

• "The kind of education and training that I most value is the practical and applied. Some of our professors asked us to relate our own issues with the course work. For example, in my graduate program in social work, we studied our own family. More than just learning material about families, we were encouraged to apply personal issues with the academic. We had a behavior class that consisted of weekly treatment cases. Vignettes on psychosocial problems were presented for us to analyze and discuss. We also talked about our job experiences, which proved to be useful."

Integrating skills, knowledge, and self.   In our view there needs to be an integration of what you know, what you can do, and the person who you are. Mere knowledge alone is not sufficient, yet without knowledge you cannot become an effective helper. If you focus mainly on acquiring skills but neglect theory and knowledge, these skills are of little importance. Furthermore, your ability to use the skills and knowledge you have is very much a function of your being sensitive to the interpersonal dimension of the helping process. You need to know yourself and your client to effectively apply helping skills. The helper who has a low degree of self-awareness is at best a skilled technician, and we doubt that he or she will make a positive difference in clients. Helping is more than technique.

We asked some practitioners what specialized knowledge and skills they saw as most important in their present job. Their comments were informal, and we did not conduct a comprehensive sample of practitioners. But these reactions do give some idea of what is most useful in education.

Most of these professionals commented on the value of internships and fieldwork placements. These supervised practical experiences had helped them learn about "the system" and how best to survive in it. The skills most people felt they needed included counseling skills, supervisory skills, communication skills, the ability to interact with different levels of management, the ability to write a proposal, organizational skills, the ability to deal with crisis intervention, and networking skills. A number of the professionals pointed out the value of self-exploratory experiences, especially groups aimed at personal and interpersonal growth. These therapeutic experiences gave them opportunities to look at themselves and to deal with their own feelings and problems, which were seen as especially helpful in preparing them to relate to clients.

Making the Most of Your Fieldwork

In the helping professions of counseling, social work, psychology, and marriage and family therapy, most graduate programs have fieldwork and internship at their core. Undergraduate programs in social work and human services also typically have a fieldwork component. These activities make possible a bridge between theory and practice. If your program is limited strictly to academic courses dealing with theory and skills, with only a few opportunities for working with clients, your learning will tend to be narrow. Of course, you need theory courses, specific knowledge, and special skills before you can meaningfully participate in fieldwork and internship placements. It is the combination of academic course work, fieldwork placement, skills training, and personal development that makes for a sound program. Students often do not derive the maximum benefit from fieldwork and supervision. We offer some practical strategies for making the most of these applied experiences.

The Value of Fieldwork Experiences

When we talk with graduates of our program, they typically mention their fieldwork as having been most significant. Most of them mention that they landed their present position as a result of the contacts they established at their fieldwork placement. In fact, most graduates report wishing they had

had even more fieldwork opportunities. Some regret not having had a broader range of experience in their internships.

As an initial suggestion, we recommend that you visit as many sites as possible before making your selection, if that is allowed in your program. Get job descriptions, and arrange interviews with selected agencies. What follows are other specific suggestions on how to get the most value out of your field placements:

- Get into a variety of placements. Do not limit yourself to one kind of population. Stretch your boundaries now, to help you to discover the kind of population you would eventually like to work with. Through your internships you may learn what you don't want to do as well as what you would like to do more of. Some students who initially want to "do counseling" exclusively later find themselves in the role of an administrator, supervisor, or consultant.
- Take courses and workshops that will prepare you for the type of work expected of you in your placement. These workshops can be a useful resource for staying on the cutting edge of new developments with specialized populations.
- Let yourself fit into the agency, instead of trying to make it fit you. Learn as much as you can about the politics of the agency by talking with people who work there, by attending staff meetings, and by asking questions. All of your learning will not result merely from interacting with clients. You can learn a good deal about an agency by being attentive and by talking with coworkers.
- Be aware of the toll that your work might have on you, both emotionally and physically. Certain aspects of your life that you have not been willing to look at may be opened up as you get involved with clients. Know that your increased awareness could lead to more anxiety in your life.
- Recognize the limits of your training, practice only within these boundaries, and put yourself in situations where you will be able to obtain supervised experience. Regardless of your educational level, there is always more to learn. It is essential to learn the delicate balance between being overly confident and doubting yourself.
- Strive to be flexible in applying techniques to the different client populations, but do so under supervision. Avoid falling into the trap of fitting your clients to one particular theory. Use theory as a means of helping you understand the behavior of your clients. Realize that diverse client backgrounds necessitate diverse communication approaches. Although it is essential to learn therapeutic skills and techniques, they should be applied in appropriate ways.
- If you have a placement that you do not particularly like, don't write it off as a waste of time. At least you are learning that working in a drug-rehabilitation center, for example, is not what you want for a career. Beyond that, it is useful to determine what you don't find productive about the placement and why. You can also think of ways to make your assignment more

meaningful, rather than just telling yourself that you'll put in your time and get your credit. There are no doubt at least a few avenues for creating learning opportunities.

• Make connections in the community. Learn how to use community resources and how to draw on support systems beyond your office. You can do this by talking to other professionals in the field, by asking fellow students about their connections in the community, and by developing a network of contacts.

• Keep a journal, recording your observations, experiences, concerns, and personal reactions to your work. Your journal is an excellent way to stay focused on yourself as well as to keep track of what you are doing with clients.

• Be open to trying new things. If you have not worked with a family, for example, observe a family session or, if possible, work with a supervisor who is counseling a family. Avoid setting yourself up by thinking that if you do not succeed perfectly in a new endeavor, you are a dismal failure. Give yourself room to learn by doing, at the same time gaining supervised experience.

• Be prepared to adjust your expectations. Don't expect an agency to give you responsibility for providing services to clients before it has a chance to know you. You'll probably start your fieldwork by being in an observing role. Later you may sit in on a counseling group, for example, and function as a coleader.

• Find ways to work cooperatively with other students and to combine your talents with theirs. Look for means of tapping into your own creativity. If you are talented musically, for example, look for a way that you might incorporate music into your field placement activities. If a fellow student has talents in the areas of dance and movement, perhaps you can combine forces in an innovative therapeutic intervention.

• Treat your field placement like a job. Approach fieldwork in much the same way as you would if you were employed by the agency. Demonstrate responsibility, be on time for your appointments and meetings, show up for all appointments with clients, and strive to do your best. Although you may be in an unpaid placement, this does not mean you can be irresponsible on the job. Often an unpaid internship can turn into a paid position.

• Think and act in a self-directed way. Don't expect the staff to do everything for you and to take all the initiative. Be active and seek ways that you can involve yourself in a variety of activities. If you merely wait for a supervisor or other workers to give you meaningful assignments, you may be less than satisfied with your placement.

The Challenge of Diversity

As we have suggested, it is a good idea to seek a placement where you will be challenged to work with a variety of clients and tasks. Your learning will be limited if you attempt to get placements with clients just like yourself or those whom you already know you can work with. If you think you want to work with children, for example, you might consider an internship working with the elderly. By working with diverse populations you can test out your interests and develop new ones. If you narrowly focus on the population or problem you want as a specialization, you are likely to close off many rich avenues of learning and also limit your possibilities of finding a job.

If you are anxious about working with clients in crisis, select a crisis clinic for one of your placements. As a part of your fieldwork for internship placement, you usually receive on-the-job training and supervision. Therefore, you might not need expertise in counseling rape victims before being accepted for such a placement. You will learn from coworkers and supervisors some interventions in working with such clients. Thus, more important than knowing how to work with a specific population or a specific problem is having a general background of knowledge and skills and being open to acquiring more specific abilities.

Helping someone different from you. Some interns make the mistake of clinging to the conviction that in order to be of help to a person they must have had the same life experience. Thus, a male counselor may doubt his capacity to effectively counsel an adolescent girl who is struggling with what she wants to do about being pregnant. A White counselor may doubt that he can work with a Black client. Or a counselor who has not experienced trauma may wonder about his ability to empathize with clients who have had traumas in their life. When these counselors are challenged by a client, they often tend to backtrack and become apologetic. We hope that you can see the value in drawing on your own life experience in working with clients who are different from you. You may not have had the same problem, yet you may be able to identify with the feelings of loneliness or rejection of your client. It is more important to be able to understand the client's world than to have had the identical problem.

One of our colleagues told us that her paralyzed client became upset and angry when she said to him "I understand how you feel." His reply was "How would you know? You can walk out of here, and I can't." On reflection, our colleague thought that she might have said: "You're right, I don't fully understand your situation. I can imagine your frustration and pain over becoming paralyzed at such a young age in a motorcycle accident. But I haven't been in your situation, so I don't know what you're thinking and feeling. I hope you'll help me understand what this is like for you, and I hope I can help you work through your own feelings about being paralyzed."

Challenging your self-doubt. Interns are often unsure, apologetic, and unwilling to credit themselves with what they are able to do. Ask yourself how you deal with your own feelings about what you know and don't know.

Consider how you might deal with a client who challenged you. At the initial session your client is surprised at your age. "Who are you to help me?" he asks. "You look so young, and I wonder if you have the experience to help me." Assume that this challenge opens up some of your own fears and doubts. Can you imagine saying any of the following things silently to yourself?

- "He's right. There are many years separating us. I wonder if I can understand his situation?"
- "This guy's attitude really makes me mad. He's not giving me a chance, and I feel attacked before I've even had a chance to know him."
- "Well, I don't feel comfortable with this confrontation, but I don't want to back down. I feel like letting him know that even though we differ in age, we might have many similarities in our struggles. I'd like an opportunity to at least explore if we can form a relationship."
- "He's right. What makes me think I have anything to offer him? Maybe I should have chosen another line of work."

Most professionals have feelings of self-doubt and question their competence at certain times and in certain situations. The purpose of your supervised fieldwork is to provide you with a rich and meaningful learning opportunity. This is a place where you can acquire specific knowledge and skills if you are willing to challenge your doubts. We hope you have the courage to face your feelings of incompetence rather than running from them or pretending that they do not exist. By seeking diverse field placements and questioning and learning from the supervision process, you can eventually develop the skills needed to put into practice the theory and methods you have learned.

Profiting from Your Supervision

Be clear in your own mind what you expect from your supervisors, and discuss the matter with them from the outset. This section suggests how to approach your supervision and actively participate in this process.

Be Open to Learning from Your Supervisors

You will limit your opportunities for learning if you assume a know-it-all stance. Be open to input not only from supervisors but also from teachers, peers, colleagues, and clients. Be willing to make mistakes and talk openly with your supervisor about these mistakes. If you are too afraid of making errors, you won't be willing to try anything new. You will be overly conscious about what you are doing and whether you are doing it "right." Take advantage of your student role. You are not expected to know everything. Give yourself permission to be a learner.

In our training of group leaders we typically find that the students approach workshops with considerable anxiety over making mistakes and looking incompetent in the eyes of their peers and supervisors. Early in the workshop we tell them: "Be active. Don't surrender to your fears of making mistakes. One sure way not to learn much in this workshop is by being extremely self-conscious and critically judging most of what you want to say or do. No matter what happens, there is something to be learned. If a group session is unproductive, you can explore what specific factors contributed to this outcome.''

When we give students these instructions, they usually react with relief, and they tell us they feel much less anxious. We let them know that we understand and empathize with the difficulty of being observed by both their peers and by supervisors.

Be able to say 'I don't know.' Being willing to admit your ignorance is important in interactions with both your supervisor and your clients. If you feel intimidated because you have to let a client know that you do not have an answer for her problem, you can say something like this: "You know, I don't know what to say about your concerns that you might be pregnant. I'm aware that you're a minor, and I'm somewhat cautious about suggesting a particular course of action. I'm also aware that you're anxious at this time and that you'd very much like me to tell you what you should do. I'd be willing to consult my supervisor and get some ideas that I can bring back to you in a couple of days.'' In this way you acknowledge to your client your limitations, but you keep the door open to providing her with information she can use in resolving her own problems.

Express your reactions. In working with both students and professionals, we often find that they have many good reactions that they keep to themselves. We typically encourage our trainees to talk out loud more often, rather than engaging in a silent monologue. In a recent workshop a group counselor was quiet during the group session. The supervisor asked her what was going on. "Well, I'm very aware that you, my supervisor, are present in this session,'' she replied. "I feel inhibited in following my hunches, because I'm wondering what you might think of what I'm doing. I'm afraid that you might be judging me and that I might not be measuring up very well.'' Her supervisor told her that this was what she should have said aloud.

In another instance one trainee continually suggested one exercise after another during a particular group-training session. Later, when he was asked why he had introduced so many different exercises in such a short session, he replied: "Well, the group seemed to be getting noplace. People seemed bored, and I felt responsible for making something happen! I was hoping to bring the group alive by trying some interaction exercises.'' We told the trainee that it would have been good to describe what he saw happening in the group. He could have talked about his feelings of responsibility and his awareness of the boredom level in the group. Instead, he ignored expressing his own important reactions in favor of trying some mechanical technique, which didn't work in the long run.

Focus on both elements of supervision. Some approaches to supervision emphasize the client's dynamics and teach you intervention strategies for dealing with specific problems. Others focus on your dynamics as a therapist and as a person and on your behavior in relationship to your client. Certainly, adequate supervision must take both of these elements into consideration. You need to understand models of helping clients, and you need to understand yourself if you hope to form truly therapeutic alliances. If your supervision is solely focused on what your client is doing or on teaching you specific techniques for what to do next, it will be lacking in a most important dimension.

Learn, but don't copy. We have observed that some trainees limit their own development by trying too hard to copy the style of a supervisor or teacher. With supervisors whom you respect, you are likely to watch them carefully and may tend to adopt their methods. It is important, however, to be aware of how easy it is to become a carbon copy of another person. To get the most from your supervision, try different styles but continually evaluate what works for you and what doesn't. You might ask yourself "What fits my belief system, both personal and theoretical? Do I have any conflicts between the theory or application of my supervisor's way and my own?"

If you pay too much attention to another person, you are likely to blur your own uniqueness. You need to be able to take what is good from your various supervisors and teachers, yet it is important to avoid being a clone. A balance is needed. Be willing to learn from others, but don't feel that you need to *be* them.

Learn to Be Assertive

Define how you want to spend your time in an agency, and get the supervision you need. Don't passively wait to be told what to do. At least think about what you would like to learn and what skills you would like to acquire. Let your supervisor know. Typically, a placement involves a written contract signed by the student and the supervisor of the agency. This contract usually spells out the number of hours to be worked per week, the activities that will be performed, the learning objectives, the opportunities for training, the expectations for the intern, and the expectations for the supervisor. Before agreeing to your contract with your supervisor, you can discuss in some detail the ways in which you think you could be of greatest benefit to the agency. You can also clearly spell out what you would like to experience and learn before you leave. You may not always get what you want. But if you are not clear what you want in the first place and are not willing to ask for it, you surely will not obtain it.

The assertion skills you practice in getting adequate supervision will be useful in your relationships with clients, and colleagues as well. Being assertive does not mean being aggressive, which alienates most people. By bulldozing your way into an agency you will needlessly put others on the defensive. Being passive/aggressive is not useful either, whether it involves rebelling against all authority, appearing bored, or consistently showing up for appointments or meetings late. Resisting in such passive ways is likely to shut you off from many chances to learn.

It helps to realize that supervisors are people, too. They get bogged down with their own demands. As their client load grows and pressures increase, they may not initiate the regular supervision sessions that they have promised. Furthermore, some practitioners do not volunteer to become supervisors but are told that they should add interns to their already heavy work load. At times their training for being a supervisor is minimal, and they are expected to "learn by doing." If you are able to understand the predicament of supervisors, you are more likely to establish a basis of communication with them. Within a climate of open communication, you can sensitively and assertively let them know that you need help. If you have a difficult case, you can say something like this: "I really feel stuck with Susan. For several weeks now, we've been getting nowhere. Every suggestion I make seems to fall on deaf ears, and she has many reasons why it won't work. I suggested termination, and she got angry with me. Now I don't know what to do. Can I meet with you for a few minutes to talk about some alternatives?" If you merely complain that your supervisor is always too busy or fails to show up for appointments, all you will get is frustration. But by being clear, specific, and persistent, you are likely to get your needs met.

Case example.   Picture yourself as an intern in this situation. Your supervisor asks you to counsel a family, consisting of mother, father, and two young boys. The supervisor tells you that the parents are primarily interested in learning how to manage their problem children and want to learn disciplinary techniques. In the supervisor's view a more important problem consists of the conflicts between the wife and husband. You have had very little course work or training in working with families, and you feel lacking in the competencies to do family counseling. Below is a sample of some of the things that might be going on inside of your head:

- "Now what am I going to do? I feel overwhelmed, but I don't want to appear like a neophyte, so I'd better take this family on."
- "I'm unprepared to counsel a family. I haven't even had a single course on family dynamics or family therapy. But if I don't agree to see the family, my supervisor might get angry and might think less of me. What should I do?"
- "The thought of dealing with this family terrifies me. I wouldn't know where to begin. I'd like to sit in on some sessions with my supervisor and observe and participate as a cotherapist. Do I dare suggest this?"

This inner dialogue gives some sense of the struggle that you might go through in dealing with a supervisor who asks you to go beyond what you consider to be the boundaries of your competence. Let your supervisor know of your concerns, and the two of you can talk about alternatives.

Deal with Inadequate Supervision

Realistically, there are times when you will have to deal with supervision that is far from ideal. How can you recognize supervision that is substandard? What assertive courses of action are open to you in dealing with it?

Recognizing the ideal supervisor.   Although there is no one way of conducting clinical supervision, research in this area suggests notions of how good supervisors generally perform their tasks. Based on their survey and integration of published research on clinical supervision, Carifio and Hess (1987) conclude that ideal supervisors

- possess appropriate levels of empathy and respect genuineness, concreteness, and self-disclosure.
- seem to embody the same personal characteristics as the ideal therapist.
- are knowledgeable and experienced both in methods of intervention with clients and in supervising trainees as they intervene with clients.
- can create a climate of openness, trust, mutual understanding, two-way communication, and collaboration in the supervisor/supervisee relationship.
- set clear and explicit goals and use these goals to guide them in using various teaching techniques.
- avoid combining personal therapy with supervision.
- are generally supportive and noncritical.
- provide direct and immediate feedback that is closely tied to an intern's behavior. This feedback is systematic, objective, accurate, timely, and clearly understood.
- are able to influence a supervisee's behavior through a variety of methods, processes, and approaches.
- are not highly directive yet are not passive either.

The chances are that you will meet and work with some supervisors who do not match up to such an ideal. Some supervisors feel ill equipped to do what is expected of them, and some may be as insecure in their supervisory role as you are in your new role as an intern.

Accepting different styles of supervision.   It can benefit you to learn how to function under a range of supervisory styles, both now as a student and later as a helping professional. One supervisor may believe that harsh confrontation is a way to cut through a client's stubborn defenses. Another treats clients as victims who are not responsible for their problems. Another provides unlimited resources of advice for clients and promotes a problem-solving orientation for every client problem. There are supervisors who foster a supportive and positive orientation and who give out "warm fuzzies" exclusively. Other supervisors thrive on crises and problems and therefore tend to escalate such situations rather than defusing them. Some supervisors work very hard at becoming friends with their interns, whereas others create a professionally aloof relationship. Be open to supervisors with various orientations and learn to incorporate their viewpoints into your style of helping. Do not be too quick to criticize a style different from yours.

If you do have trouble with a supervisor, the answer is not always merely finding a new one. In such situations you may need to discuss your expectations and goals regarding supervision with your supervisor. Rather than convincing yourself that your supervisor will not be cooperative, assume that he or she will be open to your suggestions. Later, when you accept a position in an agency, you typically do not have the option of changing supervisors. What is more, you often don't have choices in who your coworkers will be. Thus, it is important to learn the interpersonal skills necessary in working out differences while the stakes are not so high.

At this point you might write down what kind of supervisor you think would be the most difficult for you to work with, and why. What might you do if it were impractical to change positions? What strategies could you use in constructively dealing with this supervisor?

Solving problems in your supervision. You may encounter a number of problems in working with a supervisor. Communication may not be open or encouraged. Some supervisors may poorly define what they expect of you. Some may fail to show up for appointments. Others may delegate their responsibilities to their secretary. There is also the supervisor who is insecure but disguises this insecurity by being overly controlling and autocratic. Some supervisors dump too much on an intern too soon. They may delegate "dirty work" and unwanted jobs to their interns. Supervisors may be guilty of unethical practices. One supervisor had her supervisee do her work, for example, and then wrote up the proceedings as though she had seen the client. Some supervisors misuse power through a need to be seen as always right. Finally, there are supervisors who do not carry out their responsibility to give feedback. They keep the student intern in the dark and offer very little direction.

These are but a few possible conflict situations that are likely to face you in your internship. What do you think you might do if your supervisor were to give you very little feedback? Would you be willing to let the supervisor know that you wanted more response? Would you ask for it? Would you insist on it? What might you do if no feedback were forthcoming?

Borders and Leddick (1987) discuss the resistance that often characterizes the supervisee/supervisor relationship. In much the same way that resistance operates in the therapeutic relationship, it also operates in the process of supervision. Borders and Leddick indicate that the supervisory roles and functions themselves tend to be somewhat detrimental to efforts to create an open relationship. Supervisors are responsible for and will evaluate the supervisee, so that supervisees are understandably anxious about being observed and evaluated. Interns can challenge themselves by converting this resistance into productive energy. They can spend time thinking about what they want and begin to find ways to ask directly for it. They need not submit to their anxiety of being evaluated or allow themselves to be frozen by these fears.

The Value of Group Supervision

In group supervision you learn not only from your supervisor but also from fellow trainees. It is important to talk to other interns and to share experiences and struggles. If group supervision is not available to you, seek out informal contacts with others who work in your agency.

Group supervision is enhanced when you make the process a personal one. You can do this by focusing on your own reactions and sharing them in your supervision group. What clients seem to trigger you? What clients do you hope won't show up next week? What clients threaten you? What clients do you find yourself especially liking? By focusing on your relationships with your clients and your own dynamics, you can increase your self-awareness through the feedback you get from others in such a group.

It is also helpful to explore your values and attitudes in conjunction with your supervision. If you become aware that you have a tendency to seek gratitude from clients, for example, it could be useful to explore your own need for approval and your fear of rejection, either in your own personal therapy or in a group supervision session.

Supervision versus Therapy

Some have suggested that a supervisee's personal difficulties are inappropriate topics for supervision, unless these problems directly affect the intern's clinical practice. We agree that supervision and therapy should not be combined, but we do think that the two processes have much in common. Furthermore, good supervision can entail focusing on the problems and blind spots of the intern. These potential problem areas at least need to be pointed out. Supervisors are in a good position to recognize some of your blocks and countertransferences. They can work to help you at least recognize some of the attitudes, feelings, and behaviors that are likely to interfere with your handling of certain clients.

If further or more in-depth exploration is needed and if your difficulties with certain clients are rooted in your own dynamics, a supervisor may encourage you to get involved in some form of personal therapy. You should not misconstrue such a suggestion as an indication that you are not personally fit for the profession. Getting involved in the lives of clients in a placement is bound to open up some of your own psychological wounds, and unresolved conflicts are likely to surface. Be open to looking at whatever arises in you as you encounter a diversity of clients. Personal therapy along with your supervision can be an ideal combination, provided your supervisor and your therapist are not the same person. Receiving supervision from one professional and psychotherapy from another professional can yield the maximum benefit for the supervisee's personal and professional development (Carifio & Hess, 1987).

Is There Life after Graduation?

Neither undergraduate nor graduate programs typically prepare students for the jolt they experience when they leave school and enter the world of work. Professionals report anxiety, frustration, and disappointment as a result of their job's unexpected stressors and demands (Olson, Downing, Heppner, & Pickney, 1986). Goal-oriented and hard-working students may experience the blues after graduation, a condition sometimes known as "postgraduate depression." There is a void between graduation and the world of work. For so long you have had a structured life, and now you find yourself without this structure. You have looked forward to the goal of a degree for a long time, and you have put forth much energy and made sacrifices to get what you want. Now you have it, and you are somewhat depressed. You ask yourself what you might want to do.

Myths about Starting Work

In their article "Is There Life after Graduate School?" Olson and her colleagues (1986) describe six myths pertaining to the new professional, which we briefly describe:

1. "As soon as I unpack my bags, I will be settled." As a new professional you may minimize the impact of the adjustments that face you once you take your first professional job. You may underestimate how much time and energy it takes to reorganize your personal and professional life.
2. "My new associates will welcome me enthusiastically and accept me as one of them." You may expect to receive social support, professional collaboration, and approval from coworkers. Not all colleagues fulfill these expectations.
3. "I will never be an apprentice again." You may assume that you will be able to work with minimal supervision and that you will not have to go through another apprenticeship. You may find, however, that being an apprentice is a good way to enter and become a part of an organization.
4. "I will easily master the varied demands of my job." Because you were able to handle many demands as a student, you may assume that the diverse roles you will be expected to play as a professional will be easy to perform. But coordinating multiple tasks can be draining and difficult. One crucial step toward mastery of the multiple demands of a job is to admit that they cannot be immediately accomplished.
5. "I must perform perfectly, lest someone discover that I am a fraud." You may be like other new professionals who feel that they are either perfect or fraudulent. You do not need to perform all aspects of your job instantly and perfectly. Setting reasonable goals and being open to feedback can lessen the pressure on you. By consulting with former graduate peers you can form a support group and laugh together about some of your unreasonably high standards.
6. "Because I have worked so hard to get here, I will love my job." You may feel somewhat disillusioned because all aspects of your job do not meet your expectancies. It could help to realize that while you love your job, you may well not love all aspects of it.

Merely recognizing the above myths could go a long way toward helping you learn to challenge, test, and discard some of them. Even though your educational program may not have prepared you to deal adequately with the professional world, you can begin to face some of the realities that will greet you when you enter it.

Ways of Keeping Professionally Alert

We now discuss some ways of extending your education beyond graduation. Realize that your knowledge and skills will soon be outdated unless you take steps to keep abreast of new developments. Some of the current issues in the helping professions that are receiving increased attention are methods of dealing with substance abuse; gay and lesbian issues; physical and psychological abuse of children, the elderly, and spouses; acquired immune deficiency syndrome, or AIDS; and legal and ethical issues. Keeping professionally alert implies that you avail yourself of in-service and continuing-education programs. It is important to remember that your education is not completed when you finish school. The challenge is to find ways to go outside the confines of your daily work and not to become encapsulated by its boundaries.

Although many professions have mandatory continuing-education requirements for the relicensing or recertification of their members, we hope that you develop your own self-directed program and do not merely comply with the minimal mandatory requirements. You can do this by taking specialized courses and workshops that deal with particular client groups and newer techniques.

Reading is another good way of keeping yourself abreast of developments in your field. In addition to professional journals and books dealing with your specific subject of interest, novels and nonfiction works about other cultures are also of value in your continuing education.

Bugental (1987, p. 270) makes some excellent suggestions for enriching your inner life. Although he is writing primarily about the training of psychotherapists, we think that his ideals are appropriate as guidelines for other helpers who are already in the human-services field. The following are experiences that Bugental recommends:

- experience with both individual and group therapy, preferably with therapists of both sexes
- a minimum of three years of life experience in which students earn their own living in the larger world, outside of the mental-health field
- fieldwork experience in a variety of settings, such as a social agency, a mental hospital, and a public school
- a balanced study of the basics of human psychology, medical perspectives, social influences, and professional ethics
- extensive reading that portrays a wide range of human experiences and the great existential and philosophical issues of life
- relationships with mentors and models who stimulate students to reflect on their experiences and grapple with them in ways that vary from fantasy to specific action
- internships that carefully nurture the development of sensitivities and skills

By Way of Review

- Become active in getting the most from your education. No program is perfect, but you can do a lot to bring more meaning to your course of study.
- In selecting an educational program, follow your interests. Be willing to experiment by taking classes and by getting experience as a volunteer worker.
- Just as you are graded in your educational program, you will be evaluated in the professional world. Evaluation practices create stresses and strains, yet it is still possible to find meaning within the system.
- Skills and knowledge are obviously important in becoming an effective professional. But your quality as a person is an equally important determinant of your success as a helper.
- Your fieldwork courses are likely to be among the most important experiences that you will have in your program. Select these experiences wisely, and arrange for a diversity in your placements. Realize that these placements can help you decide on your professional specialization.
- Treat your field placement like a job, even if you don't get paid for your internship.
- Don't burden yourself with trying to be a perfect intern. Fieldwork experiences are designed to teach you about the skills of helping, and you can learn much from your mistakes.
- In getting the most from supervision, learn how to ask for what you need from your supervisor. It is important that you learn your limits and communicate them to your supervisor.
- Supervisors have different styles, and no one way is right. You can learn a great deal from various supervisors, but be cautious about copying their style.
- The ideal supervisor may be hard to find. Supervisors are sometimes assigned to this role with little preparation or training.
- If your supervision is inadequate, be assertive in doing something about the situation. Persist in getting what you need by taking an active and assertive stance.
- Even though supervision is like therapy in some ways, there are important differences. Personal therapy can be a useful adjunct to supervision, but it is best that the supervisor and the therapist not be the same person.

What Will You Do Now?

1. If you are an undergraduate and if you think you'd like to pursue a graduate program, select at least one graduate school to visit so you can talk with faculty members and students.

2. If you are in a training program, now is an ideal time to begin getting involved in professional organizations. You can do this by joining at least one such organization as an active student member. Joining as a student has many advantages. To help you find an organization that might fit your needs, we

have listed a number of them in Appendix D. By joining an organization you can take advantage of its workshops and conferences. Membership also puts you in touch with other professionals with similar interests, gives you ideas for updating your skills, and helps you make excellent contacts.

3. If you have a supervisor (for your fieldwork or in your job), make up a short list of questions that you'd like to discuss with him or her. What would you like to gain from supervision? Approach your supervisor before the end of the semester to discuss your desires.

Suggested Readings

American Association for Counseling and Development. *Counselor Education and Supervision.* One of the best ways to keep abreast of developments in the theory, research, and practice of counseling supervision is to read this journal. It is published quarterly by the American Association for Counseling and Development, 5999 Stevenson Avenue, Alexandria, VA 22304. Subscriptions for nonmembers are $12 per year; members of the Association for Counselor Education and Supervision, a division of the AACD, receive the journal as a benefit of membership.

Austin, M. J. (1978). *Professionals and paraprofessionals.* New York: Human Sciences Press. This is a useful source of information on the roots of the paraprofessional movement, the building of career opportunities for paraprofessional workers, and the relationships between these workers and professionals.

Borders, L. D., & Leddick, G. R. (1987). *Handbook of counseling supervision.* Alexandria, VA: Association for Counselor Education and Supervision. This practical guide to supervising internships and practicums is written primarily for supervisors who want to improve their skills. It is also a useful ''how-to'' manual for students in fieldwork courses. It includes sample evaluation and assessment forms and a chapter on ethical and legal issues. It is an excellent resource for topics such as defining goals for supervision, choosing and implementing supervision interventions, the supervisory relationship, and evaluation issues.

Kottler, J. A. (1986). *On being a therapist.* San Francisco: Jossey-Bass. This book is an ideal supplement to a fieldwork or internship course. The author introduces the many struggles involved in being a therapist. He focuses on the mixing of our personal and professional lives, the hardships of therapeutic practice, the lies that we tell ourselves, clients who test our patience, boredom and burnout, the struggle for power and influence, and ways to remain open to our personal growth.

Rogers, C. (1983). *Freedom to learn for the 80's.* Columbus, OH: Charles E. Merrill. This is an outstanding treatment of how education can foster creativity in learning. Rogers writes about freedom and responsibility in our learning. You can apply his ideas to thinking about changing your education for yourself.

Stoltenberg, C. D., & Delworth, U. (1987). *Supervising counselors and therapists.* San Francisco: Jossey-Bass. The authors develop a model of supervision that includes the needs and characteristics of trainees at each level; procedures for assessing trainees in eight areas of growth, including interpersonal skills, treatment goals, and client evaluation; and recommendations for how and when supervisors should intervene to help trainees.

The Helper in the Helping Process

Focus of the Chapter

The purpose of this chapter is to highlight the central role in the helping process of the helper's basic assumptions and belief. Studies suggest that what makes helpers effective is directly related to the helper's belief system (Combs, 1986). Your beliefs about the nature of people will have a great deal to do with the helping strategies you employ. We have found that helpers often operate without a clear awareness of their beliefs and attitudes. It is essential to recognize how you came to acquire your beliefs and how they affect what you do with clients.

This chapter also addresses the stages in the helping process, along with the main tasks that you will need to master in your role as a helper. We look at the skills and knowledge you need at the various stages of helping, along with the personal characteristics that are required to apply your skills. Our basic assumption is that the kind of person you are and the attitudes you bring to the helping relationship are the major determinants of its quality.

The Impact of Helpers' Beliefs on Their Work
Beliefs of Effective Helpers

Combs (1986) summarized 13 studies in five helping professions to identify the characteristics of the effective helper from a person-centered perspective. His survey found clear distinctions between effective and ineffective helpers. What appears to make the difference between effective and ineffective helpers is what they believe about empathy, self, human nature, and their own purposes. The 13 studies lend support to the assumption that in order to understand behavior, it is essential to understand the perceptual field (or subjective frame of reference) of the individual. Thus, to understand the dynamics of a helper's behavior, it is necessary to direct attention to the nature of the helper's personal meanings. According to Combs, the categories explored in these studies suggest at least five areas of beliefs that seem to discriminate clearly between good (or effective) and poor (or ineffective) helpers:

1. *Beliefs about the value of focusing on the client's personal world.* Effective helpers are people-oriented; that is, they focus on internal personal meanings rather than external behavioral data. They are primarily concerned with how the world appears from the vantage point of those with whom they work.
2. *Beliefs about people.* Effective helpers hold positive beliefs about individuals, seeing them as trustworthy, capable, dependable, and friendly.
3. *Beliefs about self.* The helper's self-concept is vitally related to effective practice. The studies suggest the importance of a positive view of self, confidence in one's abilities, and a feeling of oneness with others as crucial for effective helping.

4. *Beliefs about purposes and priorities.* The interventions that helpers make are based on their values. The beliefs they have about helping, the purposes of society, and their relationships with clients determine their goals and decisions.

5. *Beliefs about methods.* Research on specific counselor methods has not established that methods alone serve to discriminate between effective and ineffective helpers. The most promising research on characteristics of effective and ineffective helpers seems to lie in studies of specific traits. Characteristics of effective helpers tend to include such factors as empathy, congruence, warmth, compassion, genuineness or authenticity, and unconditional positive regard. Combs suggests that helper beliefs (such as values placed on genuineness and unconditional positive regard) have significant effects on the methods that helpers choose and provide important hypotheses for further research.

Combs concludes that if helpers' beliefs determine good and poor performance, as the studies he reviewed suggest, the focus is best placed on "becoming a counselor" rather than "learning how to counsel." In the training of helping professionals, emphasis should be given to clarifying and developing their beliefs. He adds:

> The goal of professional education from such an orientation would be helping students achieve a broad, accurate, personally relevant, internally consistent, and appropriate system of beliefs about self, others, purposes, priorities, and desirable ways of relating to the world, both in and out of professional practice [1986, p. 59].

Beliefs of Ineffective Helpers

The study by Combs focused on the issue of what makes a good helper. We now offer our view of beliefs and assumptions that are nontherapeutic. Most of the statements listed below are ones that we have heard from either students or professionals. As you review these examples of helpers' assumptions, ask yourself if you might have made some of these statements.

- "A sociopath is resistant to therapy and will never change."
- "Old people can't change. They should be given support but not challenged."
- "I'm 'color blind'—I can work equally well with any racial or ethnic group."
- "If clients don't change, it's their fault, not mine."
- "People who come to me need help, which means they're not able to direct their own life. It's my job to provide them with a high degree of structure."
- "People who are on welfare are basically lazy and really don't want to work."
- "Basically, most people don't want to change. They just want to learn how to manipulate people more effectively so they can get what they want."
- "People can't be depended on to follow through with their commitments."

- "The clients in this institution are highly resistive and want to hide their true feelings and thoughts."
- "The best way to get through the client's resistance is to employ very directive and highly confrontive techniques. You have to strip away a client's defenses."
- "If you're empathic and supportive, clients will merely use this against you by manipulating you."

We do not mean to imply that if you hold any one of these beliefs, you are necessarily ineffective in helping others. If you worked with a resistant client population over a period of years, for example, you might begin to assume that people generally resist change. If you apply this generalization to all the clients you see, they are likely to exhibit resistance in response to the messages that they pick up from you. You are fostering a self-fulfilling prophecy that reinforces your assumptions. A temporary degree of cynicism does not mean that you will remain cynical forever. You might ask yourself questions such as "How rigidly do I hold certain assumptions? Am I quick to generalize on the basis of limited experience? Is there a pattern of forming judgments about people and making generalizations? Am I willing to seriously examine the assumptions that I make, and am I open to changing some of them?" It is a positive sign if you demonstrate a willingness to question the origin of your assumptions and to modify them.

Learning to Challenge Your Assumptions

We provided a series of in-service training workshops at a state institution for the criminally insane and for mentally disordered sex offenders. Although we had the good fortune to meet and work with some dedicated and effective helpers, we also encountered some ineffective helpers. To us it seemed that their patients could do no right. Certain workers at the institution were quite outspoken in their beliefs that these patients were resistant to therapy, were not motivated to change, and were only putting in their time ordered by the court. If the patients did not talk during the sessions, they were labeled as "resistive"; if they did talk, they were often seen as being "manipulative."

In our training workshops we urged the staff members to at least suspend their judgments during the time they were providing therapy. We encouraged them to give their patients a chance to show something more of themselves than the problem with which they had become identified. Although a child molester does have severe problems, we suggested that he be viewed as something more than a person who has committed sexual crimes. If the staff members were open to discovering other facets of the patient's personality, they would discover that he had had pain and struggles in his life that the helper could identify with. We hoped that the helpers would challenge some of their assumptions that seemed nontherapeutic and be open to the possibility that they could begin to see clients and the helping process in a different light.

If you are making some of the assumptions we have described, think about how they are likely to influence the way you approach certain clients. Your beliefs about yourself, the people with whom you work, and the nature of the helping process are often more subtle than the assumptions listed above. Whether your beliefs are subtle or extreme, however, you tend to behave on the basis of them. Which techniques you employ and how you approach the helping situation are largely a function of your assumptions. If you basically do not trust your clients to understand and deal with their problems, for example, you will use strategies to get them to accept your assessment and to follow your prescriptions.

After becoming aware of the attitudes and assumptions you hold, you can decide the degree to which your attitudes are being expressed in your behavior. Then you can assess how well such attitudes and behaviors are working for you and helping your clients.

We hope you will examine the source of your beliefs about the good life, an individual's capacity to make substantial change, and the nature of the helper/client relationship. Think through, clarify, and challenge these beliefs, making them your own through a conscious process of self-examination.

You may not have clear beliefs about the helping process. You may have incorporated your beliefs in an uncritical and unconscious manner. It is possible that your beliefs are narrow and that they have not been tested to determine if they are valid or functional. If you have lived in a sheltered environment and rarely stepped outside of your social group, you may not even be aware of your narrow belief system. It is possible to live in an encapsulated environment and thereby "see" only what confirms your existing belief system.

One good way to identify and clarify your beliefs is to put yourself in situations that might prove challenging. If you have limited contact with alcoholics and see them as "weak-willed individuals," for instance, consider attending some Alcoholics Anonymous meetings. If you have limited experience with certain cultural and ethnic groups, seek volunteer experiences or fieldwork placements where you will work with a culturally diverse population. If you are aware that you hold stereotypes about old people, volunteer some time in working with the elderly. Direct contact with populations that are unfamiliar to you is the best way to learn about these people. Of course, it is essential that you approach these situations with an open mind and that you avoid simply looking for evidence to support your prior judgments. A stance of openness will enable you to develop a personal orientation to helping that will lend itself to modification as you gain experience.

Your Orientation to Helping

In this section we consider how your orientation to the helping process is largely a function of your beliefs about human nature and about how people change. There are various approaches to helping. Sometimes an orientation will be imposed on you, especially if you work in an institution that makes extensive use of a particular therapeutic model. You might work in a state facility that employs behavior-modification strategies. The entire program is likely to be geared to behavioral procedures, which may not be suited to you. Or an agency may make extensive use of a diagnostic system, and you will be expected to conduct interviews and arrive at a specific diagnostic category for each client you see. Before you accept a position in any setting, find out about its theoretical framework. If the methods of intervention are not compatible with your views of helping, you are bound to experience conflict in this institution.

Clarify your thinking with respect to questions such as "Who is responsible for change in the helping relationship? What focus is most likely to lead to change? A focus on feelings? A focus on insight? A focus on behavior? A focus on cognition? What is the best balance between providing a great deal of structure and only minimal structure? What is an appropriate balance between confrontation and support?"

At this point consider some of the components of your theoretical orientation to the helping process. Your answers to the following questions are important in understanding your behavior and functioning as a helper. Also, your interventions are related to the outcomes you hope will result from your role in the helping process.

From your perspective, who is responsible for change? Do you see yourself as primarily responsible for whether your clients reach their goals? Or do you place the primary responsibility on the clients? To what degree do you share this responsibility with clients? Do you think that you have answers to give clients who come to you, or do you see that they are capable of finding their own solutions with your assistance?

Various Focuses of Helping

Identify your beliefs about what best facilitates change. If you are not clear about what brings about change, your ability to promote it is very limited. Promoting change has a number of specific dimensions. Some helpers focus on feelings. They think that what clients need most is to identify and express feelings that have been bottled up. If this is your focus, you will be doing a lot to get your clients to emote.

Other helpers put emphasis on gaining insight. If this is what you value, much of your time may be spent in exploring the reasons for actions and in interpreting clients' behavior. You will be interested in having them understand the origins of their problem.

There are those who emphasize the behavioral aspects involved in the helping relationship. They are very much oriented to what individuals are doing now and what they will do in the near future. If this is your orientation, you may not be much concerned about having your clients develop insight or express their feelings.

Some helpers like to focus clients on examining their beliefs about themselves and about their world. If you have such a cognitive orientation, your interventions will focus clients on what they are thinking and the things that they continue to tell themselves. You will see change as a result of helping your clients eliminate faulty thinking and replace this with constructive thoughts and self-talk.

Some believe in being active and directive in the helping process, and others believe that very little intervention is necessary. If you hold to the notion that little structure is useful, then you will probably not use directive procedures. You won't give much advice and won't be locked into a problem-solving mode. If you believe in active intervention, you will do much of the talking, will provide a high degree of structure, and will make sure that the sessions keep moving.

Some helpers employ a good deal of confrontation, thinking that clients will surrender their defenses only under the pressure of being challenged. Other helpers think that support is far more useful than confrontation. Depending on your beliefs, your techniques will have the effect of either supporting or challenging.

Some helpers employ short-term strategies, and others use long-term ones. Depending on the setting you work in and on your clientele, the length of treatment will vary. Do you believe that people can be helped with only brief interventions? Do you think that long-term treatment is necessary for effective change to occur?

Some therapeutic approaches focus on the past, others on the present, and others on the future. Begin to consider whether you see the past, present, or future as being most productive in the helping process. This is more than just a theoretical notion. If your orientation includes the concept that your clients' past is an important focus for exploration, many of your interventions are likely to be designed to assist them in understanding their past. If you think that your clients' goals and strivings are important, your interventions are likely to focus them on the future. Thus, you might ask questions such as "How would you like your life to be different one year from now? What do you see that you can do now to create the kind of future you say you want in ten years?" If you are oriented toward the present, many of your interventions will focus your clients on what they are thinking, feeling, and doing in the moment. Of course, your theory will largely determine the time frame that you emphasize. It is also possible to work with the past, present, and future in an integrated fashion. You can respect how your clients' past experiences influence them today. You can also be concerned about what people are doing now and yet frequently ask them to look to what kind of future they would like to create for themselves.

Your views and beliefs about human nature are very much related to your practices and the helping strategies you will employ with your clients. For example, if you see people as basically good, you will trust that your clients can assume responsibility for the direction of their life. If you see human nature as basically evil, you will adopt a role as a helper who attempts to correct people's flawed nature. Your interventions are likely to be aimed at "straightening people out." For a moment, reflect on the following statements and begin to clarify your views about human nature:

- People need direction from an authority to resolve their problems.
- People have the capacity to find their answers within themselves.
- People create their own misery or are victims of outside circumstances.
- People are basically good and are therefore trustworthy.
- People have a basic tendency toward evil and therefore need correcting.
- People are the product of their choices; that is, they are the architect of their life.
- People won't change unless they are in pain.
- People are motivated by their goals.
- People are determined by their early childhood experiences.

Your orientation to helping will certainly develop as you gain experience in working with a diversity of clients. It is certainly not essential that your orientation be established before you begin to practice. What is vital is that you formulate your views about human nature, because these views have a crucial bearing on the way you work with clients.

Some Beliefs We Hold about Counseling

It took us some time to learn that there is no one right way to approach clients. Instead of looking for the right thing to do or say, we strive to follow what we think is an interesting path to pursue with a client. The process of trusting our own intuitions and developing our own way of working with clients is not something that is ever finally arrived at. If our hunches about a client are not correct, this quickly becomes apparent if we pay attention to the relationship. What we continually relearn is the importance of talking out loud with clients about what we think is going on between us. Also, rather than working very hard to figure out what clients should want, we ask them frequently what is it they want. We often ask: "Is what you are doing working for you? If not, what are you willing to do to change it?" If their current behavior is generally serving them well, they may reconsider their need to change a style. We still encourage them to look at the price they often pay for being the way they are, and then the decision whether to change is up to them. We do not see it as our job to decide for them how they should live their life.

If clients appear to be getting little from a counseling relationship, we still examine our part in this outcome by asking ourselves about our involvement and willingness to risk with this client. Yet we also explore with the client his or her part in the lack of progress. We recognize that we cannot make clients want to change, yet we can create a climate where together we look at the advantages and disadvantages of making changes. We see helping as a mutual endeavor, in which both parties share the responsibility for making change happen.

Three Perspectives on Human Nature

In this section we describe the basic assumptions of three views of human nature, each with differing implications for the role of the helper and for the helping process. These perspectives are the psychoanalytic, behavioristic, and humanistic approaches in psychology.

The Psychoanalytic Perspective

Sigmund Freud, the father of psychoanalysis, was a strict determinist who believed strongly that all behavior is caused. The Freudian psychoanalytic view suggests that if humans remain a mystery, it is because of inadequacies in uncovering the driving forces within them and the experiences that have influenced their behavior. It is critical in the helping process to understand the nature and functioning of these internal psychological forces. In particular, helpers investigate the ways in which early childhood experiences have shaped the adult personality (Nye, 1986).

One of the major contributions of Freudian psychology is his view of the unconscious, which is crucial to understanding behavior and the problems of personality. For Freud, consciousness is a minor part of human experience. The unconscious, which is out of awareness and also outside the sphere of conscious control, is the major part of personality. Freud believed that most psychological functioning exists in this realm. The unconscious stores up all of an individual's experiences and memories. It contains repressed material, which includes an involuntary removal of painful thoughts and feelings that are excluded from awareness. The role of the unconscious is central to the psychoanalytic approach, for unconscious processes are at the root of all personality disorders and maladaptive behaviors. From this perspective a "cure" is based on uncovering the meaning of symptoms, the causes of behavior, and the repressed feelings and experiences that interfere with healthy personality functioning.

Psychoanalysis provides helpers with a conceptual framework for looking at behavior and for understanding the origins and functions of symptoms. It can be extremely useful in understanding the ego defenses as reactions to the anxiety of living in a contemporary world. From the psychoanalytic perspective, if helpers ignore the early history of the client, they are limiting their vision of the causes of the client's present suffering and the nature of the client's present life-style. This concern with the client's early history does not mean that helpers become preoccupied with the past. The psychoanalytic approach provides a dynamic understanding of the impact of these early childhood events on the current struggles of clients (Corey, 1986b).

Although you will probably have neither the training for nor the interest in conducting psychoanalytic therapy, you can broaden your understanding of human behavior by learning about the basic concepts of this approach. Knowledge of the dynamics of behavior, the functioning of the ego defenses, the workings of the unconscious, and the ways in which present personality functioning is an expression of past events will assist you in acquiring a deeper grasp of the people you are helping.

The Behavioristic Perspective

B. F. Skinner is the father of radical behaviorism. Although Skinner acknowledges that humans are feeling and thinking organisms, he does not look within the individual's psyche for the causes of behavior. Instead, he stresses the cause-and-effect relationship between environmental conditions and behavior. One of his main contributions lies in his discovery of the ways in which the physical and social environments are critically important in determining human behavior. Skinner asserts that behavior control can be achieved by focusing on observable factors, which need to be specified in objective and detailed terms.

Skinner's view of controlling human behavior is based on the principles of operant conditioning, which rest on the assumption that changes in behavior are brought about when that behavior is followed by a particular consequence. He maintains that learning occurs only with some form of reinforcement, either positive or negative. From his perspective those actions that are reinforced tend to be repeated, and those that are discouraged tend to be extinguished. Skinner's model is based on reinforcement principles and has the goal of identifying and controlling environmental factors that lead to behavior change.

From Skinner's perspective there is not room in scientific psychology for the assumption that human behavior is the result of individual choice. He argues against any conceptualizations of individuals as free agents who shape their own destiny. Instead, the individual's behavior is determined by past and present events in the objective world (Nye, 1986). Although radical behaviorists such as Skinner rule out the possibility of self-determination and freedom, contemporary behavioral approaches are developing procedures that actually give control to clients and thus increase their range of freedom (Corey, 1986b). Many contemporary psychologists are moderate behaviorists, in that in their explanation of human behavior they include certain internal determinants such as attitudes, cognitive processes, and motives, while also focusing on determinants in the physical and social environments (Nye, 1986).

Modern behavioral approaches are grounded in a scientific view of human behavior that implies a systematic and structured approach to counseling. This view does not rely on a set of deterministic assumptions involving humans as a mere product of their sociocultural conditioning. Rather, the current view is that the person is the producer *and* the product of his or her environment (Corey, 1986b).

Contemporary behavioral approaches have undergone significant changes, and the perspective has expanded considerably. Behavioral approaches are no longer grounded exclusively in learning theory. Contemporary behavior therapy encompasses a variety of conceptualizations, research methods, and treatment procedures to explain behavior change. This approach is distinguished from other approaches by its strict reliance on the principles of the scientific method. Concepts and therapeutic procedures are stated explicitly, tested empirically, and revised continually. Treatment and assessment are interrelated, for they occur simultaneously. The following characteristics apply widely to the various behavioral approaches:

- The focus is on the current influences on behavior, not on the historical determinants.
- The stress is on overt behavior change as the main criterion by which treatment is evaluated.
- Treatment goals are specified in concrete and objective terms.
- Research is a basic part of all therapeutic procedures.
- Target problems are specifically identified, so that treatment and assessment are possible (Corey, 1986b).

Helpers who subscribe to a behavioral orientation assume an active, directive role in the helping relationship. They apply scientific knowledge to discovering solutions to human problems. Such helpers typically function as a teacher, director, and expert in diagnosing maladaptive behavior and in employing behavioral procedures that are aimed at improving behavior. Helpers are provided with a well-defined system of procedures to employ within the context of a well-defined role. Furthermore, clients also have a clearly defined role. Behavioral approaches stress the importance of client awareness and participation in the helping process. Clients are expected to be actively involved in the selection of personal goals that guide the helping process, and they must be willing to cooperate in the therapeutic activities, both during the sessions in the office and in their everyday life. They are encouraged to experiment with new behaviors as a way to generalize and transfer the learning acquired within the therapeutic situation to situations in outside life.

The Humanistic Perspective

Carl Rogers was a leading psychologist in the development of the humanistic approach to understanding human behavior and the helping relationship. Rogers (1961, 1980), the father of the person-centered approach, consistently maintained that the basic nature of the human being, when functioning freely, is constructive and trustworthy. He had little sympathy with the view that human nature is basically irrational and evil. He denied that the individual's impulses, if not controlled, will lead to self-destruction and the destruction of others. Instead he asserted that human behavior is rational and moves in a positive direction when there is a growth-producing climate. He described the constructive directions taken by clients in therapy as they become freer through learning about themselves. Rogers (1983) contended that the qualities of behavior that emerge from this process not only enhance the individual's development but also enhance others in the community and contribute to the survival and evolution of the species. What follows are the value directions that Rogers (1983) believed would be chosen by people if they were genuinely free to choose:

- People tend to move away from pretenses and defensiveness.
- They tend to move away from "oughts" and from imperatives imposed on them by others.
- They tend to move away from pleasing others as a primary goal.
- They value being themselves, rather than being what others want and expect them to be.
- They discover an increasing sense of confidence in being able to make choices for themselves and in guiding their own life.
- They value their feelings, and they accept their reactions as having worth.
- They value the process of becoming a person, rather than desiring some fixed goal.
- They value openness and are able to be sensitive to their own inner reactions and feelings, the reactions and feelings of others, and the realities of the objective world.
- They are able to accept and appreciate others for what they are.
- They value real and intimate relationships, whereby meaningful communication with others is possible.

On the basis of his many years of experience in helping, Rogers (1983, p. 266) concluded:

> I dare to believe that when the human being is inwardly free to choose whatever she deeply values, she tends to value those objects, experiences, and goals which contribute to her own survival, growth, and development, and to the survival and development of others. I hypothesize that it is characteristic of the human organism to prefer such actualizing and socialized goals when she is exposed to a growth-promoting climate.

This person-centered view has implications for the helping relationship. Rogers trusted individuals to discover what is right for themselves, and he trusted in their capacity to direct their own life. He viewed the helper as a facilitator. This role of helpers is rooted in their ways of being and attitudes, not in techniques and strategies designed to get the client to "do something." From the person-centered perspective, the helper's function is to create a climate in which the individuals being helped will feel free to openly examine all of their feelings, thoughts, and behaviors. This is done if helpers are willing to be "real" in the helping relationship, which allows clients the necessary freedom to explore areas of their life that are being either denied to awareness or distorted. It is not the helper's job to do the choosing for the client but, rather, to encourage the client to assume the responsibility and joy that comes with choosing for oneself.

This relatively brief section merely summarizes three major perspectives of human behavior and their implications for the helping process. Surely you will study these approaches in other classes. If your knowledge of these perspectives is limited, you can consult sources such as Nye (1986),

Schultz (1986), and Corey (1986b) as a way to increase your understanding of these mainstream views in the helping field. As you read and study more about these theoretical orientations, think about ways to incorporate concepts and procedures from each of them into your own personal perspective of the helping relationship.

Overview of the Helping Relationship

This section is designed to help you determine your assets and liabilities as a potential helper. We use the overall framework of Egan's (1986) helping model by describing the stages in the helping process and the major tasks facing helpers at each of these stages. We also draw from the systematic skills-training approach of Brammer (1988), Carkhuff (1983), and Ivey (1988). The skills-development model offers a general framework of the phases of the helping process and is not linked to any particular theoretical approach. You can apply any of the current theories of counseling (Corey, 1986b) to this model of helping.

Our focus is on the knowledge, skills, beliefs, and personal characteristics that are required for being an effective helper. We provide a framework that will help you assess your ability to engage others in a helping relationship. The human-relations skills we describe are crucial for all helpers.

The Stages of Helping

According to many writers of textbooks on a systematic approach to helping skills, there are three major stages in the helping process, each with particular tasks to be accomplished. In the initial stage the central task is to help clients identify and clarify those aspects of their life that are not working for them. This task may include identifying problem situations or missed opportunities for full development. Typically, people become clients when they recognize that they need outside help in understanding and coping with problems. In the second stage the helper and the client cooperatively establish goals by determining the specific changes desired. If clients hope to make actual changes, they have to be willing to go beyond talking and planning; they must carry out their plans by translating them into action. Therefore, the third stage of helping deals with the process of identifying strategies for action, choosing which combination of strategies will best meet the client's goals, and putting these plans into a realistic action program.

At each of these stages the focus is on *you as a helper.* Assess your own qualities to determine your interest and ability in helping others. Realize that the helping relationship is not a mechanical process but a deeply personal human endeavor. As a helper you will be actively involved with those you are helping by drawing on what you know, by applying skills and interventions in a timely and appropriate manner, and by using yourself as a person in creating meaningful relationships with clients or others you help. This is true whether you are involved in the counseling or the administrative aspects of the human services. If you are unable to apply some basic human-relations skills, the chances are slim that you will be able to create and maintain adequate rapport with those whom you are supposed to be helping. Although the focus of our discussion is on these skills as they apply to counseling relationships, you can still find ways of applying them to a variety of other interpersonal situations.

There are a number of ways in which you can be fully available for others in this helping relationship. You can be present with your clients as they share their experiences and problem situations. You can help them identify and overcome their own distortions. By reconceptualizing a particular problem, you can help them acquire a new perspective that will lead to action. You can help clients who see very few options to develop a variety of alternatives in coping with a given problem. You can help them distinguish between what they can do and what might be difficult for them to do, and you can challenge them to stretch their boundaries. You can encourage them to make choices for themselves and to develop the courage to accept responsibility for their decisions. By providing them with support and challenge, you can help them change.

Stage 1: Identifying Clients' Problems

At the first stage of the helping process the main task is to assist clients in defining and clarifying their problems. Helpers are expected to create a relationship in which clients can reveal their story, focus more clearly on what they want to change, and attain a new perspective in dealing with their problems.

Of course, not all of your clients will come to you voluntarily. Involuntary clients will surely have some resistance to seeking help, and they may not even believe that you can help them. A good place to begin with them is to ascertain why they are seeing you and what they expect from this relationship. Even though they were ordered to seek professional help, they did make a choice to come to you, and nobody is actually forcing them to see you. Dealing with their resistance, rather than skirting around it, is one of the best ways to begin with the reluctant client.

Establishing the relationship. If clients are to feel the freedom to talk about their problems, helpers need to provide attention, active listening, and empathy. Clients must sense your respect for them, which you can demonstrate by your attitudes and behaviors. You reveal an attitude of respect for your clients when you are concerned about their best interests, view them as able to exercise control of their own destiny, and treat them as individuals rather than stereotyping them. You actually show clients that you respect them through your behavior, such as actively listening to and understanding them, suspending critical judgment, expressing appropriate warmth and acceptance, communicating to them that you understand their world as they experience it, providing a combination of support and challenge, assisting them in cultivating their inner resources for change, and helping them take the specific steps needed to bring change about.

In addition to demonstrating respect, you help clients tell their story through your own genuineness. Being genuine does not mean acting on any impulse or saying everything that you think or feel. You can be genuine with your clients when you avoid hiding yourself in a professional role; are open and nondefensive, even if you feel threatened; are willing to share yourself and your experiences with clients; and show a consistency between what you are thinking, feeling, and valuing and what you reveal through your words and actions.

Ask yourself how well you are able to pay attention to others, to fully listen to them, and to empathize with their situation. Assess the qualities you possess that will either help or hinder you in doing what is needed to assume the client's internal and subjective frame of reference. Consider these questions:

- Are you able to attend to what clients are telling you both verbally and nonverbally?
- Do you let others tell their story, or do you get impatient and want to talk too soon? Do you encourage clients to tell stories in great detail for the sake of your curiosity? Do you have a tendency to get lost in the details of their story and miss the essence of their struggle?
- Are you able to set aside your own biases for a time and attempt to enter the client's world? For example, if you consider yourself a liberated woman, are you willing to accept the client who tells you that she is satisfied in her traditional role as a housewife?
- As your client speaks, are you able to listen to and detect the core messages?
- Are you able to keep your clients focused on issues they want to explore?
- Are you able to communicate your understanding and acceptance to your clients, and do they feel this understanding and acceptance?
- Are you able to work nondefensively with signs of resistance from your clients? Can you use this resistance as a way of assisting them to more deeply explore their issues?

Although it may seem deceptively simple to merely listen to others, the attempt to understand the world as others see it is demanding. Being respectful, genuine, and empathic are best considered as a "way of being," not as mechanical techniques to be used on clients. Consider just a few ways in which you might interfere with allowing clients to express themselves. You could strive too hard to be real and thus, in the process, actually be nongenuine. For example, you may want to prove to clients that you are a real person and that you struggle with your own problems. To demonstrate your "realness" you may take the focus away from your client and put it on yourself by telling detailed stories about your life experiences. Although you may feel better, are your clients getting what they need from the relationship?

Establishing a working relationship with clients implies that you are genuine and respectful in behavioral ways, that the relationship is a two-way process, and that the client's interests are supreme. This means that you avoid doing for clients what they are capable of doing for themselves. For example, assume that an adolescent client tells you that he wants more time with his father, yet he feels intimidated and shy around him. He is afraid to approach his father. You show respect for this adolescent client when you encourage him to risk approaching his father and teach him ways of taking this initiative. You demonstrate a lack of trust in his ability if you take it upon yourself to talk to the father, even if your client has asked you to intervene.

Part of creating a working relationship means that you can recognize the signs of resistance, both in your client and yourself. It is important to understand the many meanings of client resistance and not to interpret it as a sign of your failure as a helper. If you are focused on defending yourself against the various forms of resistance you will encounter with clients, you deprive them of opportunities to explore the meanings of their resistance.

One way of not reacting defensively to a client's resistance and of exploring its meaning is illustrated by the following example. You are seeing an involuntary client for the first time. She is extremely hostile and lets you know that she neither needs nor wants your help. She attacks your abilities as a counselor. As an effective helper you cannot indulge yourself in feelings of rejection. However, in a nondefensive way you can explore with this client her unwillingness and her difficulty in seeing you. If you are patient, you may discover that this client has some very good reasons not to trust a professional like you. She may have felt betrayed by a counselor, and she may fear that the information that she gives you will be used against her one more time.

Helping clients gain a focus.   Some people who come for help feel overwhelmed with a number of problems, and by trying to talk about everything that is troubling them in one session, they also manage to overwhelm the helper. A focusing process is necessary to provide a direction for the helping efforts, enabling both the client and the helper to know where to start. To achieve this focus, make an assessment of the major concerns of the client. You could say to a client who presents you with a long list of problems: "We won't be able to deal with all your problems in one session. What was going on in your life when you finally decided to call for help?" Other focusing questions are "At this time in your life, what seems most pressing and troublesome to you?" "You say that you often wake up in the middle of the night. What do you find yourself ruminating over?" "When you don't want to get up in the morning, what is it that you most want to avoid?" "If you could address only one problem today, which one would you pick?"

Once clients determine what concerns they are seriously willing to explore, a contract can be designed with the helper. As a helper you can be instrumental in encouraging clients to explore their key issues in terms of their experiences, feelings, and behaviors. By focusing on what is salient in the present and by avoiding dwelling on the past, you can assist clients in clarifying their own problems and opportunities for change.

Confronting clients.   Confrontation is a practice that is often misunderstood. It should not be viewed as aggressive or as destructive of a supportive relationship. Confrontation can be done in a caring and responsible way. Without it, clients often remain stuck in self-defeating behavior, and they do not develop the new perspectives and new skills needed to make changes. Confrontation focuses on discrepancies, distortions, games, excuses, resistances, and evasions of clients that keep them stuck in their problem situation.

Confronting clients effectively entails focusing on their awareness of what they are feeling, thinking, and doing. If the confrontation is successful, clients are able to overcome blind spots and develop new perspectives on their life situation, and they are also influenced to make changes based on this self-understanding. Thus, confronting aims at enabling clients to participate actively and fully in the process of helping themselves. Ideally, they will learn the art of self-confrontation.

Here are a few suggestions for making your confronting effective. First of all, earn the right to confront. Challenge clients only if you feel an investment in them and if you have the time and effort to continue building the relationship with them. Your confrontation is much more likely to be accepted if you have earned "trust points" with your clients. If you have not established a good working relationship, your confrontation is likely to be received in a defensive manner. The degree to which you can confront your clients depends on how much they trust and like you and how much you trust and like them.

Be willing to be confronted yourself. If you model a nondefensive stance in the counseling relationship, your clients will be much more willing to consider what you tell them. It is also useful to present your confrontations in a tentative manner, as opposed to issuing a dogmatic decree. Confronting is your chance not to "put down" clients but to inspire them to look at what they most want to change in themselves and what seems to be blocking this change.

Confrontation is not intended to rip away the defenses of clients; rather, it invites them to challenge their defensive ways and keep moving toward more effective behavior. Here is an example of a confrontation that would be certain to arouse a client's defensiveness and evoke resistance: "I'm very tired of hearing you complain every week about how horrible your life is. You're a whiner and a martyr, and I don't know if you'll ever change."

A confrontation that could lead to a more productive exploration of the client's difficulties is as follows: "You have said time and again that most of all you want to be successful, feel good about yourself, and feel proud of your accomplishments. Yet everything you do and say sets you up to fail and to get what you say you don't want. You have done this for a long time, and you tell me that not feeling good is very familiar to you. Your father has never given you his approval, and around him you feel dumb and insignificant. Let's talk about the possibility that your chronic failures have something to do with your relationship with your father."

Likewise, in a marital counseling session it would be unhelpful to tell a husband to "shut up and listen to what she has to say!" This confrontation might shut him up for good. It would be more helpful to describe what you saw going on between the two of them:

"You say you want your wife to tell you how she feels about you. Every time she has tried this in the last ten minutes, you have interrupted her and told her all the reasons why she shouldn't feel the way she does. Would you be willing for the next few minutes to let her talk and not think about what you're going to say in return? When she's finished, I'd like you to tell her how you're affected by what she has said."

Some clients may be talented at inventing excuses for the way they are. You can confront them to accept responsibility for what they are doing rather than inventing excuses for what they are not doing. At times clients can be helped if you are willing to confront their self-defeating beliefs and behaviors. Some clients insist on seeing themselves as victims, for example, and thus they spend much of their time wanting to blame outside forces for the misery they experience. With effective confrontation you can assist them in redirecting the focus from others to themselves. Other clients might operate on the assumption that they must have universal approval. Again, your challenge of their belief system can be instrumental in helping them see where they picked up such a belief and whether it is now serving them well.

You can also challenge clients on the strengths they possess but are not fully using, rather than limiting your confrontation to their weaknesses. It helps to be specific as you confront clients, which can be done by avoiding sweeping judgments and focusing on concrete behaviors. You can describe to clients what you see them doing and how their behavior affects you. It is also useful to encourage a dialogue with clients, and your sensitivity to their responses is a key factor in determining the degree to which they will accept your confrontations.

Here is an example of a helper's challenge to a client who is not making the best use of her strengths: "For several weeks now you've made detailed plans to reach out to a friend. You seem able to be assertive, you say that when you do reach out to people they usually like you, and you have no reason to fear that this friend will reject you. Yet you have not made contact with this friend, and you have many excuses for not doing so. Let's explore the possibility that you don't want to make this contact. What is stopping you from using your assertive skills?"

Ask yourself if you're willing to confront others. Some people are timid and apologetic when it comes to confronting. Some helpers provide plenty of unconditional positive regard and positive support but are reluctant to confront clients. If you find that you have a hard time confronting others, it is important to understand what makes it difficult for you. It could be that you very much want to be liked and approved of by your clients. If you confront them, you may fear that they will think poorly of you. Even though confronting might not be easy for you, it is a skill that you will need to acquire if you hope to move clients beyond a mere "talking-about" phase of their counseling.

Using self-disclosure appropriately. Sharing yourself can be a powerful intervention in making contact with clients. We are not encouraging an indiscriminate sharing of your personal problems with your clients. But it can be therapeutic to talk about yourself if doing so is for the benefit of the clients. Does your disclosure help them talk more honestly and specifically about themselves? Does it help them put their problems into a new perspective? Does it help them consider new alternatives for action? Does it help them translate their insights into new behavior?

Some helpers use self-disclosure inappropriately as a way of unburdening themselves. In the process they burden the client, and the client doesn't know what to do with this information. To us, self-disclosure does not mean telling clients detailed stories about your personal past or present problems. At times clients may evoke feelings in you that connect their struggles with your problems. If your feelings are very much in the foreground and inhibit you from fully attending to a client, it may be helpful for you and your client if you share how you are being affected. Depending on your relationship with the client, you might give some detail about your own situation, or you might simply reveal that what the client is struggling with touches you personally.

Perhaps the most important type of self-disclosure is that which focuses on the relationship between you and your client. If you are having a difficult time listening to a client, for example, it could be useful to share this information. However, it helps to describe your own feelings and reactions and not to judge a client. You might say: "I've noticed at times that it's very difficult for me to stay tuned in to what you're telling me. I'm able to be with you when you talk about yourself and your own feelings, but I tend to wander away as you go into great detail about all the things that your daughter is doing or not doing." In this statement the client is not being labeled or judged, but the helper is giving his reactions about what he hears when his client tells stories about others. An example of an unhelpful response would be "You're boring me!" This response is a judgment of the client, and the helper assumes no responsibility for his own part in his boredom.

How willing are you to engage in appropriate and relevant self-disclosure? Do you find it difficult to talk about yourself and what you are feeling? Admittedly, you are vulnerable when you share your own experiences, feelings, and reactions. Yet can you expect your clients to be willing to be vulnerable in front of you if you rarely show them anything of yourself? We want to stress again that we are not encouraging you to share detailed stories of your past, merely to demonstrate that you are human. Inappropriate sharing of yourself can easily distract the client from productive self-exploration. The kind of sharing that can be used by clients is letting them know how you are perceiving and experiencing them. You are bound to have many reactions to your clients in the therapeutic relationship. Selectively discussing some of these reactions can help the clients, especially if you encourage them to discuss the feedback you give them.

Some helpers seem to have an inordinate need to talk about themselves. In fact, one of their motivations for choosing a helping profession, conscious or unconscious, could be their need to address their own problems through the problems of others. They may make the mistake of pulling the focus away from the clients and directing it to their own concerns. Examine the impact that your disclosures have on others, and develop an honesty about your own motivations and behavior. If you are distracting your clients from exploring their issues, this is the time that you could benefit from your own therapy. In your therapy sessions you can put the focus on yourself and work on your concerns.

Stage 2: Helping Clients Create Goals

Egan (1986) believes that many helpers make the mistake of dwelling too long on helping clients identify, explore, and clarify their problems. Helpers who direct too much effort at the initial stage of helping may promote insights, yet they often do not succeed in getting their clients to translate these insights into new goals in life.

During the second stage the aim is to help clients devise alternative approaches to dealing with their problems. This is done by guiding clients in a brainstorming process to create perspectives that are in line with their values. Clients help in setting specific goals, which can lead to action. It is important that these goals be measurable, be realistic in terms of the resources of clients, be chosen by the clients, and be achievable in a realistic time period.

A case example.   Brian, a young worker, comes to you because he wants help in pursuing his goal of getting into college. He has put off applying to colleges for several years, and the thought of actually being accepted scares him. His job dissatisfaction is so great that it has begun to affect his personal life. In his work with you Brian discovers that he has accepted some early messages from his parents. They communicated to him that he was ignorant and would never amount to anything, and they attributed his early difficulties in school to laziness. Test results have shown that Brian was performing far below his intellectual abilities. Brian's insight that he unconditionally accepted these early messages has been important. He realizes now that he must acquire better reading and writing skills before he can successfully compete in college. As a helper, you could make a mistake by focusing mainly on Brian's feelings about his parents and himself and by endlessly exploring the reasons why he feels inadequate. At this stage Brian is aware of what has stopped him so far in accomplishing his goals. He knows specifically what he needs to do to make a change in his life. Now he has clarified a new set of goals, and his task is to identify the specific steps to take in accomplishing his goals.

A different problem that some helpers have is being too impatient and setting out too quickly to solve clients' problems. The need of helpers to solve problems for others could easily block them from hearing what clients want to communicate to them. A common mistake we observe with trainees is their tendency to want to short-circuit the exploration of feelings of clients and too readily provide them with a solution to their presenting problem. This problem-solving focus aborts the struggle of clients in expressing and dealing with feelings and thoughts and eventually coming up with alternatives that are best for them. You need to help clients understand why it is important for them to express feelings that they have bottled up for years. You need to teach them the value of searching for their own solutions.

Again, if you are too intent on providing cures for every problem, it is likely that you are focused on your own needs for being a competent helper who wants to see results. You may be uncomfortable with the client's struggle, and you may push for resolution long before client exploration has even begun. If you were the helper in the case of Brian, you would have spent no time listening and exploring his deep feelings of inadequacy. You would not have assisted him in examining what has kept him time and again from succeeding academically. With your problem-solving orientation, you would have urged him to apply prematurely for college. If Brian had not had enough opportunity to express and explore his fears and self-doubts, and if he had not acquired any insight into his own part in setting himself up to fail, he would not be likely to succeed in college.

Stage 3: Encouraging Clients to Take Action

Once the goals of the helper/client relationship have been identified, it becomes necessary to decide on the various avenues by which these goals can be accomplished. Knowing *what* you want to change is the first step, and knowing *how* to bring about this change is the next step. Clients first of all are assisted in developing and assessing action strategies for making their vision a reality. As Carkhuff (1983) stresses, people need to develop step-by-step procedures leading to their goals. After an action program is formulated, the steps need to be carried out and then evaluated. What follows is a description of the major tasks of this stage of the helping process.

Identifying and assessing action strategies. Clients often do not accomplish their goals because they rush into a single strategy that comes to mind or set these goals unrealistically high. One function of helping at this stage is to assist clients in thinking of many possible routes to achieving their goals. Together helpers and clients can come up with a wide range of alternatives for coping with problems, and together they can assess how practical these strategies are and decide on the best plans for action. Clients are helped to recognize the skills they need in order to put their goals into action. If they don't have certain skills, they can acquire them during the helping sessions or can learn about resources that are available to them.

Referring back to the case of Brian, assume that he tells you that he intends to sign up for 16 units at a nearby college. It would be appropriate for you to challenge him on how realistic his plans are. Is he taking on too much and thus setting himself up to fail one more time? You could guide him in creating a more realistic plan and assessing it. Because you know that Brian lacks fundamental skills, you could explore with him some ways to acquire these needed skills: tutoring, remedial classes, or adult-education programs. You could also discuss taking fewer units and less-demanding classes, as a way of increasing his chances for success.

At this stage of helping the focus is on asking clients to come up with clear plans of what they will do today, tomorrow, and the next day to bring about change and on what might get in the way of their plans. In choosing action strategies, clients consider their internal and external resources and limitations and then determine which strategies are best suited to their capabilities. Helpers work with them to ensure that these strategies are specific and realistic, are related to the client's goals, and are consistent with the client's value system.

Part of the helping process involves a discussion of the main costs and benefits of each strategy as well as a discussion of the possible risks involved and the chances for success. During this phase it is the helper's task to work with clients in constructively dealing with any resistance they might have to formulating plans or carrying them out. Helpers also caution clients about plans that are too ambitious or unrealistic. Helpers and clients work together to devise and implement many practical alternatives to coping with life situations.

Carrying out an action program. Clients are encouraged to see the value in becoming active in trying new behavior, rather than being passive and leaving action to chance. One way of fostering an active stance on the part of clients is to formulate clear contracts. In this way clients are continually confronted with what they want and what they are willing to do. Contracts are also a useful frame of reference for evaluating the outcomes of helping. Discussion can be focused on how well the contracts are being met and what modifications of the contract are in order.

If certain plans don't work out well, this is a topic for exploration for a subsequent session. For example, if a mother does not follow through with her plan to deal with her unruly son who attracts a lot of attention by getting in trouble in school, the counselor can explore with the mother what got in her way of carrying out those plans that she had devised in her counseling sessions. Contingency plans are also developed. The counselor might role-play different ways the mother could deal with setbacks or with her son's lack of cooperation. Clients learn how to deal with setbacks and how to predict possible roadblocks to their progress. Consider Brian's situation again. After signing up for some skill-building classes, he tells you that he feels overwhelmed in his classes, is very discouraged, and wants to quit. You can explore with him ways in which he could stick to his plan and how he could overcome his self-doubts.

Developing Helping Skills Takes Time

People are not "naturally born" helpers. Instead, helping skills are learned, practiced, and refined. As you consider what is involved in the overall process of encountering and helping clients, you might feel somewhat overwhelmed by all that needs to be done. Just as you may have felt lost when you were learning how to drive a car, how to ski, or how to play the violin, you may be intimidated by all of the variables you are expected to pay attention to, both in your clients and in yourself. You could make the mistake of being so focused on anything that your clients say and do that you forget to pay attention to your reactions as you are sitting with them. By trying too hard to catch every gesture and to understand every sentence, you can easily distract yourself from being present with clients. One supervisor gave a student sound advice when she said "If you miss something with a client, the person will no doubt bring it up again later."

On the other hand, you could be so acutely aware of yourself that you largely forget about your client. If you are so attuned to thinking about what you should do next, about saying the "right" thing, about being sure that you are "helpful," and about making sure that you are seeing results, you are bound to miss some of what a client is telling you. By being overly self-conscious and uncertain about your adequacy as a helper, you are missing making contact with your clients.

We want to offer some assurance that you don't have to be able to focus on all aspects of the helping process at one time and that you can learn these helping skills with practice and supervised feedback. We see the learning of helping skills as an ongoing process, rather than a state that is achieved once and for all.

By Way of Review

- Effective helpers can be differentiated from ineffective helpers, in part, by their belief systems. Effective helpers hold positive beliefs about people; have a healthy self-concept; ground their interventions in values; and possess traits such as empathy, congruence, warmth, compassion, genuineness, and unconditional positive regard.
- Examine your assumptions to determine whether they are helpful for clients. Clarify and challenge your beliefs and make them your own through this process of self-examination.
- In clarifying your orientation to helping, useful questions to ponder are "Who is responsible for change? What best facilitates change? Is insight necessary for change to occur? How useful are confrontation and support? What are the values of a focus on the past, the present, and the future? What is the nature of human nature, and what are the implications for practice?"
- Three perspectives on the helping process are the psychoanalytic, behavioristic, and humanistic approaches. These perspectives differ in the answers they provide to basic questions such as "What is the core of human nature? What are the inherent qualities of human beings? What are the causes of human suffering, and what are the best ways of helping people with problems? What is the most effective way to study human behavior?

- The psychoanalytic view of human nature is deterministic. People are seen as being largely determined by irrational forces, unconscious motivations, biological and instinctual drives, and certain critical events during the first six years of life. Helpers with a psychoanalytic orientation are interested in major personality change, which usually involves a long-term therapeutic process.
- The behavioristic approach stresses that humans are largely influenced by their sociocultural conditioning. However, contemporary behavioristic approaches also account for the reality that people are both the producer and the product of their environment. The helping process is characterized by concepts and procedures that are stated explicitly, tested empirically, and revised continually.
- Carl Rogers's humanistic perspective holds that human nature is basically trustworthy, a view that has implications for the role of the helper. In person-centered therapy, helpers create a climate whereby clients find the resources within themselves to help themselves.
- There are three stages in the helping process. Stage 1 consists of helping clients identify and clarify their problems. Stage 2 consists of helping clients create goals. Stage 3 involves encouraging clients to take action. Specific helper strategies are required at each of these stages. Developing these skills takes time and supervised practice. Your own life experiences play a vital role in your ability to be present and to be effective in working with clients.

What Will You Do Now?

1. Identify a few of your key beliefs and assumptions that stand out for you after you've read this chapter. As a way of examining how you acquired these beliefs and assumptions, talk with someone you know who tends to hold similar beliefs. Then seek out somebody with a different perspective. With both of these people, discuss how you developed your beliefs.

2. Review the section "Overview of the Helping Relationship," and consider the skills needed for effective helping. Select what you consider to be your one major asset and your one major limitation, and write them down. How do you see your main asset enabling you to be an effective helper? How might your main limitation get in the way of working successfully with others? What can you do to work on your weak area? You might ask someone you know well to review your statements about yourself. Do they see you as you see yourself?

3. After reflecting on the section "Your Orientation to Helping," write no more than a one-page response that describes your personal view of what helping is about. You might imagine that a supervisor had asked you to describe your views about counseling or that in a job interview you had been asked "Tell us briefly how you see the helping process." You could also

imagine that someone who is not sophisticated in your field had said to you: "Oh, you're a counselor. What do you do?"

Suggested Readings

Brammer, L. M. (1988). *The helping relationship: Process and skills* (4th ed.). Englewood Cliffs, NJ: Prentice-Hall. This book presents basic helping skills and attitudes in a clear way. The author discusses a repertoire of basic helping skills and attitudes, a wide variety of settings in which helping skills are applied, and a framework for viewing helping functions. Emphasis is given to crisis situations and prevention programs.

Carkhuff, R. R. (1983). *The art of helping* (5th ed.). Amherst, MA: Human Resource Development Press. This is a systematic approach to the helping relationship that focuses on specific skills that enable clients to grow. These skills include attending, responding, personalizing, and initiating.

Cormier, L. S., & Hackney, H. (1987). *The professional counselor: A process guide to helping.* Englewood Cliffs, NJ: Prentice-Hall. This is a readable book that describes the stages and skills of counseling. Chapters are devoted to rapport and relationships, assessing client problems, developing counseling goals, selecting counseling strategies and interventions, and special problems in counseling.

Egan, G. (1986). *The skilled helper: A systematic approach to effective helping* (3rd ed.). Pacific Grove, CA: Brooks/Cole. This is perhaps one of the best texts providing an overview of the skills used in the helping relationship. Egan gives many examples of basic communication skills needed for effective helping from the initial session to the termination of the helping process. His specific examples and illustrations clarify the tasks at each of the three stages of the helping process.

Hackney, H., & Cormier, L. S. (1988). *Counseling strategies and interventions* (3rd ed.). Englewood Cliffs, NJ: Prentice-Hall. This edition includes a new chapter on the process of clinical supervision and how beginning counselors can use it to refine their skills. It contains separate chapters on strategies for dealing with the cognitive, affective, and behavioral aspects of client problems. The focus is on assessing the counselor's and the client's influence in the helping process.

Ivey, A. E. (1988). *Intentional interviewing and counseling* (2nd ed.). Pacific Grove, CA: Brooks/Cole. This is a readable work that describes a systematic approach to skill acquisition, developed by Ivey and his associates, known as microcounseling. Chapters deal with skills needed for attending, questioning, facilitating, focusing, confronting, structuring, and influencing in the helping process. The author discusses ways of integrating these various helping skills.

Nye, R. D. (1986). *Three psychologies: Perspectives from Freud, Skinner, and Rogers* (3rd ed.). Pacific Grove, CA: Brooks/Cole. In a simple and straightforward manner, the author presents the basic ideas of Freud's psychoanalysis, Skinner's behaviorism, and Rogers's humanistic approach. The chapter on comparisons, contrasts, and criticisms is particularly useful in understanding the differences among these perspectives. This is a good source for reviewing these divergent theoretical outlooks.

Values and the Helping Relationship

Focus of the Chapter

This chapter is designed to help you clarify your values and think about how they will influence your work as a helper. Toward this end we explore how values operate in the helping relationship and process. The focus is on the critical distinction between making your values known to your clients and indoctrinating them with a particular ethical code or philosophy of life. To assist you in clarifying your values and identifying ways in which they might interfere with effective helping, we describe practical situations that you are likely to find yourself perplexed about.

Conflicts between clients and helpers often surface in situations involving gay and lesbian life-styles, family values, sex-role behaviors, religious values, the issue of abortion, and sexual values. Since cultural values are such an integral part of the helping process, we give special attention to the problems of helping multicultural client populations.

The Role of Values in Helping

We suggest that you take this self-inventory as a way of focusing your thinking on the role your values will play in your work as a helper. As you read the following statements, decide the degree to which each one most closely identifies your attitudes and beliefs pertaining to *your role as a helper.* Use this code: 3 = this statement is true for me; 2 = this statement is not true for me; 1 = I am undecided.

___ 1. I see it as my job to challenge a clients' philosophy of life.

___ 2. I could work objectively and effectively with clients who had values that differed sharply from my own.

___ 3. I see it as both possible and desirable for me to remain neutral with respect to values in working with clients.

___ 4. Although I have a clear set of values for myself, I feel quite certain that I could avoid pushing my values and unduly influencing my clients to adopt my beliefs.

___ 5. I think it is appropriate for me to express my views and expose my values, so long as I don't impose them on clients.

___ 6. I might be inclined to subtly influence my clients to consider my values.

___ 7. If I discovered sharp value conflicts between a client and myself, I would refer the person.

___ 8. I have certain religious views that I think would influence the way I work.

___ 9. I don't see that I would have any difficulty in counseling a pregnant adolescent who wanted to explore abortion as one of her alternatives.

___ 10. I have certain views pertaining to gender roles that might affect the way I counsel.

___ 11. I would not have problems in counseling a gay couple.

___ 12. I see the clarification of values as the central task of the helping process.

___ 13. My view of family life would influence the way I'd counsel a couple considering divorce.

___ 14. I would have no trouble in working with a woman (man) who wanted to leave her (his) children and live alone, if this is what my client decided for herself (himself).

___ 15. I have generally been willing to challenge my values, and I think they are largely ones that I have chosen for myself.

___ 16. I would have no trouble in working in individual counseling with a married client who was having an affair, even if the client was not willing to disclose the relationship to his or her spouse.

___ 17. I feel quite certain that my values will never become a problem in terms of my capacity to remain objective.

___ 18. I think I will work best with clients who have values that are similar to mine.

___ 19. I would have no trouble in working with clients who were culturally different from me.

___ 20. I would be very willing to share my specific values on a given issue at any time that my client asked me to do so.

There are no "right" or "wrong" answers to the above statements. The inventory is designed mainly to focus you on thinking about how your values are likely to influence the way you carry out your functions as a helper. You might take some specific items that catch your attention and talk with a fellow student about your views. As you read the rest of the chapter, assume an active stance and think about your position on the value issues we raise. A basic question is whether it is possible for helpers to keep their values out of their work.

Exposing Values versus Imposing Them

Benjamin (1987) asserts that clients ultimately have the responsibility of choosing in which direction they will go, what values to adopt, and what values to modify or discard. Through their encounters with helpers, they can learn to examine values before making choices. Benjamin contends that helpers can become resource persons if they do not conceal their values from clients or try to impose their values on them.

Patterson (in press) asserts that it is not the role of counselors to impose their values on clients. The following are some of his key arguments against indoctrinating clients or attempting to inculcate a value system or a philosophy of life in them:

• Although people do share in some universally accepted values, each individual is unique. Therefore, each person's philosophy of life is unique.

- It is the individual's responsibility to develop this philosophy of life from many sources.
- It is unrealistic to expect that all counselors will have a fully developed and ideal philosophy of life ready to be impressed on clients.
- It is doubtful that the helping relationship is the appropriate place for instruction in ethics and a philosophy of life.
- Individuals typically do not adopt a system or code of ethics from one source at a particular time.

Patterson does not think that counselors should refuse to discuss values and ethics. He believes that it is appropriate for them to make their values known when a client requests it, when they determine that it is necessary or desirable that a client be aware of these values, or when they judge that the therapeutic relationship or process will be improved by explicitly acknowledging their values.

Our Perspective on Values in the Helping Relationship

We agree with Patterson's views on the role of values. From our perspective it is neither possible nor desirable for helpers to remain neutral or to keep their values separate from their professional relationships. Although we don't see it as therapeutic or ethical to push values on clients, it is essential that helpers be clear about their values and understand how values influence their work and the direction taken by their clients. Since values have a significant impact on the helping process, it is important to openly express them when it is appropriate in the helping situation.

There are certainly those who do not agree with our position about the role of values in the helping relationship. On one extreme are those who see helping as very much a process of social influence. Some counselors, for example, have definite and absolute value systems, and they believe it is their proper function to influence their clients to adopt this view of the world. At the other extreme are helpers who are so concerned about unduly influencing their clients that they remain scrupulously neutral. Out of fear that their views might contaminate the client's decision, these helpers make it a practice not to expose their values.

Our position is that the helping relationship is not designed to indoctrinate clients or push them to adopt the frame of reference of the helper. Nor do we think that it is the helper's job to teach their clients the right way to live.

Are Your Values Showing?

As a beginning helper, you may have a tendency to push your values. If you are strongly opposed to abortion, for example, you may not even consider that your client has a right to believe differently. On the basis of such convictions, you may subtly (or not so subtly) direct your client toward choices other than abortion. We see your job as helping your client clarify her values, struggling with what is best for her and for others in her situation, and assisting her in making the best choice. It is unfortunate that some well-intentioned helpers think that their job is to help people conform to acceptable absolute standards or to straighten out their clients.

Regardless of how devoted you are to maintaining objectivity as a helper, we think that you will reveal many of your beliefs through your nonverbal language, by the things you say or don't say, by your reactions to what clients tell you, and by what you choose to focus on in a session. Your clients will learn how to "read" you in terms of your frowns, postural changes, and silences. The thoughts, feelings, and behaviors of your clients that you reinforce will give them important clues to what you think about them. If you adopt a helping style of concealing your values and reactions, you are likely to function in mechanical and routine ways. Your clients will probably demand more involvement from you, and they will want to know what your positions are on certain issues so that they can compare their thinking with your views.

Our own practice is to tell clients of some of our values that are likely to affect their work with us. To give you an idea of what we mean, we usually tell them about our bias and orientation. For example, we think that the examined life is better than the unexamined life. We operate on the assumption that people are not victims and that with awareness and hard work they can make substantial changes in their life.

Our bias is that pain is frequently a useful source to explore. If clients identify painful experiences and are willing to express them, the chances are that they will be led to significant unfinished business, which is fertile material for exploration. One of the values that we promote is self-determination, or choosing for oneself and accepting the responsibility for these choices. Although some individuals would like others to choose for them, we operate on the assumption that therapy is aimed at assisting people to find their own best decisions. These are but a few examples of the values that we are open about. Furthermore, if we have a difficult time with clients because it seems to us that they are behaving in ways that are inconsistent with their values, we confront them on this discrepancy.

Exposing your values can be very useful. This is especially true in situations where you discover that you and your clients have sharp value differences. If you know that you would have a difficult time in working objectively with a client because of such conflicts, ethical practice dictates that you not accept the person as a client. If you become aware of value conflicts once the relationship has been established, a referral might be in the best interests of your client. You could discuss the possible difficulties you or your client might have if the professional relationship were not terminated. If your client subscribed to strongly fundamentalist religious values and had a certain vision of how she should live her life as a good person, for example, you might have trouble in accepting her attitudes and choices if you did not embrace her values. You might find that you wanted to continually challenge her values and liberalize her thinking.

As another example, assume that you are seeing a homosexual client who wants to talk about his relationship with his lover and the difficulties they have in communicating with each other. As you are working with him, you become aware that it is difficult for you to accept his sexual orientation. You find yourself challenging him about this, and you are not concentrating on what he says he wants to work on. Instead you are focused on his life-style, which is totally unacceptable to you, for it goes against what you think is morally right. These reactions are so much in the foreground that you and your client recognize that you are not helping him. In such cases the ethical course of action is to refer clients to professionals who are able to work with them more objectively than you can because of your value system.

Value Conflicts with Clients

The recognition that your values cannot be kept out of the helping relation-ship makes it imperative that you be clearly aware of them and of how they should be involved in your work (Patterson, in press). We are not suggesting that you should quickly refer all clients whose value system conflicts with yours. What is essential is that you respect your clients' right to hold a set of values that might differ from yours. Even if you do not endorse their values, you may still be able to work effectively with them if you are able to refrain from pushing your values onto them. As Patterson has noted, counselors need not accept or approve of the client's values. Disagreement with the client's values does not necessarily mean that the counselor does not accept the client as a person. Patterson emphasizes that how the client's values and value problems are dealt with is the central issue in counseling. Before we discuss specific areas of potential value conflicts between coun-selors and clients, we suggest that you consider these questions:

- Am I aware of the most important values that I hold, and am I aware of how my values are likely to operate in the way I work with my clients?
- Is it possible for me to interact with my clients without making value judgments? Do I think it is even desirable to avoid making such judgments?
- Am I able to remain true to my own values and at the same time make allowances for the right of my clients to select their own values, even if they differ from mine?
- Do I have a need to push what I think is right on my friends and my fam-ily? If so, what are the implications for the way I am likely to function as a helper with my clients?
- Am I able to make the distinction between exposing my values and im-posing my values?
- Do I see it as my job to make decisions for clients, or is it my job to help my clients make their own decisions?
- How can I best determine whether a conflict between my values and those of a client dictates that a referral to another professional is in order?
- When I become aware of difficulties in working with clients because of value differences between us, what is the appropriate course of action?

Gay and Lesbian Issues

The situation.   You are doing an intake interview with a gay man, age 33. Art tells you that he is coming to counseling because he often feels very lonely and isolated. He has difficulty in intimate relationships, with men or women. Art's concern is that once people get to know him, they will not accept him and somehow won't like him. During the interview you find out that he has a lot of pain over his father, with whom he has very little contact. He would like a closer relationship with his father, yet his gayness stands in the way of a relationship with him. Art's father has let him know that he feels guilty that he "turned out that way." He just cannot understand why Art is not "normal" and why he can't find a woman and get married like his brother. Art mainly wants to work on his relationship with his father, and he also wants to overcome his fears of rejection with others with whom he'd like a close relationship. He tells you that he has accepted his gayness and would like those he cares about to accept him as he is.

Your stance.   What are your initial reactions to Art's situation? Considering your own values, do you expect that you would have any trouble in establishing a therapeutic relationship with him? In light of the fact that he lets you know that he does not want to change his life-style, would you be able to respect this decision? As you think about how you would proceed with Art, reflect on your own attitudes toward gay men. Consider if you are able to accept possible value differences, including sexual preferences. Think especially if you might be inclined to push any of your values, regardless of your stance. For example, if you have personal difficulty in accepting homosexuality on moral or other grounds, might you encourage Art to give up his ways and become heterosexual? You might focus on a number of issues in your counseling sessions with Art, some of which are his fear of rejection, pain with his father, desire for his father to be different, difficulty in getting close to both men and women, sexual preference, and values. With the information you have, which of these areas are you likely to emphasize? Are there other areas you might want to explore with Art?

Discussion.   Gay and lesbian life-styles tend to evoke much negative reaction, as you are aware from the news media. If you have a conservative value system, this issue can easily present a challenge for you if you work with gay or lesbian clients. Although you may tell yourself and others that you accept the right of others to live their life as they see fit, you might have trouble when you are in an actual encounter with clients who are struggling with personal concerns such as sexual identity, intimate relationships, loneliness, acceptance, rejection, guilt over letting parents down, and self-worth. There could be a gap between what you can intellectually accept and what you can emotionally accept. If you have negative emotional or intellectual reactions to a gay or lesbian life-style, there is a danger that you could impose your own values if you accepted these clients.

If you find that your values are such that you'd have difficulty in counseling gays and lesbians, we certainly don't think that you should apologize for your values, nor should you feel that you would have to accept homosexual clients. If you know your limitations and make an appropriate referral, you are doing both yourself and your potential clients a service in the long run.

As a way of clarifying some of your values pertaining to homosexual life-styles, take the following inventory, using this code: 3 = I agree, in most respects, with this statement; 2 = I am undecided in my opinion about this statement; 1 = I disagree, in most respects, with this statement.

___ 1. Gay and lesbian clients are best served by gay and lesbian counselors.
___ 2. A counselor who is homosexual is likely to push his or her values on a heterosexual client.
___ 3. I would have trouble working with either a gay couple or a lesbian couple who wanted to adopt children, even if they were fit parents.
___ 4. Homosexuality is a form of mental illness.
___ 5. A homosexual person could be as well adjusted as a heterosexual person.
___ 6. Homosexuality is immoral.
___ 7. I would have no difficulty in being objective in counseling gays and lesbians.
___ 8. I have adequate information about referral sources in the local lesbian and gay communities.
___ 9. I feel a need for specialized training and knowledge before I could effectively counsel gays or lesbians.
___ 10. I expect I would have no difficulty in conducting family therapy if the father were gay.

After you finish the inventory, look over your responses and see if you can see any patterns. Compare some of your responses with a survey that assessed psychological practitioners' attitudes, knowledge, concerns, and strategies in counseling lesbians and gay men (Graham, Rawlings, Halpern, & Hermes, 1984). With respect to attitudes toward lesbians and gays, the survey revealed that:

• Eighty-eight percent of the therapists agreed with the position that homosexuality is not a form of mental illness.
• Seventy-seven percent felt that a homosexual person could be as well adjusted as a heterosexual person.
• Seventy-four percent felt that lesbians and gays should be allowed to adopt children if they are fit parents.

With respect to knowledge of homosexual life-styles, the results were:

• Despite seemingly positive attitudes toward homosexuals as a group, the therapists demonstrated only scant knowledge about the subject that was available in scientific literature.

- Therapists' major concerns were about their lack of "objectivity," their lack of information about referrals to local lesbian and gay communities, and the inadequacy of training in counseling these clients. They specifically stated a need for such training.

Family Issues

A situation involving a restless mother.   Veronika has lived a repressed life-style. She got married at 17, had four children by the age of 22, and is now going back to college at 32. She is a good student: excited, eager to learn, and discovering all that she missed. She finds that she is attracted to a younger peer group and to professors. She is now experiencing her second adolescence, and she is getting a lot of affirmation that she did not have before. At home she has been taken for granted, and the members of her family are mostly interested in what she can do for them. At school she is special and is respected for her intellect.

Ultimately, Veronika becomes involved in an affair with a younger man. She is close to a decision to leave her husband and her four children, ages 10 to 15. She comes to see you at the university counseling center. Veronika is in turmoil over what to do, and she wants to find some way to deal with her guilt and ambivalence.

Your stance.   For a moment, consider your own value system. If Veronika were asking for your advice, what would you be inclined to say? What are your thoughts about her leaving her husband? her four children? Would you encourage her to "do her own thing"? Would you support her if she were leaning toward leaving her family? If Veronika were to give this matter considerable thought and then tell you that, as painful as it would be for her own growth and well-being, she needed to leave her family, what would be your stance? Would you be inclined to encourage her to bring her entire family in for some family counseling sessions? What values do you think you might push, if any? If she were to tell you that she was leaning toward staying married and at home, even though she would be resentful, what interventions might you make? If you had been left yourself, either as a child or by a spouse, how might this affect you in working with Veronika?

A situation involving a family in crisis.   A family consisting of wife, husband, and three children comes to your office. The family was referred by the youngest boy's child welfare and attendance officer. The boy, an adolescent, is viewed as the problem person in the family. The husband is in your office reluctantly. He has threatened divorce when things got difficult, but he has not followed through. The father appears angry and resistant, and he lets you know that he doesn't believe in this "therapy stuff." He says he doesn't see that there is much of a problem, either in the marriage or in the family. The mother is fearful and says that she has no way of supporting herself and her three children. She is willing to work on the relationship.

The wife tells you that she and her husband fight a lot, that there is much tension in the home, and that the children are suffering. The child who was referred is acting out by stealing. The husband makes excuses for the boy. As far as he is concerned, if his wife were to stay home more and not run around with friends, there would be no problems in the family.

Your stance. If you were sitting with this family, would you feel some hope because at least they were all in your office? Would the fact that the father had come to the session, though reluctantly, be an indication that he might be willing to work out the difficulties? Or would you feel hopeless with this family? If so, would you counsel the couple to get a divorce? In light of the fact that the children appear to be negatively affected by the couple's problems, would you suggest a separation or divorce? Consider your own values on family stability, on working hard to make a marriage work, on separating when the going gets difficult, and on divorcing and getting on with a new life. Some counselors are likely to say: ''Well, you don't seem to be making it with each other. Your kids are being hurt by your bickering, and neither of you seems very happy in your relationship. I wonder why you would want to stay together and continue hurting each other?'' Another counselor with a different bias might say: ''You know, it's your decision to make whether you will stay together or separate as a couple. I would very much hope that the two of you get clear if you are willing to work at making a go of your marriage. I hope you don't quit too soon, without exploring all the options and the consequences of your decision.''

In light of your values pertaining to the family, what might you say, and what values might you express? Would you expose your own values to this family, even if the members did not ask you? If they were to ask you what you thought of their situation and what you thought they should do, what do you think you would say?

A situation involving an affair. A couple enters your office for marital counseling. The husband has confessed to his wife that he is having an affair. This incident has precipitated the most recent crisis in their relationship. Although the wife is highly distraught, she wants to stay married. She realizes that their marriage needs work and that there is boredom between the two of them, yet she thinks it is worth it to work on their problems. They have children, and the family is well respected and liked in the community.

The husband wants to leave and live with his newfound lover, yet he is struggling with conflicting feelings and is not sure what to do. He is very confused, for he still loves his wife and children, yet he feels that he is in the ''spring of his life'' with the other woman. He is aware that he is going through a midlife crisis and each day he comes up with a different decision. His wife is in a great deal of pain and feels desperate. She has been totally dependent on him, with no means of support.

Your stance. What are your values pertaining to affairs in a marriage? Do you think that an affair is a sign of a betrayal? a troubled marriage? certain problems within the family? growth and change? a midlife crisis? personal conflicts within the person having the affair? something that just happens and can't be helped? What would you want to say to the wife? to the husband? Given your value system, would you counsel them to divorce? to have a trial separation? to work hard on saving the marriage?

In thinking about the direction you might pursue with this family, consider if you have ever been in this situation yourself in your own family. If so, how do you think this experience would affect the way you work with the couple? If the husband were to say that he was very confused, desperately wanted an answer, and was hoping that you would point him in the "right direction," would you be inclined to tell him what you think he should do? Or would you tell him that this was his struggle and he would have to find his own answer? Would you be inclined to tell the couple your values? Or would you keep them to yourself so as not to unduly influence them?

Sex-Role Identity

The situation.   Frank and Judy describe themselves as the "traditional couple." They are in marriage counseling with you to work on the strains in their relationship that arise from rearing their two adolescent sons. The couple talk a lot about their sons. Both Judy and Frank work full time outside of the home. Besides working as an elementary-school principal, Judy has another full-time job as mother and homemaker. Frank says he is not about to do any "women's work" around the house. Judy has never really given much thought to the fact that she has a dual career. Neither Judy nor Frank shows a great deal of interest in critically examining the cultural stereotypes that they have incorporated. Each of them has a definite vision of what women and men "should be." Rather than talking about their relationship or the inequalities of the distribution of tasks at home, they focus the attention on troubles with their sons. Judy wants advice on how to deal with their problems.

Your stance.   If you become aware of the tension between this couple over rigid sex roles, will you call it to their attention in your counseling with them? Do you see it as your job to challenge Frank on his traditional views? Do you see it as your job to encourage Judy to want more equality in their relationship? If you were counseling this couple, what do you think you might say to each of them? How do you think your values would influence the direction you might go? Would you encourage the couple to focus more on their relationship and less on the behavior of their sons? What bearing do your own sex-role conditioning and your own views have on what you will do?

Discussion.   Hare-Mustin (1980) has argued that therapists who work with couples and families need to clarify their own values pertaining to traditional and nontraditional family arrangements and that they should share these values with their clients. She contends that counselors should be prepared to explain to the family their views on issues such as stereotyped sex-role requirements, role functions, and the distribution of responsibilities between parents and children.

If you will be counseling couples and families, it is essential that you appreciate the fact that sex-role stereotypes are functional and, therefore, die hard. As Scarato and Sigall (1979) have observed, a woman faces a dual problem: dealing with a partner who is unwilling or unprepared to share domestic tasks and letting go of roles that have been a basic part of her identity and have given her value. Scarato and Sigall have stressed the importance of practitioners' continually evaluating their own beliefs about appropriate family roles and responsibilities, child-rearing practices, multiple roles for women, and nontraditional vocations.

Margolin (1982) has also given recommendations on how to be a nonsexist family therapist and how to use the therapy process to confront negative expectations and stereotyped roles in the family. One of her suggestions is that helpers examine their own behavior and attitudes that would imply sex-differentiated roles and status. For example, helpers can show their bias in subtle ways by looking to the husband when talking about making decisions and looking to the wife when talking about home matters and rearing children. Margolin also contends that practitioners are especially vulnerable to the following biases: (1) assuming that remaining married would be the best choice for a woman, (2) demonstrating less interest in a woman's career than in a man's career, (3) encouraging couples to accept the belief that child rearing is solely the responsibility of the mother, (4) showing a different reaction to a wife's affair than to a husband's, and (5) giving more importance to satisfying the husband's needs than to satisfying the wife's needs. She raises two critical questions for those who work with couples and families:

1. How does the counselor respond when members of the family seem to agree that they want to work toward goals that (from the counselor's vantage point) are sexist in nature?
2. To what extent does the counselor accept the family's definition of sex-role identities rather than trying to challenge and eventually change these attitudes?

Religious Values

The situation.   Your client has a strong fundamentalist background. Peter has definite ideas about right and wrong, sin, guilt, and damnation, and he has accepted the teachings of his church without question. When Peter encountered difficulties and problems in the past, he was able to pray and find comfort in his relationship with God. Lately, however, he has been suffering from chronic depression, inability to sleep, extreme feelings of guilt, and an overwhelming sense of doom that God is going to punish him for his transgressions. He consulted his physician and asked for medication to help him sleep better. The physician suggested that he seek psychological counseling. At first Peter resisted this idea, for he strongly feels that he should find comfort in his religion. With the continuation of his bouts of depression and sleeplessness, he hesitantly comes to you for advice.

He requests that you open the session with a prayer so that he can get into a proper spiritual frame of mind. He also quotes you a verse from the Bible that has special meaning to him. He tells you about his doubts about seeing you for counseling, and he is concerned that you will not accept his definite religious convictions, which he sees as being at the center of his life. He inquires about your religious beliefs.

Your stance.   Would you have any trouble in counseling Peter? He is struggling with trusting you and with seeing the value in counseling. What are your reactions to some of his specific views, especially to those pertaining to his fear of punishment? Do you have reactions to his strong fundamentalist beliefs? If you have definite disagreements with Peter's beliefs, could you be accepting of him? Would you challenge him to think for himself and do what he thinks is right? Would you encourage him to question his religion?

Assume that you have a religious orientation, yet you believe in a God of love whereas Peter believes in a God of fear. You let him know that you have differences in the way the two of you perceive religion. Yet you also say that you want to explore with him how well his religious beliefs are serving him in his life and also examine possible connections between some of his beliefs and how they are contributing to his symptoms. With these assumptions, do you think you could be helpful to Peter? Would you accept him as a client?

Now assume that you don't share any of Peter's religious values, that you are intolerant of fundamentalist beliefs, and that you see such beliefs doing far more harm than good for people. Given these values, would you accept a client like Peter? Would you be able to work with him objectively, or would you try to find ways to sway him to give up his view of the world?

Discussion.   We find that an increasing number of students are expressing interest in the relationship between religion and counseling. Many of them wonder whether the goals of religion and those of counseling are compatible. Some of them are attracted to the field of counseling because they see it as a vehicle for teaching people about the value of religion as a way to find meaning in life. Some students are concerned that their religion would not be respected by other students and professors in the counseling field. Thus, they feel that they must hide their values. Others wonder about their ability to work objectively with people who don't embrace a religion.

Quackenbos, Privette, and Klentz (1986) take the position that religion is a pervasive force in our society and yet is excluded from counseling practices. They support an integration of religious values with psychotherapy. They suggest that the clergy need rigorous training in counseling and that secular counselors also need preparation for dealing with religious issues.

Peck (1978), a psychiatrist and author of *The Road Less Traveled*, writes that psychotherapists tend to pay too little attention to the ways in which their clients view the world. He encourages counselors to be specifically aware of the view of the world held by their clients. From his perspective, this world view is always an essential part of clients' problems, and a correction of their world view is necessary if they are to get better. Peck advises psychotherapists whom he supervises to become aware of their clients' religion, even if they maintain that they do not have a religion. In this broader frame of reference a religion is a basic part of how individuals view the world and, consequently, how they decide to act.

In clarifying your values pertaining to religion and counseling, consider these questions: "Does an exploration of religion belong in counseling? Is counseling complete without a spiritual dimension? If a client's religious needs arise in counseling, is it appropriate to deal with them? Are counselors pushing their values on their clients when they decide what topics can and cannot be discussed in counseling? Do you have to hold the same religious beliefs to counsel clients who have religious struggles?

Abortion

The situation.   Connie, a 19-year-old college student, has not seriously considered using birth-control measures, because she likes the idea of being a "spontaneous person." She doesn't want to use birth-control pills because is afraid she will gain weight. She has had an abortion, which was difficult for her. Now she is pregnant again.

Connie is wondering whether she wants to have another abortion. A part of her wants that, and another part of her wants to have the child. She is thinking about telling her parents, especially since she is wondering what it would be like to have her child and live at home with them. She is also considering the option of having her child and giving it up for adoption. She is unable to sleep, feels guilty for having gotten herself into this situation again, and is very undecided. Although she has talked to her friends and solicited their advice, she has gotten many contradictory recommendations. Connie lets you know that she is not at all sure that she did the "right thing" by having the abortion a year ago. She asks you for advice on what you think she should do.

Your stance.   With the information you have, what are some things you'd say to Connie? You could pursue any number of options with her, including the following:

- You could encourage her to tell her parents and let them advise her what to do.
- You might explore her guilt with her to find out the meaning of it.
- You might suggest that she follow her inclination to have the child, especially since she felt unsure about the abortion a year ago.
- You could persuade her to have another abortion, especially since she is uncertain about what to do.
- You could encourage her to have her child and give it up for adoption.
- You might refer her to another agency or practitioner because of your values on abortion, either for or against.

Think about your values as related to abortion. Are you clearly opposed to it on moral and religious grounds? If so, would you tell her so? Would you attempt to dissuade her from having an abortion and suggest other options? Would you attempt to keep your values out of the session? If your values are that women have the right to decide whether they will have a child, would you try to persuade her to accept your view? Would the fact that she had had a prior abortion make any difference to you? If you sensed that she was using abortion as a method of birth control, would this make a difference in how you proceeded?

Sometimes we hear students say that they would refer a pregnant client to another professional because of their values. They would not like to sway the woman, and they fear that they could not remain objective. Does this apply to you? What would you do if a client of yours happened to get pregnant? Would you refer her at this point? If so, might she feel that you were abandoning her?

Sexuality

Situation involving sex in a nursing home. You are working in a nursing home. You discover that several of the unmarried elderly people are engaging in sexual intercourse. At a staff meeting several other workers begin to complain that supervision is not tight enough and that such "goings on" should not be permitted. What input would you want to have in this staff meeting? What are your thoughts about unmarried elderly people engaging in sex? Would you be inclined to promote this practice? Would you agree that more careful supervision was needed to prevent it? How would your own values affect your recommendations?

Situation involving a sex-education program. You are working in a facility for adolescents and are doing a good deal of individual and group counseling. You discover that many young teenagers are sexually active and that a number of them have gotten pregnant. Abortion is common. Many of these girls keep their baby, whether or not they get married. The agency director asks you to design a comprehensive education program for preventing unwanted pregnancy.

In thinking about the kind of program you would suggest, consider these questions: What are your values with respect to teenagers' being sexually active? What are your attitudes about providing detailed information on birth-control methods to children and adolescents? How would your own values influence the design of your program?

Assessing your sexual values. Consider your values with respect to sexuality, as well as where you acquired them. How comfortable do you feel in discussing sexual issues with clients? Are you aware of any barriers that could prevent you from working with clients on sexual issues? How would your experiences in sexual relationships (or the lack of them) influence your work with clients in this area? Would you promote your sexual values? For example, if a teenage client was promiscuous and this behavior was in a large part a form of rebellion against her parents, would you be inclined to challenge her behavior? Or if a teenage client took no birth-control precautions yet was sexually active with many partners, would you urge him or her to use birth control? Or would you encourage abstinence? Or would you recommend that he or she be more selective in choosing sexual partners?

Although you may say that you are open-minded and that you can accept sexual attitudes and values that differ from your own, we think you could be tempted to try to change clients whom you believed to be involved in self-defeating practices. It would be good to assess your attitudes toward casual sex, premarital sex, sex with many partners, group sex, teenage sexuality, extramarital sex, and homosexuality. What are your attitudes toward monogamy? What do you consider to be the physical and psychological hazards of sex with more than one partner? How would your views on this issue influence the direction you'd take with clients in exploring sexual concerns?

When you've made this assessment, ask yourself if you would be able to work objectively with a person who had sexual values sharply divergent from yours. If you have very conservative views about sexual behavior, for example, will you be able to accept the liberal views of some of your clients? If you think their moral values are contributing to the difficulties they are experiencing in their life, will you be inclined to persuade them to adopt your conservative values?

From another perspective, if you see yourself as having liberal sexual attitudes, how do you think you'd react to a person with very traditional values? Assume your unmarried client says that he'd like to have more sexual experiences but that his religious upbringing has instilled in him the belief that premarital sex is a sin. Whenever he has come close to having sexual experiences, he has been burdened with guilt. He would like to learn to enjoy sex without feeling guilty, yet he does not want to throw his values away. He is in conflict and wants your advice. What do you think you'd say to him, if your values were liberal? Would you be inclined to challenge his moral upbringing? Would you encourage him to discard his values, which seem to be bringing him grief and anxiety? Could you be supportive of his choices if they were in conflict with your values?

AIDS Education

The situation.   You are working in a community mental-health agency, and the director asks you and several of your colleagues to design a comprehensive education program to promote awareness of AIDS in the entire community. The director tells you that her goal is to do everything possible to prevent people from contracting AIDS and that she'd like people to develop a realistic understanding of the issues involved in this major health problem. She wants people to have detailed information about AIDS, and would like to see them discuss the issue at community meetings to be held in the center. Once you and your colleagues have written up a proposal, she wants your group to make a presentation to the board members of the agency, who represent a range from very conservative to very liberal.

Your group works diligently and comes up with a comprehensive program. Your proposal calls for focusing on the schools, from elementary to community college. Your group is suggesting workshops and short courses to be conducted by community workers and health-care providers. Although your program involves a frank and comprehensive discussion of all major issues pertaining to AIDS, it also calls for dealing with the topic in a manner that is sensitive to the community and that is appropriate for the target groups. Some of the key features of your proposed workshops include the following: information on the state of the disease, identification of who is at risk, psychosocial dimensions of the disease, attitudes toward those who have contracted AIDS, ethical and legal issues, medical facts and concerns, prevention of AIDS, and implications for the future. You intend to have AIDS patients talk to classes at the schools, along with physicians and other professionals with knowledge about this disease. Your program will also focus on teaching specific methods of "safe sex" and encouraging these practices.

After your group finishes presenting its findings to the board of directors, several members loudly and passionately protest on the grounds that your group is promoting immorality and interfering with their rights as parents. They don't want the schools encouraging their children to practice "safe sex" when in their home they are teaching them how to live morally decent lives. They attempt to convince you that AIDS is a natural consequence of rampant immorality that has been spreading through the country.

On the basis of your values, what arguments might you give these board members? How would you answer their opposition? Would you be willing to omit the more controversial aspects of your program? Would you be willing to make room in your program for advocates of abstaining from sexual relationships outside of marriage? Would you be willing to give equal time to representatives who opposed your point of view? Your values will certainly enter into the picture as you develop your views toward your responsibilities in either dealing with or attempting to ignore the AIDS crisis.

Counseling and education are seen as crucial in stopping the spread of AIDS. Both the American Psychological Association (APA) and the American Association for Counseling and Development (AACD) have recommended that education and counseling about AIDS be available to people who enter clinics for family planning, prenatal counseling, sexually transmitted diseases, and drug abuse (Thiers, 1987).

Cultural Values and Assumptions in the Helping Process
The Trend toward Cultural Awareness in Helping

In order to function effectively as a helper, you need to remain aware of clients' cultural attributes and to realize how cultural values operate in the helping process. There is a growing sensitivity to ethnic and cultural issues in the human-services professions. The following are some of the recent developments: (1) There is a trend toward cross-cultural courses and other means of acquiring knowledge about working with minority clients. (2) There is a concern for adapting techniques and interventions in ways that are relevant for culturally diverse populations. (3) There is an increasing recognition of the need for helpers to know themselves if they hope to understand clients from different cultures. (4) There are implications for practice in the value orientations and differing basic assumptions underlying Eastern and Western therapeutic systems.

The need for a multicultural emphasis. The helping professions have yet to fully address the special issues involved in working with people of various cultures. Many of the clients whom you will work with bring with them specific values, beliefs, and actions conditioned by their race, ethnicity, gender, religion, historical experiences with the dominant culture, socioeconomic status, political views, life-style, and geographic region.

A multicultural perspective on the helping process takes into consideration all of these aspects of a pluralistic society. Such a perspective respects the needs and strengths of diverse client populations, and it recognizes the experiences of these clients. Carefully examine the cultural appropriateness of your intervention strategies, and strive to obtain the knowledge, skills, and competencies that will enable you to function effectively in a multicultural society.

Cultural tunnel vision. Our work with students in a human-services training program has shown us that many of them have cultural "tunnel vision." They have limited cultural experiences, and in some cases they see it as their role to transmit their values to their clients. We find that many students lack awareness of the difficulty of dealing with clients who have a cultural background different from their own. Some students have made inappropriate generalizations about a particular group of clients. For example, helpers often assert that minorities are unresponsive to professional psychological intervention because of a lack of motivation to change or a "resistance" to seeking professional help. Minority clients are likely to be influenced either positively or negatively by their perceptions of the initial attitudes and expectations of helpers they encounter (Lorion & Parron, 1985). Regardless of your cultural heritage, it is essential that you honestly examine your own expectations, attitudes, and assumptions about working with various cultural and ethnic groups. You need to understand and accept clients who have a different set of assumptions about life, and you need to be alert to the likelihood of imposing your world view. In working with clients with different cultural experiences, it is important that you resist making value judgments for them.

Cormier and Hackney (1987) note that values and life-styles of clients from other cultures might well differ from the predominant values of your culture. If you possess cultural tunnel vision, you are likely to misinterpret many patterns of behavior displayed by clients who are culturally different. Unless you understand the values of other cultures, you are likely to misunderstand these clients. Because of this lack of understanding, you may label certain client behavior as resistant, you may make an inaccurate diagnosis of a particular behavior as maladaptive, and you may impose your own value system on the client. For example, many Hispanic women might be resistant to changing what you view as dependency on their husband. If you work with Hispanic women, you need to appreciate that they are likely to live by the value of remaining with their husband, even if he is unfaithful. Hispanic tradition tells these women that no matter what, it is not appropriate to leave one's husband. If you are unaware of this traditional value, you could make the mistake of pushing such women to take an action that will violate their belief system.

Western and Eastern Values

Most of the theories and practices of the helping process that you have learned are grounded in Western assumptions. But many of the clients you will work with have a cultural heritage associated with Eastern values. In short, some of the interventions you have learned will be of questionable relevance if you do not modify your techniques. Indeed, as Cormier and Hackney (1987) observe, the skills and strategies of most models of professional helping are derived from counseling approaches developed by and for White, middle-class, Western clients, and therefore they may not be applicable to clients from different racial, ethnic, and cultural backgrounds. The Western model of helping has major limitations when it is applied to minority groups such as Asian Americans, Hispanics, Native Americans, and Blacks. Seeking psychological professional help is not typical for many of these groups. In most non-Western cultures, in fact, informal groups of friends and relatives provide a supportive network. Informal helping consists of the spontaneous outreach of caring people to others in need (Brammer, 1985).

A comparison of Western and Eastern systems shows some striking differences in value orientations. Saeki and Borow (1985) and Ho (1985) discuss some of these contrasts. Western culture places prime value on choice, the uniqueness of the individual, self-assertion, and the strengthening of the ego. By contrast, the Eastern view stresses interdependence, underplays individuality, and emphasizes the losing of oneself in the totality of the cosmos. From the Western perspective the primary values are the primacy of the individual, youth, independence, nonconformity, competition, conflict, and freedom. The guiding principles for action are found in the fulfillment of individual needs and individual responsibility. From the Eastern perspective the primary values are the primacy of relationships, maturity, compliance, conformity, cooperation, harmony, and security. The guiding principles for action are found in the achievement of collective goals and collective responsibility.

Behavioral orientations are also different. The Western view encourages expression of feelings and striving for self-actualization, whereas the Eastern view encourages control of feelings and striving for collective actualization. There are also differences in therapeutic practices between these systems. Western approaches emphasize outcomes such as improving the environment, changing one's coping behavior, learning to manage stress, and changing objective reality in other ways to improve one's way of life. Eastern approaches emphasize acceptance of one's environment and inner enlightenment.

We recently presented a series of workshops in Hong Kong for human-services professionals. It gave us the opportunity to rethink the challenges of applying Western approaches to working with non-Western clients. Almost all the participants in these workshops were Chinese, but some of them had obtained their graduate training in social work or counseling in the United States. These professionals were challenged with retaining the values that were basic to their Chinese heritage, yet they were faced with the task of integrating a counseling viewpoint with their values.

In talking with these practitioners, we learned that their focus is on the individual in the context of the social system. In their interventions they pay attention to the family and do not focus primarily on the individual's interests. They are learning how to balance a focus on personal growth with what is in the best interest of the family and society. They are able to respect the values of their clients, who are also mostly Chinese, yet at the same time they are able to challenge their clients to think of some ways to change. Many of the helping professionals in Hong Kong told us that they had to demonstrate patience and understanding with their clients. They saw it as essential to form a trusting relationship with their clients before engaging in confrontation. Although this necessity is true of counseling in general, it seems especially important for non-Western clients.

Case example. An Asian student is seeing you because he continues to get "B" and "C" grades, which is a source of embarrassment to his family. He is in great difficulty because he feels that he is letting his family down and actually bringing shame to the family by what he considers his "academic failure." If you were working with this student, how would you help him deal with his feelings of guilt and failure and at the same time be cognizant of his cultural values? Would you challenge your client? Would you try to change his reactions to his family? Would you help him become more self-accepting? Would you tend to focus on the issue of what constitutes academic success, or would your focus be on what constitutes "bringing shame to the family"?

Challenging Your Stereotypical Beliefs

Although you may think that you are without bias, stereotypical beliefs could well affect your practice. Stereotyping involves assuming that some aspects of the behavior of an individual will be typical of most other members of his or her cultural group. This assumption leads to statements such as "Asian-American clients are emotionally repressed." "Black clients are suspicious by nature and will not trust professional helpers." "Native Americans have very low motivation." Cormier and Hackney (1987) indicate that such statements reflect a myth of uniformity, the notion that all people from a cultural group are alike. Helpers need to realize that there will be variations within cultures, just as there are among cultures.

Although cultural differences among groups are obvious, we think that it is important not to go to the extreme of focusing exclusively on the differences that can separate us. In working with the mental-health professionals in foreign countries, we have become even more convinced that there are some basic similarities among the peoples of the world. There are universal experiences that can bind people together. Although the circumstances of one's pain differ, most people experience the pain of making decisions and attempting to live with integrity in their world. It is essential to be respectful of the real cultural differences that exist, and it is equally critical that we not forget the common denominators that all people experience.

Challenging Your Cultural Assumptions

Helpers often make cultural assumptions that they are unaware of. We give a few examples of assumptions that could interfere with effective helping in multicultural situations. By reflecting on these you can begin to see ways to challenge your assumptions as you work with any client.

Assumptions about time. If your clients are primarily concerned with survival issues or making it through on a day-to-day basis, they are not likely to take well to a 50-minute-hour appointment that is made weeks in advance. They are expecting to get expert help and advice now on what they can do to better cope with their problem situation (Cormier & Hackney, 1987).

Kottler (1986) writes of being surprised when he was a visiting professor at a university in Peru that his students were not as compulsive about arriving on time as he was. When he was ready to begin class at 9 A.M., he found himself standing before an empty room. He would be interrupted every few minutes by students casually strolling into class. Kottler's students taught him to appreciate whatever was happening at the moment. He learned that in Latin cultures there is a great respect for the present but less concern for the future. Many people in these cultures are not ruled by the clock and simply will not be rushed. This trait does not mean, however, that they are uncooperative or resistive to authority. Rather, it means that time will wait; and if not, who cares?

Assumptions about self-disclosure. Self-disclosure is highly valued in traditional counseling. Most helpers assume that no effective helping can occur unless clients reveal themselves. This assumption ignores the fact that self-disclosure is foreign to the values of some cultural groups. For example, some European ethnic groups stress that problems should be kept "in the family." According to Sue and Sue (1985), those Asian Americans who are described as the "most repressed of all clients" may well be holding true to their cultural background. A different perspective on this issue is given by Patterson (1985), who contends that the inability to self-disclose is something to be overcome, not accepted. For him, unless clients are willing to verbalize and communicate their thoughts, feelings, attitudes, and perceptions, there is no basis for empathic understanding by the helper.

We generally agree with Patterson that unless clients challenge the obstacles to disclosure, they will be unable to participate in the helping relationship. However, you can recognize and appreciate that some of your clients will struggle in letting you know the nature of their problems. This struggle in itself is a useful focus for exploration. Rather than expecting such clients to "let it all hang out," you can demonstrate respect for their values and at the same time ask them what they want from you. With your support and encouragement, they can sort through their values and conditioning pertaining to self-disclosure and decide the degree to which they want to change.

Assumptions about nonverbal behavior. Clients can disclose themselves in many nonverbal ways, and thus it is a mistake to rely solely on what clients talk about. Mainstream Americans often feel uncomfortable with silence, and thus they tend to fill in quiet gaps with words. In some cultures, in contrast, silence indicates a sign of respect and politeness. You could misinterpret a quiet client's behavior if you did not realize that she might be waiting for you to ask her questions. There are no universal meanings of nonverbal behaviors. Thus, it is essential that you acquire sensitivity to cultural differences in order to reduce the probability of miscommunication, misdiagnosis, and misinterpretation of behavior (Wolfgang, 1985).

You may have been systematically trained in attending and responding skills, which include keeping an open posture, maintaining good eye contact, and leaning toward your client (Egan, 1986). Although you have learned certain skills as a way to create a positive helping relationship, clients from some ethnic groups may have trouble in responding positively or understanding the intent of your posturing. You have probably been taught that good eye contact is a sign of presence and that the lack of such contact is evasive. Yet Devore (1985) cautions that Asians and American Indians may view direct eye contact as a lack of respect. In some cultures lack of eye contact may even be a sign of respect and good manners. Attneave (1985) writes that American Indians consider a direct gaze as indicative of aggressiveness; in cross-gender encounters it usually means sexual aggressiveness. Thus, you can make a mistake if you prematurely label clients as "resistive" or "pathological" if they avoid eye contact and do not respond to your invitation of attending behavior.

Assumptions about trusting relationships. Anglo Americans tend to form quick relationships and to talk easily about their personal life. This characteristic is often reflected in their helping style. Thus the helper expects that the client will approach their relationship in an open and trusting manner. Doing this is very difficult for some clients, however, especially given that they are expected to talk about themselves in personal ways to a stranger. Among many cultures it takes a long time to develop meaningful relationships. What is more, you will have to *earn* the trust of these clients before they will confide in you.

Assumptions about self-actualization. A common assumption that helping professionals make is that it is important for the individual to become a fully functioning person. But some clients are more concerned about how their problems or changes are likely to affect others in their life. You will recall that in the Eastern orientation one of the guiding principles is the achievement of collective goals.

Assumptions about directness. Although the Western orientation prizes directness, some cultures see it as a sign of rudeness and as something to be avoided. If you are not aware of this cultural difference, you could make the mistake of interpreting a lack of directness as a sign of being unassertive, rather than as a sign of respect. Some Latin-American cultures value finding indirect ways for asking for what you want.

Assumptions about assertiveness. If you are operating from a Western orientation, you will assume that your clients are better off if they can behave in assertive ways, such as telling people what they think, feel, and want. Some training programs teach participants coping skills that involve taking an active stance toward life.

As is true of directness, being assertive is not always viewed as appropriate behavior. Thus, you could offend certain clients by automatically assuming that they would be better off if they became more assertive. For example, you might work with a woman who seems to you very unassertive. She rarely asks for what she wants, she allows others to decide her priorities, and she almost never denies a request or demand from anyone in her family. If you work hard at helping her become an assertive woman, it could very well create conflicts within her family system. If she changes her role, she may no longer fit in her culture. Therefore, it is crucial that both you and your client consider the consequences of making too many such changes.

Given all of these faulty assumptions, we hope you see the importance of challenging some of the views about clients that you take for granted. One way to respect your clients is to ask them to tell you about themselves and listen to their underlying values. We are not suggesting that you merely listen in an accepting way, for you can still challenge clients who are culturally different from you. For example, the client who expresses little emotion can be asked if this is a problem for him or if this is something that he might consider changing. You could ask another client if she sees any problem with not being assertive or direct. Perhaps she may change certain aspects of her cultural conditioning yet retain other aspects that she deems important. Asking your clients what they want from you is a way of decreasing the chances that you will impose your cultural values on them.

Attributes of Effective Multicultural Helpers

Effective helpers do not impose their values and expectations on their clients from differing cultural backgrounds, they avoid stereotyping clients, and they do not force clients to fit a uniform counseling approach (Cormier & Hackney, 1987). Sue (1981a, 1981b) and Sue and his associates (1982) have identified essential components of effective multicultural helping in three areas: beliefs and attitudes, knowledge, and skills.

First of all, effective helpers understand their own values and assumptions of human behavior and recognize that those held by others may differ. They seek to examine and understand the world from the vantage point of their clients. They are able to share the world view of their clients, rather than being culturally encapsulated. They are able to identify and understand the central constructs of their clients, and they avoid applying their constructs inappropriately with their clients. They monitor their functioning through consultation, supervision, and continuing education. They can appreciate diverse cultures, and they feel comfortable with the differences between themselves and their clients in terms of race and beliefs. If necessary, they are willing to refer a client because of their limitations in multicultural counseling.

Second, culturally effective helpers possess certain knowledge. They understand the impact of oppression and racism on the helping professions and on their personal and professional lives. They understand that external sociopolitical forces may have influenced culturally different groups. They possess knowledge about the historical background, traditions, and values of the groups with whom they are working. They understand how the value assumptions of the major theories of counseling may interact with the values of different cultural groups. They know how to help clients from varied backgrounds make use of indigenous support systems.

Third, effective helpers have acquired certain skills in working with culturally diverse populations. They are truly eclectic. They use skills, methods, and goals that are appropriate to the experiences and life-styles of the clients. They modify and adapt conventional approaches to counseling in order to accommodate cultural differences. They are able to send and receive both verbal and nonverbal messages accurately and appropriately. They are able to make out-of-office interventions when necessary by assuming the role of consultant and agent for change.

By Way of Review

- Ethical practice dictates that helpers seriously consider the impact of their values on their clients and the conflicts that might arise if values are sharply different.
- Ultimately, it is the responsibility of clients to choose in which direction they will go, what values they will adopt, and what values they will modify or discard.
- It is neither possible nor desirable for helpers to remain neutral or to keep their values separate from their professional relationships.
- It is not the helper's role to indoctrinate clients or to push them to adopt the value system of the helper.
- At times, it can be useful for helpers to expose their values to their clients, yet it is counterproductive to impose these values on them.

- Simply because you do not embrace a client's values does not mean that you cannot effectively work with the person. The key is that you be objective and respect your client's right to autonomy.
- There are numerous areas in which your values can potentially conflict with the values of your clients. You may have to refer some clients because of such differences.
- Your values will influence your stance toward education and counseling pertaining to the spread of AIDS. The type of educational program that you are likely to design will probably be a reflection of many of your basic values.
- In order to function effectively with clients of various cultures, it is essential that you know and respect specific cultural differences and realize how cultural values operate in the helping process.
- A multicultural perspective on the helping process takes into consideration specific values, beliefs, and actions related to race, ethnicity, gender, religion, socioeconomic status, life-style, political views, and geographic region.
- Be aware of any tendencies toward cultural tunnel vision. If you have limited cultural experiences, you may have difficulties in relating to clients who have a different view of the world. You are likely to misinterpret many patterns of behavior displayed by such clients.
- There are some striking differences in value orientations between the Western and the Eastern systems. These differences have important implications for the process of helping.
- In working with people from other cultures, avoid stereotyping and challenge your assumptions about the use of time, self-disclosure, nonverbal behavior, trusting relationships, self-actualization, directness, and assertiveness.
- Effective multicultural helpers have been identified in terms of the specific knowledge, beliefs and attitudes, and skills they possess.

What Will You Do Now?

1. Write down some of your central values pertaining to the helping process that you might be most inclined to discuss with a client. Under what circumstances might you want to share and perhaps explore your values and beliefs with your clients? Can you think of situations in which you think it might be counterproductive for you to do so?

2. Consider a personal value that could get in the way of your being objective in working with a client. Take a value that you hold strongly, and challenge it. Do this by going to a source who holds values opposite to your own. If you are strongly convinced that abortion is immoral, for instance, consider going to an abortion clinic and talking with someone there. If you have difficulty with a gay or lesbian life-style, because of your own values, go to a gay organization on campus or in your community, and talk with people there.

3. Find a way to connect up with a person or persons from a different culture in order to find out more about their way of life. Make up a brief list of questions that would help you learn more about their culture.

Suggested Readings

American Association for Counseling and Development. *Counseling and values*. This is the official journal of the Association for Religious and Value Issues in Counseling (ARVIC), a division of the American Association for Counseling and Development (AACD). Regular membership in ARVIC is open to members of the AACD. The journal is published three times yearly, at a subscription rate of $12 for nonmembers. Contact ARVIC, 5999 Stevenson Avenue, Alexandria, VA 22034.

Axelson, J. (1985). *Counseling and development in a multicultural society*. Pacific Grove, CA: Brooks/Cole. This is a very useful survey of issues pertaining to culture and counseling, including profiles of various cultural groups. Especially useful are the chapters on traditional approaches to counseling, eclectic approaches to counseling, the culture of the counselor, and the interaction of counselor and client.

Hart, G. M. (1978). *Values clarification for counselors*. Springfield, IL: Charles C Thomas. This book for human-services workers explores the nature of values and the ways in which people can be assisted in examining their own values. The author discusses a three-stage model for clarifying values.

Levine, C. (1987). *Taking sides: Clashing views on controversial bioethical issues* (2nd ed.). Guilford, CT: Dushkin Publishing Group. This book deals with a variety of ethical and value issues: Is abortion immoral? Should doctors withhold the truth from dying patients? Can suicide be rational? Should insurance companies be allowed to screen for antibodies to the AIDS virus?

Peck, M. S. (1978). *The road less traveled: A new psychology of love, traditional values and spiritual growth*. New York: Simon & Schuster (Touchstone). This is a best-selling book for both the lay population and professional helpers. The author focuses on the role of spiritual values in the helping process. Special attention is given to the topics of discipline, love, growth and religion, and grace.

Pedersen P. (Ed.). (1985). *Handbook of cross-cultural counseling and therapy*. Westport, CT: Greenwood Press. This is an outstanding reference work that will give you a good overview of cultural values and implications for the practice of counseling.

Rogers, C. (1980). *A way of being*. Boston: Houghton Mifflin. This work contains a series of updated writings of Rogers's personal experiences and perspectives. There are many ideas pertaining to values, attitudes, and beliefs of helpers.

CHAPTER 5

Common Concerns Facing Beginning Helpers

Focus of the Chapter

As a helper you will encounter a range of special concerns throughout your career, but some problems will be particularly pressing when you begin helping others. One challenge you will face is learning how to deal effectively with the feelings some of your clients have toward you and the corresponding feelings that are evoked in you. Even experienced helpers show interest in learning creative ways to deal with difficult clients, especially those who exhibit a great deal of resistance. As a beginning helper you are likely to be threatened by resistance to your interventions. In this chapter we address important issues of transference, countertransference, resistance, and managing your own feelings as you work with difficult clients.

Because the AIDS crisis shows no signs of easing, counseling and education to stop the spread of the disease are becoming a priority in many of the helping professions. AIDS presents a special concern for helpers. We encourage you to think about your role and responsibility in dealing with the issues surrounding this crisis.

The chapter will probably raise more questions than it answers. We are not interested in providing easy solutions to the many difficult situations that you will encounter in the helping relationship. Our purpose is to introduce you to a range of difficult situations that you will be involved in as you help others.

Transference and Countertransference
Dealing with Transference Issues

Transference is the unconscious process whereby clients project onto their helper past feelings or attitudes they had toward significant people in their life. Transference typically has its origins in the client's early childhood, and it constitutes a repetition of past conflicts. Because of the client's unfinished business, there is a distortion of the way you as a helper are perceived. You may be viewed with a mixture of positive and negative feelings, and at different times the same client may express love, affection, resentment, rage, dependency, and ambivalence. You are likely to experience transference feelings from clients even if you are limiting your practice to brief counseling and to crisis intervention. What is essential is that you understand what transference means and that you know how to deal with it skillfully. Transference evokes reactions in the helper. These reactions can become problematic when they result in countertransference, the helper's unrealistic and exaggerated reactions to the client's transference. Below are some examples of transference situations that you are likely to come across. Ask yourself what your response might be to a client's feelings toward you and what feelings are likely to be evoked in you.

Clients who make you into something you are not. Some clients will want you to be the mother or father whom they never had but always wanted. These clients may have visions that you will take care of them and that you will solve all their problems. They see you as an all-knowing being who can pull them out of the quandary they are stuck in. In considering clients who make you into a parent and want you to adopt them, ask yourself these questions: "Do I look to others to be the parents I never had? How comfortable or uncomfortable am I with clients who attribute to me traits such as being all-knowing and all-wise? How do I feel when someone expects me to make decisions for them? To what degree do I make it my responsibility to pull clients out of stuck places? What might I get for myself by assuming the role of parent for such clients?"

Other clients may immediately distrust you because you remind them of a former spouse, a critical parent, or some other important figure in their life. For example, consider the female client who is assigned to a male therapist and lets him know that she has no regard for men. All the men in her life have been untrustworthy, and since her therapist is male, he, too, will betray her. If you had a client who prejudged you on the basis of earlier experiences, how might you react? Are you able to recognize your client's behavior as transference reactions, and are you able to deal with them nondefensively? How might you go about showing this client that you are a different person from people in her past?

There are clients who will not let themselves get emotionally close to you because they feel that as a child they were abandoned by people they cared for. They are taking some past experiences and superimposing them on the relationship with you. Assume a client of yours comes from a divorced family. She tells you that for many years she has seen it as her fault that her parents divorced. She is somehow convinced that there was something wrong with her that caused her parents to separate. Because she was abandoned in the past and remembers the pain of that time in her life, she is leery of letting you into her life. She fears that if she gets too close to you, you, too, will abandon her. In working with such a client, consider these questions: "Is there much I can do to convince her that I do not intend to abandon her? What are my reactions to being told that I am going to be like her parents? What might I do in such a situation?"

Clients who see you as a superperson. Consider having this person as a client. He uses all sorts of superlative adjectives to describe you. He sees you as always understanding and supportive and as someone who seems perfect in all areas of living. He cannot imagine that you might have personal difficulties. He is sure that you have the perfect marriage, that your children are perfectly happy, and that you have the perfect career. He tells you that he would be devastated if he ever found out that you were not all that he sees you as being. Furthermore, this client gives you full credit for any changes that he might have made. To what degree might you be inclined to believe some of what such a client tells you about yourself? To what degree might you feel burdened by his perception? What do you think you might have to do to live up to his ideal? How would you deal with his giving you total credit for his improvement?

Clients who make unrealistic demands on you. Some clients make no decisions without first calling you to find out what you think. They want to know if they can call you at any time. These are the clients who time and again want to run over the allotted time for their session. They want you to see them for no fee, with only the promise of paying later when they are in a better financial position. They feel close to you and would like to include you in their social life. They demand that you be always patient with them even when they do little to change. They expect you to accept them no matter what their behavior is during the session. They want you to affirm them and convince them that they are special in your eyes. Even though you may intellectually understand the nature of these unrealistic demands on you, how do you imagine such demands would affect you emotionally? In what ways could you help such clients see the connection between how they treat you and how they treated some significant person in their past? In what ways would you want to treat them differently than significant persons in their past treated them?

Clients who displace anger onto you. Some clients come into the sessions and lash out at the helper with displaced anger. They are annoyed with a helper who dares to become impatient. These clients are basically telling helpers that since they are supposed to be helping, they have no right to express their own feelings. As a helper, do you give yourself room to have and to express feelings you have toward your client? How can you express your reactions to clients in a way that is therapeutic and does not cause them to become closed? How do you react to clients who project anger onto you that you do not think you have earned?

Clients who easily fall in love with you. Some clients will make you the object of all of their verbal affection. They may tell you that there is nobody in the world whom they feel as much affection for as you. They may see you as the ideal person and want very much to become the person they see you as being. They are convinced that they could find a resolution to their problems if only they found a person like you who would love and accept them. How might you respond to being the object of adulation? Could you be tempted to believe everything favorable that these clients tell you and even solicit such ego-gratifying feedback? Could your client's reactions distort or enhance your self-perceptions?

Working with Transference Therapeutically

These illustrations of transference demonstrate how essential it is for you to gain awareness of your own needs and motivations. If you are unaware of your own dynamics, you will tie into your clients' projections and get lost in their distortions. You are likely to avoid focusing on key therapeutic issues and instead to focus on defending yourself.

It is a mistake to think that all feelings that your clients have toward you are simply signs of transference. At times clients may be realistically angry with you because of something you do or say. Their anger does not have to be an irrational response triggered from past situations. If you answer your phone continually during a session with a client, for example, she may become angry with you over the interruptions and your lack of presence. Her anger could be a justifiable reaction and not one that should be "explained away" as a mere expression of transference.

Likewise, clients' affection toward you does not always indicate transference. It could be that they genuinely like some of your traits and enjoy being with you. Of course, many helpers are quick to interpret positive feelings as realistic and negative feelings as distortions. You can err by being too willing to accept unconditionally whatever clients tell you or by interpreting everything they tell you as a sign of transference.

In a group setting we have found it useful to have the participants recognize their transference reactions to one another and to the group leaders. At the beginning of a group we ask members to pay particular attention to people in the room whom they notice the most. We accomplish this by asking questions such as the following:

- Are you finding yourself drawn to some people more than to others?
- Are there some people who seem especially threatening to you?
- Are you finding yourself making quick assumptions about others and forming hasty impressions? For example, "He looks judgmental." "She is intimidating me." "I think I can trust him and will like him." "I definitely want to stay away from her." "It looks as if these three people are in a clique."

We pay particular attention to members who have strong reactions to another person whom they hardly know. We use these transference feelings by assisting clients to work through their reactions in the group. By doing so they often gain insight into ways in which they are behaving outside of the group. This insight includes coming to an understanding of how they reacted to important figures in their childhood and how they now act around people who are important to them.

Dealing with Countertransference Issues

The other side of transference is countertransference, or unrealistic reactions that helpers have toward their clients, which may interfere with their objectivity. Simply having feelings toward a client does not automatically mean that you are having countertransference reactions. Certainly you may feel deep empathy and compassion for some of your clients, which may be a function of their life situation. Countertransference occurs when your needs become too much a part of the relationship or when your clients trigger old wounds in your life that may not have healed. Just as your clients will have some unrealistic reactions to you and will project onto you some of their unfinished business with significant people in their life, so will you have some unrealistic reactions to them. Your own vulnerabilities will be opened up as you are drawn into some of the transference reactions of those you help.

Your countertransference can have both positive and negative effects on the helping process. If your own needs or unresolved personal conflicts become entangled in your professional relationships and destroy your sense of objectivity, this is negative countertransference. If you use your own feelings as a way of understanding yourself, your client, and the relationships between the two of you, these feelings can be a positive force. Even though you may be insightful and self-aware, the demands of the helping profession are great. The emotionally intense relationships that develop with your clients can be expected to bring your unresolved conflicts to the surface. Because countertransference may be a form of identification with your client, you can easily get lost in the client's world, and thus your value as a helper becomes limited. Below are some illustrations of countertransference.

- *"Let me help you."* Your client has gotten a raw deal from life. No matter how hard he tries, things typically go sour in spite of his best efforts. You find yourself going out of your way to be helpful to this client and even consider having him move in with a relative of yours.
- *"I hope he cancels."* You are intimidated by a client's anger directed at you or others. When he cancels a session, you find yourself very relieved.
- *"You remind me of someone I know."* Your clients will often remind you of a significant person in your own life. Put yourself in each of these following situations and imagine how you would respond:
  - You are a middle-aged therapist, and your husband has left you for a 20-year-old woman. You are faced with a female client who is having an affair with a middle-aged married man. Next, consider that your client is the middle-aged man who is having an affair with the much younger woman.
  - You have been a rape victim, and your client discloses that she has been raped. Or your client informs you that he has raped someone.
  - You have been abused as a child, and your client tells you that he has abused some of his own children.
  - You have just dealt at home with a very rebellious teenage daughter, and your first client for the day is a rebellious, acting-out boy.
- *"You are too much like me."* Some of your clients are bound to remind you of some of the traits that you would rather not acknowledge in yourself. Even if you do recognize certain traits, you may find it disconcerting to work with clients who talk about problems and situations that are very much like your own. A client may be a compulsive workaholic, for example, and you may see yourself as working too hard. You might find yourself spending a lot of energy getting this client to slow down and take it easy.
- *"My own reactions are getting in my way."* Sometimes your clients will express pain and show tears. This anguish may make you uncomfortable, because it reminds you of some past or present situation in your life that you would rather avoid. You may intervene by attempting to stop the client's feelings.

No one is immune to countertransference. It is therefore crucial that you be alert to its subtle signs and that you not be too quick to pin the blame for your reactions on your clients. For example, you may find that certain clients evoke a parental response in you. Their behavior can bring out your own critical responses to them.

You will probably not be able to eliminate countertransference altogether. But you can learn to recognize it and deal nondefensively with whatever your clients evoke in you. In this way you can use your feelings as an instrument in your therapeutic work and as a way to further understand yourself. Some signs that you would do well to pay attention to in recognizing your own countertransference are as follows:

- You become easily irritated by certain clients.
- You feel intense anger toward a person you hardly know.
- With some clients you continually run overtime.
- You find yourself wanting to lend money to some unfortunate clients.
- You feel like adopting an abused child.
- You quickly take away pain from a grieving client.
- You regularly feel depressed after seeing a particular client.
- You feel excited knowing that a certain client is soon to arrive.
- You tend to become very bored with a certain client.
- You are aware of typically working much harder than your client.
- You get highly emotional and get lost in the client's world.
- You become aware of giving a great deal of advice and wanting to have clients do what you think they should do.
- You are quick not to accept a certain type of client, or you suggest a referral with little data.
- You find yourself lecturing certain kinds of client.

This list is not all-inclusive, and you can become more aware of your own manifestations of countertransference by focusing on yourself in your supervision sessions. Rather than talking exclusively about a client's problem, you can spend some time talking about how you feel when you are in a session with the client. A good way to expand your awareness of potential countertransference is by talking with colleagues and supervisors about your feelings toward clients. This can be especially helpful if you feel stuck and don't quite know what to do in some of your sessions. Part of what could be stalling you is feelings that you are reluctant to acknowledge. It is well to remember that helping others change will certainly also have the effect of changing you. If you want your being to be untouched, it is well to consider another line of work.

Dealing with Difficult Clients

Professional helpers and students alike are concerned with how to handle difficult clients. They hope to learn techniques for making these clients less difficult, for such clients tax them personally and professionally. There are no simple techniques, however, no tricks that you can pull out of a bag. You can, however, pay attention to what certain difficult clients evoke in you and why they stir these reactions. In our classes and workshops we explore the examples of difficult behavior that participants present to us, and we emphasize coming to an understanding of the functions that resistive and defensive behaviors serve for clients. We examine the payoffs of clients' defensive styles and attempt to understand how their resistance is a way of protecting them against anxiety. However, the focus is not just on the dynamics of difficult clients. Instead, we help students or helpers to become aware of and understand their own reactions to resistance, and we teach them ways of constructively sharing their reactions with clients.

Common Forms of Resistance

Clients can be creative in demonstrating a variety of resistances. Although dealing with client resistance to the helping process is sometimes painful, doing so is often the best way to establish an effective and genuine relationship. Resistance generally makes good sense, and clients often have some realistic reasons for their resistance. The people whom you help may have had negative experiences with professional helpers and with community agencies. They are likely to approach you with a "show-me" attitude. By taking their resistance seriously and exploring its sources, you are demonstrating respect for them. You are beginning to establish the foundations of trust, which is essential for any form of helping.

Albert Ellis (1985, 1986) has described many forms that resistance takes as counselors work with what he calls "difficult customers." Rational-emotive therapy (RET) acknowledges that some resistance is a normal reaction, since there are fears attached to the process of change. It also recognizes that resistance is caused by a variety of factors within the client (such as irrational thinking) but that the counselor's attitudes and behavior can also produce much client resistance. What follows is an adapted description of the common forms of resistance as detailed by Ellis (1985, 1986).

- *Healthy resistance.* All forms of resistance are not to be considered dysfunctional, and some resistance to personality change and therapy is a normal reaction that serves some useful purposes for clients.
- *Resistance motivated by a client/therapist mismatch.* At times clients and therapists are not compatible. Clients may simply not like a therapist, for any number of reasons.
- *Resistance stemming from clients' transference disturbances.* Ellis (1985) quarrels with the psychoanalytic notion that love/hate problems between clients and therapists are manifestations of a transference relationship. For Ellis, clients' strong feelings of love and hate toward their therapist could be based on reality factors that have little to do with their childhood experiences. RET takes the view that disturbed transference relationships are usually sparked by some irrational beliefs of the client (Ellis, 1986). For example, a female client might argue "Because my analyst is helpful and fatherly to me in some ways, he *must* be a complete father to me, and he *must* love me dearly!"
- *Resistance caused by counselors' relationship problems.* Counselors are not immune to having their relationship difficulties. They may not like some of their clients; they may have countertransference difficulties and

therefore be biased against some clients; and they may be insensitive to their clients' feelings and may not know how to maintain a good therapeutic relationship. The resistance that clients show in these cases is largely brought about by the counselor's difficulties.

• *Resistance related to counselors' moralistic attitudes.* Some counselors assume a moralistic stance, condemning both themselves and others for "evil" acts. These helpers who damn their clients for their wrongdoings manage to help their clients to damn themselves. Such clients will typically resist any attempts at helping.

• *Resistance related to fear of disclosure.* Clients often find it difficult to talk about themselves freely, especially if they view their thoughts, impulses, feelings, and actions as shameful. Such clients who resist because of their shame are usually telling themselves an irrational belief, such as: "It's wrong to lust after my mother; I *must* not behave that wrongly. I can't admit that I do feel that way." "If I told my therapist that I lust after my sister, he would think I was a sex fiend and wouldn't like me. I have to be liked by my therapist and would be a shit if even he didn't like me" [Ellis, 1985, p. 12].

• *Resistance created by fear of discomfort.* One of the most stubborn forms of resistance stems from low frustration tolerance, or what RET calls discomfort anxiety. Some clients demand that they achieve pleasure immediately. They have irrational beliefs, which lead to discomfort anxiety: "It's *too hard* to change, and it *must* not be that hard. It's *awful* that I have to go through pain to experience therapeutic gain. I *can't tolerate* the discomfort of working hard. The world is a *horrible place* when it forces me to work so hard. Life *should be* easier." RET shows clients ways to substitute long-range hedonism for short-range hedonism. It teaches that there is rarely any gain without pain.

• *Resistance due to secondary gain.* Many clients resist change because the payoffs that they get from their problems seem considerable. When clients improve, they sometimes discover hidden penalties. Some men learn to express their emotions, for example, only to be ill rewarded by society. They may then relapse into their old and familiar stoical ways.

• *Resistance stemming from feelings of hopelessness.* There are clients who resist because they are convinced that they cannot change their dysfunctional behavior. Although they may make good progress in their counseling, if they show any regression they are likely to irrationally conclude that they are indeed hopeless.

• *Resistance motivated by fear of change or fear of success.* Some symptoms, such as shyness or fear of public speaking, protect clients against possible failure. Their shyness keeps them from being rejected, and their fear of speaking in public keeps them from making a fool of themselves in front of others. If they gave up their symptoms, they would open themselves to the chance of failure and disapproval. Some clients tell themselves that this would be so "catastrophic" or "awful" that they want to cling to their symptoms.

The foregoing description of some of the common kinds of resistance shows that although clients come to counseling for help because they are plagued with a variety of symptoms of emotional disturbance, they often stubbornly resist efforts on the helper's part. This resistance is at least partly due to what the helper does or does not do. More often, however, clients have their own reasons for resisting the help that they have sought.

Types of Difficult Client

Ellis (1985) has written about how to deal with the resistance of your most difficult client—you. His main point is that therapists rarely function at an ideal level; rather, they are human and very fallible. Therapists, like their clients, all too often fall prey to irrational beliefs and accept assumptions that they have not questioned. When counselors encounter resistant clients, for example, they often assume that it is their own fault and that if they were the perfect counselors that they should be, their clients would be cooperative.

In many respects we agree with Ellis when he contends that dealing with your resistance (and your countertransference) is likely to be your greatest challenge as a helper. Rather than constantly paying attention to what your clients do or fail to do, focus on your reactions to your clients, and see what these reactions tell you, both about yourself and your client. You make resistance all the more difficult to deal with in clients when you demand perfection of yourself and labor under irrational beliefs about how the world must be fair.

If you want to be therapeutic with difficult clients, you need to develop patience and give such clients room to maneuver. Regardless of which specific behavior a client exhibits, it is essential that you understand your own countertransference. Certain clients are more difficult for you because they evoke countertransference reactions. Keep this in mind as you review the list of difficult clients below. The list is not all-inclusive, but it does illustrate a sample of the major concerns that helpers discuss with us.

Involuntary clients.   You may not have the luxury of seeing clients who freely come to you for your help. Some will be sent by the court, others will be sent by their parents, others will come in under duress with a spouse, and others will be referred by another helper. The point is that involuntary clients are likely to have little motivation for change and to see little value in the help that you offer. For example, Herman attends a class for those found guilty of driving under the influence. His main motivation in coming to this class is to satisfy the judge's order. He figures that coming to class is better than going to jail. Although he is willing to come to the sessions, he tells you that he doesn't see that he has a problem. Rather, his intoxication was due to a series of unfortunate circumstances. There is not much he sees that he wants to change.

In your role as a helper, you could become either defensive or apologetic. We see it as a mistake to apologize for the fact that an involuntary client is sitting in your office. In Herman's case, he is responsible for being in his situation. It is *he* who needs to accept the consequences of his decisions and behavior. If you work harder than he does, there is little left for him to do. We see nothing wrong with your making some stipulations about how the two of you will spend your time. It helps to remember that when you have an involuntary client, you often have an involuntary helper. With some exploration of his resistance and willingness on your part to provide information about the services you offer, it is possible to melt resistance. Sometimes clients are reluctant to seek help because of their misconceptions about what the helping process entails. You can confront him with the reality that no one dragged him in to see you. Ultimately, he decided that it would be a better deal to come to see you than to accept the consequences if he did not. Together you can make a contract setting out how you are willing to spend your time with him.

Silent and withdrawn clients. Clients who say very little are bound to evoke your anxiety. Imagine the following client sitting in your office. He looks down at the floor much of the time, responds politely and briefly to your questions, and does not volunteer any information. For you the session drags on, and you feel as though you are a dentist pulling teeth. You might ask "Do you want to be here?" He will reply curtly "Sure, why not?" If you ask him what is going on in his life and what he wants to talk about, he will tell you that he doesn't know.

Do you feel that you need to do something to make this client talk? Are you taking his silence personally? Are you thinking of all sorts of ways to draw him out? Before your ego becomes too involved and you are unable to see his problem, it is useful to attempt to put his silence in some context. You might ask yourself, and even at times your client, what the silence means. His silence could have any one of the following meanings: He is frightened. He sees you as the expert and is waiting for you to ask a question or tell him what to do. He feels dumb; he may be rehearsing every thought and critically judging his every reaction. He is responding to past conditioning of "being seen but not heard." His culture may put a value on silence. He may have been taught to listen respectfully and merely to answer questions. Furthermore, your client may be quiet and invisible because this pattern served to protect him as a child. In other words, all forms of silence should not be interpreted as stubborn resistance and a refusal to cooperate with your attempts to help.

Silent clients can affect you in many ways. You may begin to judge yourself, thinking that if you knew the right things to say and do, your client would open up and talk fully. You could make a mistake by doing the talking for your client or by constantly drawing him out. It might be helpful to say something such as "I notice that you are very quiet in this group. You seem to pay attention to what other group members are saying, yet I very rarely hear from you. I'd like to know more about how it is for you to be in this group. Is your silence something that bothers you, or is it OK with you?" If this client does not interpret his silence as a problem, then maybe you will be working in vain if you try to change him. This silent group member will have many reasons for being quiet. If he sees his silence as a problem, you can explore with him the ways in which this behavior is problematic. It could be a mistake to continually draw him out by asking him what he is thinking and feeling. If you assume the responsibility for bringing him out, he never has to struggle with the forces that are keeping him quiet.

Talkative clients.   The opposite of the client who says nothing is the one who seems never to stop talking. Some clients tend to get lost in telling stories. They jump from one topic to another. They take great care in providing you with every detail so they won't be misunderstood. They often get lost in relating their stories, and you wonder what the point of the story is. Instead of talking about how they are affected by a particular situation, they give you much irrelevant information.

Consider the case of Bertha. When she is in your office, she goes on and on and on. Any attempt you make to stop her results in her telling you that she wants to be sure that you know what she is saying. She gets very involved in ''he-said'' and ''she-said'' monologues. Bertha's defense is to keep talking, for then she doesn't have to stay long enough to experience any feelings or insights. If she slows down and experiences some of the things she is talking about, she is likely to feel anxiety.

In working with Bertha, you might feel intimidated. Although she is talking about painful situations, she is doing so in a very detached and rehearsed style. You might have reservations about interrupting her, out of fear of cutting her off. One of your functions is to help Bertha gain awareness into how her behavior serves as a defense. A few examples of some helpful comments are:

- ''I notice that when you speak of your relationship with your mother, you have tears in your eyes. Yet you quickly move away from your tears when you start talking *about* her instead of how you feel when you are with her.''
- ''I have trouble following what you're saying, and I wonder why you're telling me all of this.''
- ''Let's stop right here, and you tell me what you're feeling at this moment.''
- ''You're making a real effort to give me a lot of details so that I can understand you better, but I'm getting lost, and I'm not understanding you. I want you to know that I do want to understand you, but I can't when you go into so many details.''
- ''If you had to express in one sentence all that you've been trying to tell me, what would you say?''

If you are having reactions to a talkative client like Bertha, such as noticing that you have a hard time staying with her, it could be therapeutic to deal with your own reactions. Chances are that Bertha is affecting many people in her life in much the same way as she is affecting you. This is an opportunity for her to get feedback on how she comes across and for her to determine if she wants to do anything different. If you chronically suppress your reactions and pretend that you are listening with unconditional positive regard, she will soon pick up that you are not present for her. Also, by not dealing with her, you are reinforcing her talkativeness.

Overwhelming clients. Some of your clients have so many problems that they feel chronically overwhelmed. Not only do they keep themselves overwhelmed, but they may overwhelm you as well. Disaster seems to lurk constantly around the corner. Such clients often have an endless reserve of problems, as if they thrived on having and creating problems. They come in each week and excitedly begin with "Just wait until I tell you what happened to me this week." Although some of the situations they describe are terrible, you suspect that they get some sense of pleasure out of reporting these incidents. A sample of the way some clients continue to overwhelm themselves can be seen from Ruth's statements:

"I've just got to tell you everything that happened this week. I got an 'F' on one of my term papers, I'm having trouble getting financial aid, and if I don't get this aid, I can't stay in college. My daughter is having all sorts of problems with her boyfriend, and she comes to me late at night and wants to talk. Of course I listen, and then I get up in the morning feeling like a dishrag. Then I don't have the energy to get through the day. My son is having problems at school. His counselor called me to tell me that he is truant much of the time. I had to go down to the school, and I surely didn't have time for that with all the things that went wrong last week. The toilet got stopped up, and of course I was the one who had to take care of that. Oh, by the way, the garbage disposal broke again, and there was a flood in the kitchen. I feel I have to handle everything, and all by myself. When my husband comes home, all he does is plop himself in front of the TV, watch the sports, and drink beer. I just don't see how I can hold up everything. I've got to be a terrific student, the one who repairs leaks, the counselor to my kids, and on top of that I should be understanding of my husband who doesn't want any more pressure when he comes home. Oh, I don't know where to begin. Everything seems to be pulling at me at once."

Although this may sound a bit dramatic and exaggerated, some of your clients will sound like this. As you listen, you may have a hard time making an impact. If you don't intervene actively and forcefully, yet sensitively, Ruth will not only overwhelm herself, but you, too, will be at your wit's end. You will not know where to begin, and you are likely to feel burdened with all of her problems and think that you must solve them.

As with other forms of resistance, you need to explore with Ruth the ways in which she contributes to her problems by overwhelming herself. It can be helpful to tell her something like this: "Ruth, I know there are many things that you feel are pressing on you today. But we have only an hour, and we realistically can't attend to everything that has gone on with you all week. Why don't you sit quietly for a moment and reflect on what it is that you most want from this session? Select the one concern that is most pressing to you at this time." By focusing her, you are a catalyst in helping her to avoid being lost, being drowned in a sea of problems.

'Yes, but' clients.   You will encounter clients who are exceptionally talented at inventing reasons why your interventions just won't work. As a helper faced with such clients, you quickly feel de-energized. No matter what insights or hunches you share or what suggestions you make, the end result is the same: the client quickly retorts with an objection. Some illustrations of the "yes, but" syndrome follow:

HELPER: "Have you considered telling your wife some of what you've told me?"

CLIENT: "Yes, but you don't know my wife." "I agree that it might help, but my wife would be very threatened." "But my wife will never change!" "I'm willing to talk to her, but I don't think it would help."

HELPER: "Every time I suggest something, you come back with plenty of reasons why my suggestion wouldn't work. I wonder if you really do want to change?"

CLIENT: "Yes, but you just don't understand my situation." "You expect so much of me. I try, but things just don't work out." "Of course I want to change, but there are just so many things that keep me from changing. Only God knows how hard I try!"

When you are trying to help such clients, there is a danger of becoming too easily discouraged. It doesn't take much to get irritated with them. Even though you are willing to help this client, he is determined to prove to you that he cannot be helped. Eventually you are bound to feel helpless and to be inclined to give up. When you sense that you are working harder than your client is working, it may be time to renegotiate with him what he wants.

Clients who blame others.   Some clients assume a stance of being a victim and a martyr. They chronically blame circumstances and other people for everything that happens to them. Carrie is a good illustration of a client who is quick to find fault in the universe for her unhappiness but slow to recognize her part in contributing to her misery. She views herself as having no control over her life. She seems to refuse to consider her role in creating her own unhappiness, largely because she is so attuned to finding fault outside of herself. Just a few of the outside factors that she sees as being responsible for her misery are these: her husband does not understand her; her children are selfish and inconsiderate; she always feels miserable a few days before her period; she feels terrible when there is a full moon; she has severe allergies, which keep her from doing what she wants; she really can't lose weight, because she is too depressed. And on and on it goes.

As long as Carrie puts the focus of her problems outside of herself, no change is possible in her life unless others change. If you allow her to talk continually about these others "out there," you have no power as a helper, because most of what she talks about is not in the room. It is possible for you to work with her to change, but you cannot work with all of the variables apart from her. You cannot control the moon, nor can you change some of the people in her life.

It would not be surprising if Carrie were to annoy you. You might engage in a lot of argumentation with her, challenging her on all of the ways in which she makes herself a martyr. If she continually refused to look at her own role, you might be tempted to refer her. As with most of these forms of resistance, it is important to keep clear within yourself and not get lost in the attempt to sway her. You can challenge her, share your reactions with her, listen to her, and ask her what she is willing to do to get what she says she wants.

Clients who deny needing help. Difficult clients in another category do not see that they have a problem. Such clients may come to a marital counseling session to help their spouse but be unwilling to see their part in the troubled marriage. In fact, they may well deny that a problem even exists in the marriage. You can waste much valuable time by trying to convince these clients that they indeed have a problem when they insist otherwise. The denial of these clients is serving a function, for as long as they don't admit the problem, they don't have to cope with it.

Take Roy. If you ask him what he wants from you, he will probably reply "My wife wanted me to come to counseling, and I'm here for her sake." You may be better able to get through his resistance if you take his word for it and accept his view that he is problem-free. By asking him how he is being affected by his wife's problems, you may eventually get to problems that he wants to deny. Another alternative is to ask him how it is for him to come to your office. If he replies by saying "Oh, it's fine," you could respond "What were you thinking as you approached the office?" Or you could ask: "You say you're here to help your wife. What are some of the areas that you think she needs help with?" Or you could say: "You tell me that you don't have any problems and that your wife made you come here today. Could *that* be a problem for you?"

Some of the students we work with in a counseling program are quick to say how much they want to help others but not so quick to identify issues in their own life. We have heard such students talk about their problems in the past tense. They are ready to admit that they had problems, but they maintain that they have dealt with and solved these problems. In some of your classes you have probably had opportunities for experiential and personal-growth activities. At this time think about how open you were to exploring any facets of your life with others. Were you willing to look at your own life in an honest fashion? How much did you resist? How motivated were you to listen to and reflect on feedback that others gave you? If you find it difficult to own up to potential problems in your life, do you think you will be able to effectively challenge clients to make an honest assessment of what troubles them?

Moralistic and judgmental clients. Some of your clients will appear to be self-righteous and judgmental. Such clients question you continuously about your interventions. They have a view of the world that they believe is absolutely right, and they wish that everyone else believed as they do.

Consider this illustration of a father who is in a family-therapy session with you. He has views and convictions about everything. In the session he has comments for each family member. To his wife he says: "The trouble with you is that you're trying to do too much. How can you make meals, take care of the kids, pay the bills, go to school, and work part time? Why don't you knock off all this other stuff and stay home where you belong? What the hell good is going to college anyway?" To his son he says: "You wouldn't have half the problems you do if you put your nose to the grindstone. The idle mind is the devil's workshop. You surely have plenty of free time, and you waste most of it." To his daughter he says: "Why don't you go to church more often? You're not living the way I brought you up. Besides, what will the neighbors think?"

Of course, many judgmental individuals are far more subtle than the father depicted above. Even though their proclamations may not be as sharp as his, they may be thinking very much as he does. When we work with clients who seem self-righteous and tend to judge others harshly, we sometimes ask them to give in to their tendency to lecture and provide a very stern lecture. This gives us some material to work with therapeutically. We sometimes ask such clients to reflect on what or whom their statements remind them of. They have often unconsciously incorporated a critical parent whom they now carry around inside of themselves. The therapeutic challenge is to help these clients see what their judgments of others do to their relationships. Such moralism usually has the effect of distancing them from others. If they can come to see this, they can then assess whether any modification of their behavior is necessary.

Dependent clients. Client dependency comes in many forms. There are clients who don't make any move without first checking it out with you; those who continuously want you to tell them what you think of them; those who would like to call you at all hours of the day and night; those who want to become your friend; and those who want you to tell them what to do, how to do it, and when to do it.

If you have many clients whom you perceive as dependent, look at your possible role in fostering and maintaining their dependency on you. You might encourage clients to call you at any time, for example, without thinking that they will take you at your word. You might encourage them to call you before a job interview or right after the interview, so they can let you know how it went. It is important that you look at the ego gratification that you get from their dependence. These clients usually fear making decisions. For them, choices represent a threat. If they make the "wrong" choice, they are stuck with the responsibility. Along with accepting that we have choices comes the anxiety of using our freedom constructively and in a responsible manner. Many clients want to escape from their freedom by making you responsible for choosing for them. In some ways they expect you to fill their parents' shoes. They are likely to develop transference reactions toward you and treat you as an authority. If you buy into their manipulations and nuture their dependent tendencies, you are merely reinforcing their vision of themselves as helpless. They are bound to resent you if they consistently put you "up there" and themselves "down there."

Passive/aggressive clients.   Certain clients have learned to defend themselves from hurt by dealing with people indirectly. They use hositility and sarcasm as a part of their style of resistance. Whenever they do or say anything, they are highly evasive. If you want to give your reactions, they are likely to retort: "Well, you really shouldn't feel this way. When I made that remark, I was just kidding. You take me too seriously."

Some common signs of passive/aggressive clients are as follows: They often arrive late. They say little. You see reactions on their face, yet they assure you that everything is fine. They giggle when you talk. They raise eyebrows, frown, sigh, shake their head, look bored, and show other nonverbal reactions but deny that anything is going on with them. They chronically draw attention to themselves, and when they have the attention, they do little with it. They tend to be seductive in many ways.

Passive/aggressive clients may be hard to deal with. You may feel that you have been hit, but you won't know what hit you. It is hard to deal directly with this kind of behavior because of its elusive quality. However, you will certainly have reactions to clients who make hostile remarks, who offer much sarcasm, and who seem to engage in hit-and-run behavior. One way of cutting through this indirect behavior is to be aware of what it brings up in you and to give your reactions. What is important in dealing with this behavior is to avoid making judgments about it. You are more likely to avoid further hostility when you describe the behavior you see and tell the clients how their behavior is affecting you. It is also useful to ask them if they are aware of their behavior and to tell you what it means.

Some possible questions to consider are "Do certain hostile clients remind me of any people in my life? What do I feel like when people are not direct and I sense that there are some things they are not telling me? Is it timely and appropriate for me to give my reactions to the hostility I perceive in my clients?"

Intellectualizing clients.   Individuals who block out any feelings and present themselves in highly detached ways are another type of difficult client. Any time they get close to an emotion, they give a minilecture. They constantly try to figure out why they have a problem. They are adept at self-diagnosis and theorizing abstractly about the nature of their dysfunctions. They have learned that as long as they "stay in their head," they are safe. If they allow themselves to feel jealousy, pain, depression, anger, or any other emotion, they are not safe. To avoid experiencing anxiety, they have learned to insulate themselves from feelings.

Don't attack these intellectualizing clients and insist that they get to a feeling level. You can surely let them know how it is for you to be with them when they show little affect, but it is not helpful to try and strip away their defense. When they feel ready to let go of their defenses, they will do so. Think about the ways in which you are affected in dealing with a man who remains very cerebral. If you are successful in getting him to give up his defense, will you be able to help him? Will you be able to be present for this person when his resistance melts and he gets in touch with years of bottled-up feelings? Will you be overwhelmed with his pain and run from it? If you are not there when he expresses his fear, will this prove to him that people will let him down when he releases his emotions?

Emotionalizing clients. The opposite of the client who intellectualizes is the client who thrives on dramatic displays of emotion. Such people are quick to weep, have no trouble in "getting into feelings," and seem to thrive on catharsis. Their behavior may put you in a bind. As they sit in your office and exude feeling, you may have trouble in trusting their emotions. You may become annoyed, feel manipulated by them, or somehow feel that they are play acting.

We are not suggesting that clients who genuinely express emotions are resisting. We are talking about the difficult clients who have made a defense out of getting stuck in emotional material. When you are with such clients, reflect on what they bring out in you. It is possible that some of your highly emotional clients could remind you of selected people in your life who manipulated you with their emotions. For example, a sister might have succeeded in making you feel guilty when she cried and stormed out of the room. Now as you work with clients who exhibit some of these behaviors, you may feel a lack of compassion for them and, in turn, wonder whether you have a problem with empathy.

Handling Resistance with Understanding and Respect

Learn to respect resistance and understand its meaning. It serves a purpose, and it will help both you and your client if you can understand its context. Realize that some resistance in clients is perfectly normal and makes good sense. Why should your clients automatically trust you? Chances are that many of them have had negative encounters with helpers, and as they approach you, they wonder whether you will be trustworthy. You don't get clients' respect immediately, nor do credentials on your office wall really earn genuine regard. Instead, your clients will come to trust you, and thus let down some of their walls, if you also let some of your barriers down. Part of respecting resistance means that you appreciate that the defenses your clients have created serve a function in their life. If they give up their defenses, what will be left? If you succeed in enabling them to surrender much of their resistance, are you willing to stick with them to create new resources for coping? Sometimes your interventions will take the form of helping clients block out some aspects of reality. People need certain defenses in order to psychologically survive. Uncovering a client's defenses is often inappropriate, and supportive interventions are called for. This is especially true in crisis-intervention situations, when you are expected to deal with an immediate problem in a relatively short time.

In addition to understanding the context that surrounds the client's various forms of defensive behavior, pay attention to your countertransference that is evoked by this resistance. Avoid labeling your clients and thus entrenching their resistive styles. Don't assume that your client merely wants to annoy you. You cannot afford to have a fragile ego as a professional helper. Give your clients some rope, and don't respond to their resistance with resistance of your own. Be patient with people in your office, since they are coming to you for help in changing aspects of their life that are not working for them. Resistant clients often have the effect of making you feel incompetent, thus bringing out feelings of inadequacy and anger. If you too quickly become annoyed with difficult clients, you are likely to cut off avenues of reaching them. Perhaps one of the best ways for you to identify sources of your countertransference is by opening yourself to personal counseling or some other form of self-exploration.

AIDS: A Special Concern for Helpers

AIDS already affects a wide population and will certainly become an increasing problem. As a helper you will inevitably come in contact with people who have AIDS, with people who have tested positive as carriers of the virus, or with people who are close to AIDS patients. You simply cannot afford to be unaware of the many issues that have emerged from the AIDS epidemic. You will not be able to educate those with whom you come in contact unless you are educated about the problem yourself.

We have decided to include this section because of the ignorance and fear surrounding the AIDS crisis, both among the general population and members of the helping professions. There are conflicting reports and evidence about this disease. The changing nature of information about AIDS and misinformation about the ways in which the disease is spread result in apprehension among helpers. Our intent is not to provide you with all the relevant facts about AIDS but, rather, to encourage you to explore your own attitudes, values, and fears about working with AIDS patients.

The Helper's Role and Responsibility in the AIDS Crisis

Resistance within the helper. The AIDS crisis has created anxiety among many medical personnel and mental-health professionals. This fear brings such helpers into a real conflict. They have dedicated their life to helping those in need, yet they have a variety of reasons to justify their unwillingness to help people afflicted with the AIDS virus or AIDS-related problems. Never before have mental-health professionals had concern that they would be infected with a fatal disease that their clients were carrying. Thus, these helpers often resist close contact with those who have been infected.

Overcoming your resistance through education. Mental-health providers may say "I don't know anything about this disease, and I'm not competent to deal with people who are affected by the problem." If you find
yourself identifying with this statement and feeling somewhat overwhelmed,
it is not necessary to remain this way. There is no reason to remain ignorant,
because you can get the basic information you need about this disease. As
a minimum step you can do some reading. You can also attend a workshop
on AIDS or contact one or more of the many clinics that are being started
all over the country as a resource for learning what you need to know.

In addition to this basic information about AIDS, it is imperative that you
have skills in crisis intervention. People who come to you because they have
discovered that they are carriers of the AIDS virus are typically highly anxious. Both those who have tested positive and those who have contracted
AIDS are typically in need of short-term help. They need to find a system
to support them through the troubled times they will endure. Not only can
you be of support by listening to them and helping them deal with their immediate feelings, but you can be instrumental in assisting them to find a
broader network. This may take the form of a support group at the agency
where you work, and it can also include a support system among friends
and family members who will be able to show their presence and concern.

Special Needs of Clients with the AIDS Virus

The stigma of AIDS. In addition to clients who have manifested the more
severe symptoms of AIDS, you will see clients who have discovered that they
have the virus within them. They live with the anxiety of wondering whether
they will come down with this incurable disease. Most of them also struggle
with the stigma attached to AIDS. They live in fear not only of developing
a life-threatening disease but also of being discovered and thus being rejected
by society in general and by significant persons in their life.

The stigma is attached to the fact that most of those in the United States
who have contracted AIDS are either sexually active homosexual or bisexual
men or present or past abusers of intravenous drugs. Among the mainstream
population, there is still a general negative reaction toward people who are
homosexual or bisexual. Typically, people who develop AIDS are afflicted
with a double-edged stigma, one due to their life-style and the other due
to the disease, which is often seen as the result of their homosexual activities.
People afflicted with AIDS often stigmatize themselves and perpetuate
beliefs such as "I feel guilty and ashamed." "I feel that God is punishing
me." "I am a horrible person, and therefore I deserve to suffer." "I am to
blame for getting this disease."

In addition to feeling different and stigmatized, those with AIDS typically
have a great deal of anger. They often feel left alone and without support.
This feeling is frequently grounded in reality. In some cases family members
actually "disown the outcast." Patients often feel a sense of disillusionment,
for after getting better for a time, they become sicker. They also feel isolated.
For some this isolation is expressed through their feeling of utter rejection

by others: "I'm gay, and now I've got AIDS. No one wants anything to do with me." It is hard for them to see any meaning in their plight, and thus they often give in to depression. Consequently, they develop anger at having a life-threatening condition. They express this anger by asking over and over: "What did I do to deserve this? Why me?" This anger is sometimes directed at God for letting this happen, and then they may feel guilty for having reacted this way. Anger is also directed toward others, especially those who are likely to have given them the virus. Those at risk often feel anger toward health professionals.

How You Are Affected as a Helper

If you are involved in providing help and support for people who have developed AIDS, all of these clients will be dying, and this will certainly have an impact on you. Reflect on the following questions:

- Your clients may well displace some of their anger onto you. How do you think you will handle such anger?
- How might the hopelessness that your clients feel affect you? Can you think of ways in which their despair could lead you to feel that your work with them is futile?
- As your clients bring up unfinished business with key people in their life, how might this affect you?
- What specific values might you hold that could make it difficult for you to be objective in working with people who have AIDS? Are you open to examining and changing these values?
- Your clients are likely to bring up the issue of meaning in their life now that they are afflicted with a disease that prevents them from doing many of the things that gave them meaning. How might their crisis in discovering meaning have an impact on you? Many times these clients will say: "I simply cannot see any point in living anymore. I can't do anything. All I have to look forward to is suffering." What would you have to offer to them?
- If they bring up their fears of dying or what lies beyond death, do you see yourself as able to assist them in giving expression to their fears? Will their fears trigger your own fears?
- Since many AIDS patients are relatively young, how do you think losing them is likely to affect you?
- In working with clients who are at risk for contracting AIDS, you cannot avoid talking about sexually explicit topics. How do you feel about being able to discuss such topics?
- If you do a good deal of work with AIDS patients and their family members, what concerns do you have about burnout? What are some ways in which you could prevent burnout?
- Do you see yourself as willing to ask for support from others as you work with this difficult population? Are you willing to talk with others about how you are personally affected by this work?

The Helper's Role in Educating the Public

Regardless of what type of helper you happen to be, one of your most important functions is to dispel myths and misconceptions about AIDS and to help people acquire realistic knowledge and attitudes. To be able to carry out this function effectively, you need to be able to differentiate between fact and fiction about this disease. Information about some aspects of AIDS seems to be changing daily, so that facts we provided here might be outdated by the time this book is published. Therefore, as we have stressed, it is imperative that you keep up with the latest research in this field.

Education of various target groups is the key in preventing sharp rises in the number of AIDS victims. In order to be able to educate various segments of the population, you will need to be aware of their characteristics. This includes an awareness of the values, mores, and cultural background of the various groups you serve. In attempting to change the habits of racial, cultural, and religious groups, you are likely to run up against considerable resistance unless you are able to "speak their language." Furthermore, in educating the general public, it is important to realize that people with AIDS can easily become the scapegoat of people's projections of their unconscious fears and hatred. Thus, people who are highly intolerant of those who are different from them often engage in denial and seek a target for their resentments. Any educational program must be directed toward minimizing denial and homophobia.

Because information is changing rapidly, it is difficult for people who are at risk to trust what they hear from the medical profession. They may be defensive about further education because they don't believe what is presented to them. They may also remain in a state of denial because they do not want to change their sexual life-style. These difficulties will challenge you to find a meaningful way to provide education. A few key elements of the educational effort are listed below:

* Take steps to understand AIDS yourself.
* As a helper, explore your own attitudes, and eliminate those beliefs that make it difficult for you to make contact with those who need your help.
* All sexually active Americans need to know the basic facts about this disease and how to avoid the risk of infection.
* Emphasis must be on prevention. A comprehensive sex-education program, for all age groups, is essential if AIDS is to be prevented.
* Rather than thinking in terms of "safe sex," it is helpful to consider practices that are "unsafe," "relatively safe," and "safe." If people are going to be sexually active, they will not be safe, and they need to recognize the risks of infection.
* Community efforts need to be made to care for people with AIDS. Part of your job as a helper could be directed toward organizing and mobilizing people in the community to become active, to serve in various capacities as volunteers, and to work toward the goal of helping one another.

- In developing educational programs, keep in mind the special needs of minority groups. Certainly, many minorities are not responsive to education as it is typically presented. Alternatives to the usual means of education might include training ministers to work with their congregations, using a spokesperson or a role model whom young people can relate to, creating videos with educational goals, and using AIDS victims as resource people to teach others about the disease.

An important ethical issue that practitioners face pertains to the limits of confidentiality with clients who have the AIDS virus. For further reading on this issue, consult Gray and Harding (1988), Kain (1988), and Posey (1988).

By Way of Review

- Effective helpers must become aware of transference on the part of clients and countertransference on the part of helpers. Neither of these factors is to be eliminated but is to be understood and dealt with therapeutically.
- Countertransference refers to the unrealistic reactions that therapists have toward their clients, which are likely to interfere with their objectivity. One way of becoming more aware of your potential for countertransference is by experiencing your own therapy. Another way is by focusing in your supervision sessions on yourself and your reactions to clients.
- Resistance takes many forms, and it is necessary to understand the ways in which it serves as a protection for clients. Not all resistance stems from stubbornness on the part of the client. Some is caused, or at least contributed to, by the attitudes and behaviors of helpers.
- The goal in a helping relationship is not to eliminate resistance but, rather, to understand what functions it serves and to use it as a focus for exploration.
- There are many types of difficult clients. Some of these clients will evoke your own countertransference reactions. It is important to avoid reducing clients to a given label.
- AIDS is a special concern for all those in the helping professions. You cannot afford to be unaware of the many issues arising out of the AIDS crisis. You will not be able to educate those with whom you come into contact unless you possess current and accurate information yourself.

What Will You Do Now?

1. Select the most difficult client whom you can imagine working with and reflect on the reasons that this client would present problems for you. What makes this client a difficult one? What do you think you'd do if you actually had this person as a client? What might you do if you felt that you could not work with him or her?

2. Reflect on the kinds of resistance that you see within yourself. How open are you to accepting your faults and your limitations? If you were a client in counseling, what resistances do you imagine that you might develop to changing? What do you think it would be like if your clients were very much like you? Talk with a friend about this subject as a way of confirming (or contradicting) your views.

3. Imagine that you are doing an intake interview with a man who tells you that he has just found out that he has tested positive for the AIDS virus. He is seeking counseling to deal with his high anxiety over fears of death and is in a crisis state. What might you feel? If you know very little about the disease, go to an AIDS information center at school or a community center and ask for reading materials. Talk with someone about this disease, especially its social and psychological aspects. Find ways to challenge any values of yours that could render you ineffective in helping victims.

Suggested Readings

Bugental, J. F. T. (1987). *The art of the psychotherapist.* New York: Norton. The author hopes to help therapists of various orientations give priority to the subjective world of the client as well as to their own subjective world. He draws on a wide variety of clinical examples and personal reflections to describe the art of psychotherapy.

Ellis, A. (1985). *Overcoming resistance: Rational-emotive therapy with difficult clients.* New York: Springer. A highly interesting and easy-to-read treatment of the main forms of resistance. Ellis discusses cognitive, emotive, and behavioral techniques for overcoming resistance. An especially useful chapter is "How to Deal with the Resistance of Your Most Difficult Client—You."

May, R. (1983). *The discovery of being: Writing in existential psychology.* New York: Norton. This book is of value for helpers other than counselors and therapists. May has some insightful material on transference and resistance in the therapeutic process.

CHAPTER 6

Self-Exploration and Personal Growth

Focus of the Chapter

Professional Help for the Helper

Developmental Themes and Life Choices

By Way of Review

What Will You Do Now?

Suggested Readings

Focus of the Chapter

We have been stressing the value of self-awareness throughout this book. In this chapter we look at the circumstances under which professional help could be of special value for helpers. Our central point is that self-exploration is a process, not a final product to be attained once and for all. This process entails making an assessment of your personal assets (strengths) and liabilities (weaknesses). If helpers expect their clients to make an honest self-assessment, they themselves must be committed to this same quest for self-awareness.

We include a detailed discussion of major life themes at the stages of development from infancy through old age. Our hope is that you will reflect on critical turning points in your own life, along with significant decisions that you've made at these junctures. By drawing upon your own life experiences, you are likely to be in a better position to appreciate the struggles of your clients. As a way of facilitating your exploration of your personal struggles, we provide many cases that illustrate the problems that clients are likely to bring to you. We focus on how your awareness of your life experiences can be a useful instrument when you intervene to help your clients.

Professional Help for the Helper

The Value of Self-Exploration

There are several reasons why it is a good idea for you to experience personal counseling or psychotherapy as a part of your training program. We do not assume that therapy is just for treatment purposes or for curing deeply rooted personality disturbances. We see personal therapy as an avenue for continuing to deepen your self-understanding. This kind of professional help can be a factor in stimulating you to assess your motives for becoming a helper. You can look at your needs and how they relate to your work.

In addition, if you expect to counsel others, it is good to know what the experience of being a client is like. Through the process of therapy you can get a firsthand knowledge of what your clients are likely to experience.

Another reason that we encourage you to seek some form of personal counseling is that if you are like most people, you have certain blind spots, unfinished business, and old conflicts that might hamper your attempts to work effectively with clients. Personal therapy is one way to come to grips with such unresolved situations. Therapy can aid you in seeing how these past conflicts are affecting you in the present. Furthermore, it will illuminate your own areas of transference and countertransference. You will become aware of patterns in your reactions to certain events or types of people. If you felt that no matter how much you did it was never quite enough to win your mother's approval, for example, you may now be very finely attuned to the judgments of women who remind you of your mother. If you allowed your father to completely affirm or deny your value as a person, you may be very sensitive to what male authority figures think about you. You may give them the power to make you feel either competent or incompetent. As a child, if you often felt rejected and on the outside, you may now create situations in which you feel like the one who is left out and just does not fit. In your own therapy you will be able to explore some of the ways in which you unconsciously set up situations that repeat past situations that have been a source of pain to you. A woman who was rejected by her father, for example, finds that in every relationship with a man the end result is that she feels rejected by him. Thus, she recreates an old familiar scene with every significant man she meets. In her therapy she can come to understand her role in the continuation of this pattern of rejection.

As a helper you can perhaps learn nothing more important than the ways in which you carry old feelings from the past into present situations. You have a set of convictions that structure your life, and you are intent on confirming these assumptions even though some of them are self-defeating and no longer functional. Again, it is not so much a matter of "doing away" with your unrealistic feelings but of bringing to consciousness some of your behavior patterns and reactions. If you recognize these patterns, there is a good chance that you can change some of your reactions that at one time were functional but have now ceased to serve you. When someone in your family got angry, for example, people got hurt either physically or emotionally. As a child you made a decision that anger was a useless emotion, that you would never show this feeling, and that you would not even allow yourself to feel angry. This decision could have protected you at the time, when you felt helpless and did not know how to cope with destructive expressions of anger. However, your extreme denial of anger now interferes in your significant relationships at home and at work. People find it difficult to trust you, since you never express negative reactions to anything. If you have this trouble in accepting your own anger, you are certainly going to have difficulty in allowing your clients to express their anger and deal constructively with it.

Many professional training programs recognize the value of some form of personal therapy or self-exploration for the trainees. Whether this personal-growth experience is conducted one-to-one or in a group setting, the focus can still be on the helper as a person. We have found that many beginning helpers would rather focus on the dynamics of their clients than on looking at themselves.

Some training programs require a lengthy process of therapy for trainees. Psychoanalytic practitioners usually have to undergo several years of personal analysis. This requirement is based on the assumption that the psychoanalyst's reactions and problems can stand in the way of dealing with the client's problems. Analysts must be aware of how their conflicts can be triggered by certain clients, so that they can guard against disturbing effects. Psychoanalysts view countertransference as an inevitable part of the therapeutic relationship. Of course, they view transference reactions of clients as the most important material to be explored in therapy. If trainees allow themselves to become clients, they experientially learn what it feels like to have a range of feelings toward their therapist. The therapy process alerts them to specific ways in which their feelings can work both for and against them as helpers. In addition, by experiencing many of the difficulties of being a client, they develop more sensitivity and compassion for the struggles of their own clients.

Professional help is useful not only for trainees but also for practicing professionals. At times, experienced practitioners can use the challenge to reevaluate their beliefs and their behaviors. Furthermore, they may experience a crisis situation or an impairment for a period of time. Periodic self-review with the help of another professional can be a way of getting unstuck.

We encourage both beginning helpers and those with many years of experience to pay attention to what they are giving to their work and getting from it. We find it hard to understand why so many helping professionals see themselves as beyond getting any help for themselves, even in times of personal crisis. It is as though some helpers think that they should be able to work out any problem they have by themselves. Although they claim to value the therapeutic process for others, they do not attribute the same value to receiving help from others. Kottler (1986) describes this resistance as follows: "For a group of people who spend their whole lives engaged in the practice of helping, we seem to exhibit a lot of resistance to getting it for ourselves" (p. 126).

Helper, Know Thyself

In applying to an educational program in the helping professions, you may well have been asked to write a brief autobiography. As a part of this personal paper, you may have been asked to address questions such as the following: "What are your reasons for pursuing work in this program? What have been some of the most significant turning points in your life? How have you dealt with any crises that you might have encountered? What did you learn about yourself from dealing with these crises? In terms of working with clients, what personal experiences and learning can you draw on?" These programs take note of the fact that who you are will greatly affect your capacity to deal effectively with clients.

One way we train beginning helpers is to assist them in focusing on their own development as a person. We assume that helpers must first know themselves if they hope to be instrumental in aiding clients to learn about themselves. Another of our assumptions is that helpers cannot take clients any further than the helpers have gone in their own life. Because of our belief about the importance of helper self-understanding, we structure our training sessions for group counselors around personal themes. We ask the trainees to read about certain life themes, to think about their own development and turning points, and to recall key choices they have made at different times in their life. Some of these themes include dealing with childhood, adolescent, and adult struggles; love and intimate relationships; loneliness and solitude; death and loss; sexuality; the choice of a life-style; and meaning in life. These are some of the main themes that clients will bring into counseling sessions. Helpers will be affected by the problems that clients discuss in these areas. If helpers themselves have limited awareness of their own struggles with these themes, they are not likely to be very effective with their clients. In training workshops the participants can discover what impact their life experiences have on their clients and, in turn, how their clients' life experiences affect them. We ask you to reflect on how the themes we discuss pertain to your life.

Developmental Themes and Life Choices

We assume that you have had, or will have, a course in human growth and development that spans infancy through old age. This section deals with developmental themes at these various phases of life. The idea is not to teach you about the stages of development but, rather, to use key concepts of these stages as illustrations of problems that you are likely to encounter with clients. Our emphasis is on you and your earlier life experiences and how they are likely to influence the way in which you work with people who come to you with their problems.

We describe the eight stages of development from infancy to old age by pointing out the psychosocial tasks for each phase. We also briefly describe potential problems in personality development if these tasks are not mastered. With each stage of development we present a case illustration to give you some practice in thinking about how to approach given clients. We also encourage you to recognize how your own development in each of these areas can be either an asset or a liability as you help others. How well have you mastered some of the major psychosocial tasks at each period of your development?

One of the more useful models of the stages of human growth and development is Erik Erikson's (1963, 1982) psychosocial perspective. Erikson describes human development over the entire life span in terms of eight stages, each marked by a particular crisis to be resolved. For Erikson, *crisis* means a turning point in life, a moment of transition characterized by the potential to go either forward or backward in development. These moments point to both dangers and opportunities. From a positive perspective, crises can be viewed as challenges to be met rather than as catastrophic events that simply happen to you. It is also possible to fail to resolve the conflicts and thus regress. To a very large extent an individual's current life is the result of earlier choices. Life has a continuity.

Infancy

Trust versus mistrust.   In infancy (the first year of life) the basic task is to develop a sense of trust in self, others, and the environment. The core struggle at this time is between trust and mistrust. If the significant persons in an infant's life provide the needed warmth and attention, the child develops a sense of trust. This sense of being loved is the best safeguard against fear, insecurity, and feelings of inadequacy. Children who receive love from parents or parental substitutes generally have little difficulty in accepting themselves.

If there is an absence of security in the home, personality problems tend to occur later. Insecure children come to view the world as a potentially hostile place. They have a fear of reaching out to others, a fear of loving and trusting, and an inability to form or maintain intimate relationships. Rejected children learn to mistrust the world and view it largely in terms of its ability to do them harm. Some of the effects of rejection in infancy include tendencies in later childhood to be fearful, insecure, jealous, aggressive, hostile, and isolated.

Case example.   Imagine that a child with a history of being abused is brought to you for counseling. As a result of her experiences, she is very frightened and distrustful of the world. Some of her experiences stir up your own memories of difficult periods in childhood. Although you were never physically abused, you suffered much psychological cruelty from two alcoholic parents. Your reason for going into this profession was to make the world a better place. In working with children like this you become aware that some of your old cynicism and distrust of the world, which you thought you had successfully dealt with, now resurfaces. You find it increasingly difficult to counsel abused children.

This case illustrates how your personal involvement can render you ineffective in working with a child's pain that reminds you of your own pain. This is especially true if you have not resolved your early conflicts between trust and mistrust. However, such early experiences do not necessarily have to be a liability. If you are aware of your vulnerability in trusting and have worked through this negative conditioning to the point that you are now able to trust, your experiences can be an asset. By drawing on your own experiences, you can empathize with abused children and assist them in learning to trust the world.

Reflections and application.   As you reflect on the developmental tasks during this stage, think about the kind of foundation you had during your earliest years and how these experiences either prepared you or handicapped you for the tasks you face in your life now. Particularly consider what you learned about trusting the world. Most of the decisions you made in infancy were unconscious and preverbal. Nevertheless, such decisions were powerful shapers in the way you viewed the world later. Consider these questions: "Do you have difficulty in trusting others? Are you able to trust in yourself and your ability to make it in the world? Do you have fears that others will let you down and that you have to be very careful about how much you show of yourself?"

Early Childhood

Autonomy versus shame and doubt.   The most critical task of early childhood (ages 1–3) is to begin the journey toward autonomy by progressing from being taken care of by others to being able to care for one's own needs. Children who fail to master the task of establishing some control over themselves and coping with the world around them develop a sense of shame and feelings of doubt about their capabilities. Parents who do too much for children hamper their proper development. If parents insist on keeping them dependent, these children will begin to doubt the value of their own abilities. During this period it is essential that feelings such as hostility, anger, and hatred be accepted rather than be judged. If these feelings are not accepted, children may not be able to accept their feelings later on. They will become adults who feel they must deny all of their negative feelings.

Case example.   Your supervisor has asked you to colead a group of involuntary clients. There is much anger being expressed in the room. You find that you are working very hard to deflect this anger. At one point you tell a male client that he doesn't have to get so angry. He responds by shouting "You don't understand me, so why don't you just shut up!" You feel scared and instinctively leave the room.

Reflections and application.   If you were the helper in this situation and thought about why it was so hard for you to be the recipient of intense anger, you might come up with several answers. You grew up in a sheltered and protected environment. Since your parents made all of your decisions, you never had to struggle with deciding for yourself. You experienced your parents as very loving and kind. In your family nobody ever got angry. Even when your parents unexpectedly divorced, no one expressed anger or hurt. Basically, you were taught messages such as "Be happy and look at the brighter side of things." "Don't get angry." "We will always be there for you." "If you can't say something nice, don't say anything at all."

Some helpers have trouble in recognizing or expressing angry feelings. Thus, they also have trouble in allowing their clients to have these "unacceptable" feelings. They might talk their clients out of these feelings. If any of this situation fits you, are you able to see any alternatives besides withdrawing from anger? One way you could behave differently is to remain in the room and deal with the fears that are evoked in you as a client directs his anger toward you. A situation such as this confronts you with some feelings and attitudes that get in the way of your dealing with clients.

Preschool Age

Initiative versus guilt.   During the preschool years (ages 3–6) children seek to find out what they are able to do. They imitate others; they begin to develop a sense of morality; they increase the circle of people who are significant to them; they learn to give and receive love and affection; they learn basic attitudes regarding sexuality; they begin to learn more complex social skills; they take more initiative; and they increase their capacity to use and understand language. According to Erikson, the basic task of the preschool years is to establish a sense of competence and initiative. If children are allowed realistic freedom to choose their own activities and make some of their own decisions, they tend to develop a positive orientation characterized by confidence in their ability to initiate and follow through. If they are unduly restricted or not allowed to make decisions for themselves, they develop a sense of guilt and ultimately withdraw from taking an active stance toward life.

Parental attitudes toward children are communicated both verbally and nonverbally. Thus, children often develop feelings of guilt based on negative messages from their parents. Strict parental indoctrination tends to lead to rigidity, severe conflicts, remorse, and self-condemnation. Children may pick up subtle messages that their body and their impulses are evil, for example, and thus they soon begin to feel guilty about their natural impulses and feelings. Carried into adult life, these attitudes can prevent them from enjoying sexual intimacy.

During this period the foundations of sex-role identity are laid. Children begin to form a picture of appropriate masculine and feminine behavior. The models that children have are important in determining whether their self-concepts are healthy. Many people seek counseling because of problems they experience in regard to their sexual identity. Some men have a lot of confusion about what feelings and behaviors are appropriate for them. Some men resist doing anything that resembles feminine behavior. Some women clients have submerged their identity totally in the roles of mother and housewife. At some point they may want to broaden their conception of what is appropriate for them as women. Yet their early conditioning may make the expansion of their self-concept somewhat difficult.

Case example.   You are doing an intake interview with Paula, age 14, who was sent to you by her parents. Paula has had an abortion, is sexually promiscuous, is regularly abusing drugs, and is failing in school. You gather information about her developmental history, and it appears that many of her present problems originated during her preschool years. The parents tell you that Paula was a model child who never gave them any trouble. They were strict disciplinarians. The children she was allowed to play with were all selected by her parents. Since Paula was an unusually pretty child, the parents worried about her sexual development. They basically communicated a distrust of boys. During the preschool years, when most children are given some freedom and some room for making decisions, Paula was highly controlled by her parents. She had no room to maneuver. Since no freedoms were granted to her, she never had the opportunity to develop self-responsibility. Her mother went to work when Paula was 12 years old, and she immediately began to take advantage of being on her own several hours a day. It was then that she made friends whom her parents disapproved of. With time she became increasingly rebellious toward the rigid climate in her home. She seemed determined to become everything her parents did not want her to be.

On the basis of the above knowledge about her situation, there are a number of directions in which you might proceed as Paula's counselor. You could become an ally of her parents and take the role of attempting to "straighten her out." You can see that she is heading down a destructive path, and you could attempt to influence her to give up her irresponsible ways of behaving.

From another perspective, you could become Paula's ally. You have empathy for her situation, in that you see her oppressive background as largely contributing to her present behavior. You could decide to bring in the family, since you see the problem as being related to the parents' need to control. Do you think you could make sure that everybody in the family was being listened to? Would you be tempted to take sides?

Reflections and application.   As you reflect on the case of Paula, how do you think you'd fare as a helper in this situation? What do you think you would do? Might you focus on the parents? on Paula? on both? Are you aware of any of your attitudes that would influence your interventions? How might your own struggles for independence with your parents affect you? If you have children, how might your relationship with them influence the way you'd work with Paula or her parents?

As you read and apply the developmental tasks of this stage to your own life, look for patterns in your present attitudes and behavior that could be traced to your preschool years. Pay special attention to how these preschool patterns operate today in your life, either positively or negatively. Also, note how your life experiences either contribute to or detract from your ability to be helpful to Paula. Consider some of these questions: "Do you have a clear sense of your own sex-role identity? Are you the kind of woman or man you want to be? Where did you acquire your standards of femininity or masculinity? Are you comfortable with your own sexuality? with your body? with giving and receiving in a sexual relationship? Are there any unresolved conflicts from your childhood that affect you today? Do your present behaviors and current conflicts indicate areas of unfinished business?

Middle Childhood

Industry versus inferiority.   For Erikson, the major struggle of middle childhood, or the school years (ages 6–12), is between industry and inferiority. The central task is to achieve a sense of industry; failure to do so results in a sense of inadequacy. Children need to expand their understanding of the world and continue to develop an appropriate sex-role identity. The development of a sense of industry includes focusing on creating goals, such as meeting challenges and finding success in school. Children who encounter failure in their early schooling often experience major handicaps later in life. Those children with early learning problems may begin to feel worthless as a person. Such feelings often dramatically affect their relationships with their peers, which are also vital at this time. Problems that can originate during middle childhood include a negative self-concept, feelings of inferiority in establishing and maintaining social relationships, conflicts over values, a confused sex-role identity, dependency, a fear of new challenges, and a lack of initiative.

Case example. José and Maria are a middle-age couple who come to you for marital counseling. One of the issues that has caused trouble in their marriage is the fact that José continually changes jobs, and as a result they are always financially strapped. Maria insists that her husband seeks jobs that are far below his capabilities. José basically agrees with Maria. During the interview you learn that he had many academic difficulties in elementary school. His parents were migrant farmers, and as a result he attended many different schools. When he started school, he did not speak English, and he recalls that his teachers were not understanding of him. Most of the time he felt like a failure and an outcast, he hated school, and he decided that he was unintelligent. As the years went on, his feelings of inadequacy progressed. He always reacted with surprise when some of his teachers told him that he was performing below his abilities. Even though he realizes that he is not stupid, he has decided that it is too late to overcome some of these earlier obstacles. Out of his fear of failure and limited self-confidence, he avoids pursuing jobs that are more challenging and that could be potentially more satisfying.

Assume that you are a White, upper-middle-class counselor. You are impatient with José, for you see him blaming the system and making chronic excuses for his failures. You have a hard time understanding why he has not overcome the obstacles that he faced so long ago. If this is your frame of reference, do you think that you would be able to provide him with encouragement to explore his deeper problems, such as self-doubt and inadequacy?

On the other hand, consider that you feel for José's situation and understand how his early experiences in grade school are continuing to affect his self-confidence. You could work with him on modifying his self-limiting assumptions and changing some of the decisions he made about himself as an early learner. With José you formulate a plan for change that includes participating in remedial courses in adult education. The crux of your work involves getting him to see that his early failures stemmed from unfortunate circumstances and not from the fact that he was unintelligent.

Reflections and application. If you had a client like José, how might your own life experiences either hinder or enhance your ability to counsel him? What were some of the highlights of the first few years in school for you? In general, did you feel competent or incompetent as a learner? Did you see school as an exciting place to be or as a place that you wanted to avoid? What were some of the specific ways in which you felt that you were successful or that you were a failure? What attitudes did you form about your competence as a person during your early school years? Think of some significant people in your life at this time who affected you either positively or negatively. Attempt to recall some of their expectations for you, and remember the messages they gave you about your worth and potential. What connections do you see, if any, between the assumptions you made then and the assumptions that influence your life today?

Adolescence

Identity versus role confusion.   Adolescence (ages 12–18) is the time for testing limits, and there is a strong urge to break away from dependent ties that appear to be restricting freedom. Although many adolescents feel frightened and lonely, they often mask their fears with rebellion and cover up their need to be dependent by exaggerating their degree of independence. Much of adolescents' rebellion grows out of the context of wanting to determine the course of their own life. Adolescence is a critical time for integrating the various dimensions of one's identity. For Erikson, the major developmental conflicts of adolescents center on the clarification of who they are, where they are going, and how they are getting there. He sees the core struggle of adolescence as identity versus role confusion. The struggle involves integrating physical and social changes. There are many pressures at this time in life. Adolescents may feel pressured to make career choices early, to compete in the job market or in college, to become financially independent, and to commit themselves to physically and emotionally intimate relationships. Peer-group pressure is a major force, and it is easy to lose one's self by conforming to the expectations of friends. With the increasing stress experienced by many adolescents, suicidal ideation is not uncommon.

During the adolescent period a major part of the identity-formation process consists of separation from the family system and establishment of an identity based on one's own experiences. The process of separating from parents can be an agonizing part of the struggle toward individuation. Although adolescents may adopt many of their parents' values, to genuinely individuate they must choose these values freely as opposed to blindly accepting them.

Case example.   Adam is referred to you by the school counselor. When you ask him what brings him to your office, he first tells you abruptly that his counselor has made him come to see you. After overcoming his initial resistance, he eventually tells you the following about his problems:

"I used to be a good student, but about a year ago I lost interest in school because I felt the pressure of having to get "A"s in all my classes. I want to go to college, but I'm afraid I won't make it because I've been failing some of my classes. My parents are very disappointed in me. We used to have a great relationship, but now I don't even want to talk to them. I'd much rather stay in bed than get up and go to school. My friends tell me I've become a bore to be around, and I don't want to be around them either. What really hurt me was when my girlfriend broke up with me. When I'm not at school, I spend most of my time alone in my room listening to music. I don't know anymore what I want to do. There's nothing I look forward to, and sometimes I wish I could go to sleep and never wake up."

Reflections and applications. If you were Adam's counselor, how able would you be to hear his hopelessness, his feelings of desperation, and his possible suicidal intentions? Would you want to cheer him up and tell him that he is just going through a phase and that things are bound to get better? Would you get lost in his feelings of hopelessness by remembering some of your own unhappy adolescent years? If someone you know well has committed suicide, how might that affect your ability to work objectively with Adam? Did you ever feel a sense of hopelessness and a belief that your future would never be any better? Feelings of hopelessness and suicidal thoughts are among the most difficult issues that you will have to explore with your clients. It will probably be most difficult to remain objective and not get lost in the client's hopelessness. You may feel afraid when your clients express the depths of their despair and their desire to end it all. At these times you will feel much pressure and responsibility in wondering what to do in order to be helpful. At some point in your life you may have lost a sense of meaning and not seen much hope for change or reason to continue living. How you recognized and dealt with these feelings will greatly influence the way you intervene with clients who see little hope.

Take a few moments to review some of your adolescent experiences. How did you feel about yourself during this time? In reviewing these years, how might your experiences work for or against you in dealing with Adam? Think about your degree of independence from your parents during your adolescence. Focus on what gave meaning to your life. Also ask yourself questions such as "At this time in my life, did I have a clear sense of who I was and where I was going? Were my values my own, or did I merely unquestionably accept the values of my parents? What were some major choices that I struggled with during my own adolescent years?" As you review this period, focus on the ways in which your adolescent experiences affected the person you are today.

Early Adulthood

Intimacy versus isolation. According to Erikson, we enter young adulthood (ages 18–35) after we master the adolescent conflicts over identity. Our sense of identity is tested anew in adulthood, however, by the challenge of intimacy versus isolation. The ability to form intimate relationships depends largely on having a clear sense of self. One cannot give to another if one has a weak ego or an unclear sense of identity. Intimacy involves a sharing, a giving of ourselves, a relating to another based on our strength, and a desire to grow with that person. If we think very little of ourselves, the chances are not good that we will be able to give meaningfully to others. The failure to achieve intimacy often results in feelings of isolation from others and a sense of alienation. Erikson's concept of intimacy can be applied in any kind of close relationship between two adults. Relationships involving emotional commitments may be between close friends of the same or the opposite sex, and they may or may not have a sexual dimension.

During their 20s young people are challenged to make many critical choices. They wrestle with the choice of clinging to security or leaving those things that bring a secure existence. They struggle with the costs and benefits of developing relationships with a few people. Career choice becomes an important part of this time of life. Whether to marry and to become a parent is another issue. Young people are creating dreams and wondering about how they can translate their dreams into real life. Because of the many areas of choice pertaining to work, education, marriage, family life, and life-style, it is not uncommon for them to wonder what it is they really want. At this time of life some allow others to decide for them what their standards and choices will be.

Case example. Becky, 23, comes to you for counseling on the urging of a concerned friend. She tells you that she has been in a relationship with a young man for over five years, yet she has never really been satisfied with it. Although she has tried to break off with him a number of times, she typically resumes seeing him when he begins to "treat her so nice" and when she begins feeling guilty. If she were to give him up for good, she fears, she would have no man in her life. She concludes that having him is better than having nobody. In most aspects of her life Becky has allowed her parents to make her choices for her. Under parental pressure she pursued a teaching major and is currently in student teaching. She discovered that she really is not interested in teaching, yet she doesn't trust herself to follow her own interests. Becky has a great deal of talent in dancing, and she wanted to become a professional dancer. She abandoned this idea because she could tell her parents did not support this choice. She is aware that she has been both financially and emotionally dependent on her parents. Although she would like to choose for herself, she stops herself from doing so out of her fear of making poor decisions. Many of her high school and college friends have gotten married, and she picks up signals from her family to find a "nice boy" to marry. At this time in her life she feels a great deal of pressure within herself to please her parents, yet she realizes that she cannot please both them and herself.

Reflections and applications. Put yourself in the position of being Becky's counselor. Imagine that although you are Becky's age, you have had a very different kind of life from hers. You had few problems in establishing goals and following them. You knew what you wanted to do, and you pretty much did it. With a minimum of help from your parents you attained most of your goals. If this were the case, do you think you'd be able to empathize with her? Would you be able to identify with any of her struggles and thus help her find a way to move ahead?

If you are a middle-aged or older person, what decisions did you make in early adulthood, and how do you think those decisions would influence the way you work with Becky? Do you have any regrets about the choices you made? If you are unhappy about some of these choices, might you be inclined to be another person who would influence her to move in a particular direction?

Think especially about what you want in close relationships. What do you expect of others in intimate relationships? What do you think you can contribute to these relationships to enhance them? From a career point of view, what have you most looked for in your work? How do you think your own struggles or lack of them would affect you in working with clients like Becky who have problems in deciding for themselves what they want to do personally and vocationally?

Middle Adulthood

Generativity versus stagnation. Middle adulthood (ages 35–60) is a period when people reach the top of the mountain and become aware that they must begin the downhill journey. They might painfully experience the discrepancy between the dreams of their younger years and the harsh reality of what they have actually accomplished with their life so far. According to Erikson, the stimulus for continued growth during middle age is the core struggle between generativity and stagnation. Generativity includes more than fostering children. It includes being creative in one's career, finding meaningful leisure activities, and establishing significant relationships in which there is giving and receiving. During this time people become more aware of the reality of death, and they may reflect more on whether they are living well. It is a time for reevaluation and a time when people are at the crossroads of life. They may begin to question what else is left to life, and they may establish new priorities or renew their commitments.

During middle age there is sometimes a period of depression. When people begin to see that some of their visions have not materialized, they may give up hope for a better future. Some women who married and made a family their main priority may begin to wonder if this is all there is to life. At this time many women will choose to return to college or to work full time or to combine the triple roles homemaker, student, and worker. Some men begin to wonder if they want to stay in their career. They may have to cope with depression when they realize that they have not reached some of their important dreams.

As is true with any stage, there are both dangers and opportunities during this time. Some of the dangers include slipping into secure but deadening ruts and failing to take advantage of opportunities for enriching life. Many individuals experience a midlife crisis, when their whole world seems to be unstable. A few of the events that lead to such a crisis include the realization that youthful dreams will not come about; an illness or the onset of the aging process; the death of one's parents; the realization of one's ultimate aloneness in this life; the realization that life is not always fair and just; a marital crisis or the break-up of a long-established relationship; children's leaving the nest; the losing of one's job; and other major changes. A problem of this period is the failure to achieve a sense of productivity, which then leads to feelings of stagnation. What is important is that individuals realize the choices they have in their life and see the changes they can make, rather than giving in to the feeling that they are a victim of life's circumstances.

Case example. Ernie, age 44, has been referred to you by his minister. Ernie, who has been married for 24 years, has done everything with his wife. They have never spent a night apart. He did not make any close friends, either male or female, because his wife is very jealous and is threatened by any attempts to do so. He has totally surrendered to his wife's exaggerated fear of his having an affair. Ernie says that until recently there were no grounds for her fears. Although he had not questioned his marriage and life before, he finds himself growing more and more disenchanted with the boredom and predictability of his life. He feels caught in a rut, yet he hesitates to get out. Although he has a good job, it, too, has lost its appeal. He feels a lack of excitement in his work in much the same way that he feels a dullness about his marriage. He hates to go to work, and he hates to come home. He complains about a lack of sleep, waking up in the middle of the night, and ruminating about his life situation.

A few months ago he found that he enjoyed talking to one of the women at work. She listened to him, and they shared some common concerns. They developed a friendship, which he carefully kept a secret from his wife. Eventually Ernie and his friend became involved in a sexual relationship. Although he finds his time with her exciting and very much values her as a friend, he cannot imagine himself leaving his wife to live with her. She is also married, and she has several small children. He says that he still loves his wife, yet he is not ready to quit seeing the other woman. Although Ernie feels caught in deadening ruts at home and at work, he is not ready to quit his job or seek a divorce. He is in much turmoil, for as he puts it, he is going against his own values. He comes to you because he is in a great deal of pain and does not know what to do next.

Reflections and application. If you were counseling Ernie, what life experiences of yours do you think might help you in understanding him? If he were to ask you what you think he should do, how might you answer him? Assume that you have been hurt by an affair, and consider your capacity for remaining objective as you work with Ernie. He wants someone to tell him what to do. Would you be willing to provide him with answers? Which of the following themes in his life would you tend to focus on: His affair? His marriage? His dissatisfaction with his job? The meaninglessness in his life?

If you have reached middle adulthood, what struggles and decisions could you draw on as a resource? If you have not yet reached middle age, what would you most want to be able to say that you have accomplished in your life by this time? What would you hope to have in your relationships? What would you want from your work? How might you go about keeping yourself alive and avoid the trap of falling into predictable ruts?

Late Adulthood

Integrity versus despair.   During this period of life (about age 60 and beyond) some of the core developmental tasks include adjusting to retirement, finding a meaning in life, being able to relate to the past without regrets, adjusting to the death of a spouse or friends, accepting inevitable losses, maintaining outside interests, and enjoying grandchildren. Erikson sees the central struggle of this age period as one of integrity versus despair. People who succeed in achieving ego integrity are able to accept that they have been productive and that they have coped with whatever failures they faced. Such people are able to accept the course of their life, and they do not endlessly ruminate on all that they could have done, might have done, and should have done. Instead, they are able to look back without resentment or regret and see their life in perspective. Although they may not welcome the notion of death, they can view it as natural. In contrast, some elderly people fail to achieve ego integration. These people fear death. They develop a sense of hopelessness and feelings of self-disgust. They are able to see all that they have not done, and they often yearn for another chance to live in a different way. These people may feel that they have let valuable time slide by.

Case example.   Mr. Wellman was picked up by the police after he was found wandering around, lost and disoriented. He was brought to the geriatrics ward where you work as an intern. You notice that he is unkempt and is talking incoherently. After some time on the ward he improves to the point of being able to join a therapy group. In this group he recalls many sad times in his life. He talks about his regrets. About two years ago he lost his wife, who died after a long illness. He feels lost without her, and he says that most of his will to live vanished after she died. Her medical bills ate up his savings. Because the company Mr. Wellman worked for went bankrupt, he is left with few benefits for his old age. He has five children and 15 grandchildren, but he has no contact with any of them, because they are spread around the country. One of his major regrets is that he never really established meaningful ties with his children or grandchildren, and now he feels that it is too late. At age 74 he just does not see much sense in going on with his life. He never took the time to develop hobbies or friends. He finds life at this time to be boring and meaningless.

What help do you think you would offer Mr. Wellman? Would you agree that his state is hopeless and that there is little he can do to change at this late time in his life? Or do you see hope for him? Even at his age, are there chances for new beginnings? If so, how might you assist him in considering alternatives that he could pursue?

How often might you be able to listen to people like this without getting depressed? If you had an elderly parent who was similar to Mr. Wellman, how would working with him affect you?

Reflections and application.   If you haven't reached old age, imagine yourself doing so. Think about what you would like to be able to say about your life. Focus especially on your fears of aging and also on what you hope you could accomplish by this time. What kind of old age do you expect? What are you doing now that might have an effect on the kind of person you will be as you grow older? What are some things that you would like to do during your later years? Can you think of any regrets that you are likely to express? As you anticipate your growing older, think about what you can do today to increase the chances that you will be able to achieve a sense of integrity as an older person. Are you cultivating interests and relationships that can become a source of satisfaction in later years? If you find yourself postponing many of things that you would like to do now, ask yourself why. Assess the degree to which you are satisfied with the person you are becoming today. If you let valuable time slip by and do not act on opportunities, the chances are greater that you will experience despair during your later years. Finally, assess your present ability to work with elderly clients. If you yourself have not reached this age, what experiences could you draw on as a way of understanding the world of an elderly client? Even though you might not have had some of the same experiences, do you see ways in which you can relate to some of their feelings that are very much like your own?

By Way of Review

- Professional help is of value in increasing a helper's self-awareness. Healthy individuals who want to help others can profit from professional assistance, especially in gaining increased insight into their own personal issues that could intrude in their work.
- Personal therapy can illuminate our own areas of transference and countertransference. Your experience with the therapeutic process can increase your awareness of certain patterns of thinking, feeling, and behaving.
- If helpers realize that they are in distress or that they are experiencing conflicts in their life, they should be open to using therapy.
- At each stage of life there are choices to be made. Your earlier choices have an impact on the kind of person you are now.
- From infancy through old age specific tasks and specific crises can occur at each stage of life. Review your own developmental history so that you have a perspective in working with the developmental struggles of your clients. You will be in a better position to understand your clients' problems and to work with them if you have an understanding of your own vulnerabilities.

What Will You Do Now?

1. Write down a list of resources for personal growth and ways of increasing your self-awareness. Think of some avenues that would promote self-exploration on your part. Are you inclined to do something that will encourage you to reflect on the quality of your life?

2. Think of specific things that you'd want from both a supervisor and a therapist. On a sheet of paper, put what you'd most want from your supervisor on the left side. Imagine that you were to seek out a therapist for personal and professional growth, and write down on the right side what you'd most want from your therapist. Compare your list.

3. Review the highlights of the section on developmental themes and life choices. Remember a time in your life that was either the most difficult (painful) or the most exciting (joyful). What was this like for you? What did you learn from these experiences? If this time occurred during childhood, talk with someone who knew you well as a child about what he or she remembers of you. What are the implications of these experiences in your own life for you as a helper? How might some of your life experiences affect you as you work with others who are like you? different from you?

Suggested Readings

American Association for Counseling and Development. *Journal of Counseling and Development.* This journal publishes articles that have broad interest for counselors, counseling psychologists, and other human-service professionals who work in schools, colleges, community agencies, and government. Published ten times a year, the journal features articles that integrate published research, examine current professional issues, apply research to practice, and describe new techniques or innovative programs and practices. Subscriptions for nonmembers are $40 per year; AACD members receive the journal as a benefit of membership. Contact AACD, 5999 Stevenson Avenue, Alexandria, VA 22304.

Black, C. (1981). *It will never happen to me!* New York: Ballantine. The author shows how family dynamics influence the development of children of alcoholics and how these dynamics continue to affect the person during adulthood. This is must reading for anyone who wishes to understand these patterns.

Corey, G., with Corey, M. (1986). *I never knew I had a choice* (3rd ed.). Pacific Grove, CA: Brooks/Cole. The themes dealt with in this book are very useful as self-exploration material. The focus is on our capacity to choose the kind of existence we want. Some of the themes explored are childhood, adolescence, adulthood, the body, sex-role identity, sexuality, love, intimate relationships, loneliness and solitude, death and loss, and meaning and values.

Erikson, E. (1963). *Childhood and society.* (2nd ed.). New York: Norton. Using a modified and extended version of psychoanalytic thought, Erikson describes a psychosocial theory of development with a focus on the critical tasks of each of the eight stages of development.

Erikson, E. (1982). *The life cycle completed.* New York: Norton. In this book Erikson updates his psychosocial theory of life-span development.

Levinson, D. J. (1978). *The seasons of a man's life.* New York: Knopf. A description of growth patterns from the viewpoint of the entire life span.

Sheehy, G. (1981). *Pathfinders.* New York: Morrow. A description of the developmental themes and choices of the stages of adulthood. Some topics explored include the capacity for loving, friendship and support systems, male and female strengths, life's purpose, coping and mourning, and the view from the top of the mountain.

Managing Stress

Focus of the Chapter

It is unrealistic to think that we can eliminate stress from either our personal life or our professional life. Yet we do not have to be the victims of stress, for we can recognize how we are being affected by it and can make decisions about how to think, feel, and behave in stressful situations. We can become aware of our destructive reactions to stress and learn constructive ways of coping with it. In short, we can learn to manage and control stress rather than being passively controlled by it.

If you choose one of the helping professions, you will have to contend with hazards throughout your career. As you well know, the demands on you as a student often create stress. In addition, a fieldwork placement or a class that involves an emotional focus is likely to bring out your anxieties. This stress, of course, is not necessarily negative. Painful awareness can be a vehicle for growth and self-understanding. We want to reassure you that this emotional involvement is a normal process.

When you leave your program and get involved in practicing on a full-time basis, new stresses will stem from the nature of your work and from the professional role expectations for care givers. Unfortunately, practitioners in a training program are typically not warned about the hazards of the profession.

In writing about the distressed professional, Kilburg (1986) observes that most helpers begin their career with little or no information about what they will really experience when they enter the field. Nor are professionals generally prepared to assume the variety of difficult roles that they will be expected to play. As a result they find that they must cope with high levels of stress and failure. They feel great pressure to perform well. Frequently, the lives and welfare of human beings depend on the decisions and recommendations they make. All of this work-related stress can result in serious psychological, physical, and behavioral disorders.

Typically, helpers are not good at asking for help. Many of them have been socialized to think of others, and they have difficulty accepting their own need for help. Thus, they often give to the point of depletion. This resistance to recognizing the need for help is put cogently by Kilburg (1986, p. 25):

> Professionals can be their own worst enemies. Trained to be independent, creative, assertive, and hard driving, they do not readily acknowledge that they are in trouble or need assistance. More often, their combination of socialization and personality characteristics leads them to struggle on with a problem long after many other people would have at least sought consultation from family members or friends. Solitary battles are the most destructive for anyone because of the ease with which one loses perspective.

If you are considering a career as a counselor, you may be looking forward to helping people find a resolution to the problems they face and deal constructively with pain in their life. You are likely to be thinking about the expected satisfaction that comes with knowing that you can be an agent of change for your clients. Yet you may not be fully aware that the commitment to being a therapeutic agent for others is fraught with difficulties. As we saw in the last chapter, the process of working with clients may open you up to some of your own deepest personal struggles and unfinished business. It also seems impossible to us that you can work intensely with clients week after week and not be affected by their pain. When old pain surfaces and present struggles become overwhelming, it is essential that you seek help for yourself. There is a steep price for numbing yourself to this pain, and you need to recognize that the nature of your work makes it difficult to hide from yourself.

It is important to sensitize yourself to both the external and internal factors that contribute to negative physical and psychological reactions. We will present a variety of strategies for coping with stress, and we encourage you to develop your own set of strategies for managing stressful experiences. We are merely introducing you to the subject of stress management and urge you to select at least one book in the Suggested Readings at the end of this chapter to use as your guide.

Sources of Stress for Helping Professionals

Work-related stress for helping professionals is caused by two sets of factors. *Environmental sources* of stress include the physical aspects of the work setting or the structure of the position itself. A major stressor is the reality of having too much work to do in too little time. Another potential environmental source is the quality of working relationships with colleagues. Dealings with coworkers and supervisors can be a source either of support or of stress. Of course, certain client behaviors such as suicidal tendencies and depression are highly stressful. There are also *individual, or personal, sources* of stress, such as your attitudes and personal characteristics as a helper. To understand the dynamics of the stress you will experience as a human-services professional, you must understand both the external realities that tend to produce stress and the individual contribution that you make to stress by your perception and interpretation of reality.

Work stress, or job stress, is the condition that exists when the environmental demands of work exceed your personal capabilities for effectively coping with the situation. Before you continue reading, we suggest that you complete the accompanying Work-Stress Profile (Rice, 1987)* on pp. 134–138 and score yourself on the various scales. The inventory will give you some sense of how much job stress you live with.

If you are not now working, do your best to answer these items by thinking about how you would most probably respond in a work situation. If you have worked in the past, you can draw on that experience. If you have a fieldwork placement, you can reflect on your experiences in that setting as a way to assess how stress is likely to affect you as a professional.

---

*From *Stress and Health: Principles and Practice for Coping and Wellness,* by P. L. Rice. Copyright © 1987 by Wadsworth, Inc. Reprinted by permission of Brooks/Cole Publishing Company, Pacific Grove, California 93950.

Work Stress Profile

This scale provides some information on work stress. Instructions for scoring and interpreting the scale appear at the end.

The following statements describe work conditions, job environments, or personal feelings that workers encounter in their jobs. After reading each statement, circle the answer that best reflects the working conditions at your place of employment. If the statement is about a personal feeling, indicate the extent to which you have that feeling about your job. The scale markers ask you to judge the approximate percentage of time the condition or feeling is true to the best of your knowledge.

NEVER = not at all true of your work conditions or feelings
RARELY = the condition or feeling exists about 25% of the time
SOMETIMES = the condition or feeling exists about 50% of the time
OFTEN = the condition or feeling exists about 75% of the time
MOST TIMES = the condition or feeling is virtually always present

	NEVER	RARELY	SOME-TIMES	OFTEN	MOST TIMES
1. Support personnel are incompetent or inefficient.	1	2	3	4	5
2. My job is not very well defined.	1	2	3	4	5
3. I am not sure about what is expected of me.	1	2	3	4	5
4. I am not sure what will be expected of me in the future.	1	2	3	4	5
5. I cannot seem to satisfy my superiors.	1	2	3	4	5
6. I seem to be able to talk with my superiors.	5	4	3	2	1
7. My superiors strike me as incompetent, yet I have to take orders from them.	1	2	3	4	5
8. My superiors seem to care about me as a person.	5	4	3	2	1
9. There is a feeling of trust, respect, and friendliness between myself and my superiors.	5	4	3	2	1
10. There seems to be tension between administrative personnel and staff personnel.	1	2	3	4	5
11. I have autonomy in carrying out my job duties.	5	4	3	2	1

12. I feel as though I can shape my own destiny in this job.
    [5] [4] [3] [2] [1]

13. There are too many bosses in my area.
    [1] [2] [3] [4] [5]

14. It appears that my boss has "retired on the job."
    [1] [2] [3] [4] [5]

15. My superiors give me adequate feedback about my job performance.
    [5] [4] [3] [2] [1]

16. My abilities are not appreciated by my superiors.
    [1] [2] [3] [4] [5]

17. There is little prospect of personal or professional growth in this job.
    [1] [2] [3] [4] [5]

18. The level of participation in planning and decision making at my place of work is satisfactory.
    [5] [4] [3] [2] [1]

19. I feel that I am overeducated for my job.
    [1] [2] [3] [4] [5]

20. I feel that my educational background is just right for this job.
    [5] [4] [3] [2] [1]

21. I fear that I will be laid off or fired.
    [1] [2] [3] [4] [5]

22. In-service training for my job is inadequate.
    [1] [2] [3] [4] [5]

23. Most of my colleagues are unfriendly or seem uninterested in me as a person.
    [1] [2] [3] [4] [5]

24. I feel uneasy about going to work.
    [1] [2] [3] [4] [5]

25. There is no release time for personal affairs or business.
    [1] [2] [3] [4] [5]

26. There is obvious sex/race/age discrimination in this job.
    [1] [2] [3] [4] [5]

NOTE: Complete the entire questionnaire first! Then add up all the values circled for questions 1–26 and enter here. → [   ]

Total 1–26

27. The physical work environment is crowded, noisy, or dreary.
[1] [2] [3] [4] [5]

28. Physical demands of the job are unreasonable (heavy lifting, extraordinary periods of concentration required, etc.).
[1] [2] [3] [4] [5]

29. My work load is never-ending.
[1] [2] [3] [4] [5]

30. The pace of work is too fast.
[1] [2] [3] [4] [5]

31. My job seems to consist of responding to emergencies.
[1] [2] [3] [4] [5]

32. There is no time for relaxation, coffee breaks, or lunch breaks on the job.
[1] [2] [3] [4] [5]

33. Job deadlines are constant and unreasonable.
[1] [2] [3] [4] [5]

34. Job requirements are beyond the range of my ability.
[1] [2] [3] [4] [5]

35. At the end of the day, I am physically exhausted from work.
[1] [2] [3] [4] [5]

36. I can't even enjoy my leisure because of the toll my job takes on my energy.
[1] [2] [3] [4] [5]

37. I have to take work home to keep up.
[1] [2] [3] [4] [5]

38. I have responsibility for too many people.
[1] [2] [3] [4] [5]

39. Support personnel are too few.
[1] [2] [3] [4] [5]

40. Support personnel are incompetent or inefficient.
[1] [2] [3] [4] [5]

41. I am not sure about what is expected of me.
[1] [2] [3] [4] [5]

42. I am not sure what will be expected of me in the future.
[1] [2] [3] [4] [5]

43. I leave work feeling burned out.
[1] [2] [3] [4] [5]

44. There is little prospect for personal or professional growth in this job.
[1] [2] [3] [4] [5]

45. In-service training for my job is inadequate.
[1] [2] [3] [4] [5]

46. There is little contact with colleagues on the job.
[1] [2] [3] [4] [5]

47. Most of my colleagues are
unfriendly or seem uninterested
in me as a person.   [1]   [2]   [3]   [4]   [5]

48. I feel uneasy about going to work.   [1]   [2]   [3]   [4]   [5]

NOTE: Complete the entire questionnaire first!
Then add up all the values circled for
questions 27–48 and enter here.   →   [   ]
Total 27–48

---

49. The complexity of my job is
enough to keep me interested.   [5]   [4]   [3]   [2]   [1]

50. My job is very exciting.   [5]   [4]   [3]   [2]   [1]

51. My job is varied enough to
prevent boredom.   [5]   [4]   [3]   [2]   [1]

52. I seem to have lost interest in my
work.   [1]   [2]   [3]   [4]   [5]

53. I feel as though I can shape my
own destiny in this job.   [5]   [4]   [3]   [2]   [1]

54. I leave work feeling burned out.   [1]   [2]   [3]   [4]   [5]

55. I would continue to work at my
job even if I did not need the
money.   [5]   [4]   [3]   [2]   [1]

56. I am trapped in this job.   [1]   [2]   [3]   [4]   [5]

57. If I had it to do all over again, I
would still choose this job.   [5]   [4]   [3]   [2]   [1]

NOTE: Now go back and add up the values for
questions 1–26. Do the same for questions
27–48. Enter the values where indicated.
Then add up all the values circled for
questions 49–57.   [   ]
Total 49–57

Last, enter those sums for each of the following
groups of questions and add them all together to get a
cumulative total.

QUESTIONS:	1–26 Inter-personal	27–48 Physical Conditions	49–57 Job Interest	TOTAL 1–57
TOTALS:	[ ]	+ [ ]	+ [ ]	= [ ]

The first scale measures stress due to problems in interpersonal relationships and job satisfaction or dissatisfaction, as the case may be. The second scale measures the physical demands of work that wear on the person daily. The third scale measures job interest and involvement. For each of the scales, you can gain some sense of how much job stress you live with relative to the original test group by locating your scores on the scale provided below. On each scale, a high score means more job-related stress. If you are high in one of the areas, say interpersonal stress, it could be of some help to pay attention to the interpersonal aspects of your job.

	Low ← Stress →		← Normal Stress →		High ← Stress →
Interpersonal	.. 39 .... 43 46	.... 51 .... 54 57	.... 62 .... 68 .... 75..
Physical	.. 35 .... 40 44	.... 48 .... 52 55	.... 58 .... 62 .... 67..
Interest	.. 13 .... 15 17	.... 18 .... 19 21	.... 23 .... 25 .... 27..
Total	.. 91 ... 101 ... 111	... 117 ... 123 ... 134	... 141 ... 151 ... 167..
Percentile	.. 10 .... 20 30	.... 40 .... 50 60	.... 70 .... 80 .... 90..

The work stress profile has been tested in a sample of 275 school psychologists. The three scales are virtually identical to those identified in other work stress scales. The reliability of this scale is quite high. For the total scale, the reliability is .921. Reliabilities for the three subscales are .898, .883, and .816, respectively. A reliability of 1.00 indicates perfect reliability. The high reliability shown by this scale may be due in part to the fact that it was tested on a single occupational group. Additional studies with other occupational groups will be needed to determine if the scales are stable across a variety of occupations.

Stress Associated with Working in Organizations

Since you may well work for some kind of organization, it is useful to reflect on the major sources of frustration, dissatisfaction, and stress that are likely to be a part of this work. Some writers have pointed out increasing evidence from accounts by human-services professionals that the initial years of employment are highly stressful. In a longitudinal study of the first two years of employment for public-service employees, Cherniss (1980) found that the professionals reported anxiety, frustration, and disappointment about their job's unexpected stressors and demands. Those who were not able to cope with these demands tended to have negative professional attitudes and were on a path toward burnout.

We asked some former students who entered the helping professions to identify some of the main frustrations and stresses they were facing as a part of their job. Most of them identified as key stressors the slowness of the system, the resistance of administrators and fellow staff members to new ideas, and unrealistic expectations and demands. One young woman in her mid-20s commented:

"I get frustrated with the slow process of the system. New ideas are often overlooked. My age is a source of frustration when working with other people who will not take me seriously. Because of my age, I sometimes have difficulty gaining credibility. My biggest source of dissatisfaction, however, is watching a child that I have worked with and have seen improve go back into the system (or family) and regress to where they started."

A young social worker observed: "My greatest frustration is with the administration and its lack of support, common purpose, or teamwork."

A woman who manages the volunteer staff of student interns reported: "I am most frustrated when the staff is resistant to new ideas. Dealing with governmental bureaucracy is another major source of stress. They make it very difficult to get things done."

A social worker who is a consultant to senior managers of a bank said that she became frustrated with executives who want her to "fix" their employees but are not willing to see their part in the employees' problems.

Agencies often make demands that are unrealistic, especially an insistence that problems be solved quickly. For those who work with clients sent by the courts or those on probation, for instance, the helper is under pressure to see that behavioral changes take place in a specified time, so that more people can be seen, which means more funding.

Stress Associated with Client Behavior

Two researchers found similar results when they surveyed therapists' perceptions of stressful client behavior (Deutsch,1984; Farber, 1983a). In both studies the therapists reported that suicidal statements brought about the most stress. A comparison of the most stressful client behaviors follows.

Deutsch's findings
1. suicidal statements
2. anger toward the therapist
3. severely depressed clients
4. apathy or lack of motivation
5. client's premature termination

Farber's findings
1. suicidal statements
2. aggression and hostility
3. premature termination of therapy
4. agitated anxiety
5. apathy and depression

Therapists reported other sources of stress in the Deutsch study: not liking clients, seeing too many clients, an inability to help, self-doubts on the therapist's part about the value of therapy, conflicts with colleagues, feelings of isolation from colleagues, overidentification with clients and failure to create a balance between empathy and professional distance, inability to leave client concerns at work, sexual attraction to a client, and absence of appreciation from clients.

At this time you might think about those client behaviors that would represent the most stress to you. Look over the following list of client behaviors and rate them according to this scale: A = this would be highly stressful to me; B = this would be moderately stressful to me; C = this would be only mildly stressful to me; D = this would not be a source of stress to me.

___ 1. I am seeing a client who seems unmotivated and is coming to the sessions only because he was ordered to attend.

___ 2. One of my clients wants to terminate counseling, yet I think that she is not ready for termination.

___ 3. A client is very depressed, sees very little hope that life will get better, and keeps asking me for help.

___ 4. One of my clients makes suicidal threats, and I have every reason to take his threats seriously.

___ 5. This particular client is angry with me for not doing enough to help her situation.

___ 6. With this client I feel a great sense of identification, almost to the point of overidentifying with him.

___ 7. My client tells me that he (she) is sexually attracted to me, and I am not sexually attracted to him (her).

___ 8. My client tells me that she (he) is sexually attracted to me, and I am sexually attracted to her (him).

___ 9. My client is very demanding and wants to call me at home for advice on how to deal with every new problem that arises.

___ 10. This client almost never expresses any appreciation to me, but she often lets me know that I am not doing enough for her and that I don't seem to care enough about her.

After you've made your ratings, assess what patterns emerge. What specific behaviors seem to be the most stressful for you? How does stress affect your self-esteem, both on a personal and professional basis? How would you imagine that having to deal with such behaviors on a frequent basis would affect you? What are you likely to do to cope with these sources of stress?

Negative Outcomes of Work Stress

Three types of negative personal outcome stem from work stress: physical symptoms, psychological symptoms, and behavioral symptoms. On the basis of your own experiences, how does stress at work affect you? What physical signs tell you that you are being stressed? For example, do you feel tension in certain parts of your body? How are you affected emotionally? Does this stress affect your ability to sleep? Do you tend to withdraw or get depressed? What do you actually do behaviorally when you are under stress at your job? Think about how your job performance is affected when you feel under stress.

Physical Symptoms

Various physiological reactions prepare you for dealing with emergency situations. The heart beats faster, the blood pressure increases, and the muscles tense for action. There is an alarm reaction, or the "fight-or-flight" response. If this reaction is chronically triggered and you are constantly "on alert," you have a greater chance of developing one or more of the various psychophysiological disorders such as coronary artery disease, ulcers, and severe headaches. According to Rice (1987), there is adequate research attesting to the negative impact of stress on the cardiovascular and gastrointestinal systems. It is difficult to make the connections between work, stress, and health, because workers bring some of their physical problems with them to the job. But it is clear that work conditions can intensify a variety of health problems. Some of the more common physical symptoms of work-related stress are headaches, fatigue, insomnia, muscular tension, nausea or upset stomach, weakness in body parts, diarrhea or indigestion, light-headedness, teeth grinding, respiratory problems, sweating, increased heart rate and blood pressure, pain in the heart or chest, trembling or nervous tics, cardiovascular disease, and ulcers.

Psychological Symptoms

Rice (1987) lists the following psychological symptoms of job stress: anxiety, tension, confusion, and irritability; feelings of frustration, anger, and resentment; emotional hypersensitivity and hyperactivity; suppression of feelings; reduced effectiveness in communication; withdrawal and depression; feelings of isolation and alienation; boredom and job dissatisfaction; mental fatigue and lower intellectual functioning; loss of concentration; loss of spontaneity and creativity; and lowered self-esteem.

Behavioral Symptoms

Some of the behavioral manifestations of job stress that are identified by Rice (1987) are procrastination and avoidance of work; lowered overall performance and productivity; increased alcohol and drug use and abuse; efforts at sabotage on the job; overeating as an escape; undereating as a withdrawal; loss of appetite and sudden weight loss; aggression, vandalism, and stealing; deterioration of relationships with family and friends; tendency toward depression; and attempts at suicide.

After reviewing the physical, psychological, and behavioral symptoms of stress, go back over these lists and underline those that are characteristic of you when you experience stress. What do you see that you can do to manage this stress in better ways than you are now doing?

The Impact of Stress on Your Personal Life

The sources of stress that we identified earlier seem to have a negative impact on helpers' ability to form spontaneous and comfortable relationships with friends, and to decrease their emotional involvement in their own family. The stress associated with the intense personal contact required by therapists in their work apparently results in their wanting to pull back from relating meaningfully with family and friends (Guy & Liaboe, 1986). As Kottler (1986, p. 38) warns us: "Much of the pressure that has been building all day long as clients have come in and dumped their troubles finally releases as we walk through the door. If we are not careful, our families will suffer the emotional fallout."

An Integrated Model for Coping with Stress

The general framework of this section follows the model for coping with stress presented by Matheny, Aycock, Pugh, Curlette, and Cannella (1986). These authors designed a major study that attempted to synthesize the research on methods of coping. They define coping as "any effort, healthy or unhealthy, conscious or unconscious, to prevent, eliminate, or weaken stressors, or to tolerate their effects in the least hurtful manner" (p. 509). Their model includes both *preventive* and *combative* strategies. Although we will be using their framework as a basis for this discussion, we will also be drawing from other authors and from our own experiences.

Preventive Strategies

There are three general strategies for preventing stress: (1) avoiding or reducing stressors, (2) altering stress-inducing behavior patterns, and (3) developing coping resources.

Avoiding or reducing stressors.   One fundamental way to prevent stress is to avoid stressors. You can escape stressors by physically removing yourself from the stressful situation. Although stress accompanies the pursuit of some of your key goals, many stresses are unnecessary for your success, and these you can seek to avoid. This might entail changing jobs, getting out of a destructive relationship, or taking some other action directed at a stressor to reduce its stressfulness. For example, a mental-health worker told us that he had come to feel trapped in his 40-hour-a-week job as a counselor in a community agency. He was feeling the stresses of a heavy caseload and was fragmented by his many tasks. Rather than merely complaining about his job, he arranged to cut back to half time so that he can spend more time at home with a new baby and can pursue other professional interests. Even though he had to do some convincing of administrators at his agency in order to cut back his hours and still retain his position, and even though his family will have to adjust to less income, he was not willing to continue to feel overwhelmed and do nothing about it.

You may not be able to take such extreme measures as this person did. If you find yourself in a similar situation and cannot afford to reduce your work hours or do not want to leave your job, you can still look for ways to reduce situations that cause you needless stress. If you don't, you may eventually stop functioning effectively and lose your job. You can look for better ways to control your work schedule, for example. Although you may not be able to avoid taking on difficult clients, you can avoid scheduling the more difficult ones back to back.

Modifying stress-inducing behaviors. A second preventive strategy is to work toward modifying specific behaviors that produce stress. This strategy includes decreasing "Type A" behaviors such as excessive competitiveness, continual rushing, and hostility. Approaches to altering stress-inducing behavior patterns includes a variety of methods known as cognitive restructuring. As we have said, much of your stress is determined by your beliefs about events. Sometimes you actually create your stress by clinging to outworn beliefs. If you can change self-destructive thinking into constructive thinking, you will go a long way toward eliminating needless stress. Working on a cognitive level involves efforts to reframe situations or events in such a way as to reduce their stress value. Reframing can be directed at changing the meaning of an event. Assume, for instance, that one of your clients discontinues coming for help. If you interpret this termination as a sign of your professional ineptitude, this event will certainly be a source of stress. Rather than making yourself totally responsible for your clients' outcomes, consider their role in making their therapy a success or a failure. If you hold to the conviction that you must be successful with every client, your belief will lead to much frustration. By challenging this belief and substituting more realistic beliefs, you can alter stressful events. Remember that the goal of coping is to help you appreciate that you do not have to be the victim of stress. As you increasingly realize that the ways in which you think, behave, and feel do contribute to your stress level, you are in a position to reduce this stress. We cover the topic of cognitive restructuring in more detail later in this chapter.

Developing resources for coping. A third approach to prevention consists of developing coping resources. One of these resources is a sense of physical health, which to a large extent depends on sound nutritional habits, regular physical exercise, getting enough rest, and the like. Psychological assets are other resources for coping, such as a sense of control, a belief in oneself, and confidence. Other resources include cognitive assets, such as functional beliefs and academic competencies, and social support, including a network of friends. You can do a lot to prevent stress by learning specific skills in the areas of assertiveness, time management, and relaxation. Resistance to stress is increased by an openness to change, a willingness to make commitments, and an appreciation that you can control your life. If you allow stress to overwhelm you and convince yourself that there is little that you can do to change things, then stress will control you.

Combative Strategies

The integrative model of coping (Matheny et al., 1986) outlines five combative strategies: (1) monitoring stressors and symptoms, (2) marshaling one's resources, (3) lowering stressful arousal, (4) acting to eliminate or weaken stressors, and (5) learning to tolerate those stressors that cannot be eliminated. We briefly describe each of these coping strategies below.

Self-monitoring.   Before you can change your behavior in stressful situations, you must first be aware of which situations those are and how you react to them. Although simply monitoring your stress may be of limited value, it is a prerequisite to using other methods of stress management. Becoming aware of what stresses you is the first step toward modifying your way of dealing with stress. Self-monitoring will probably reveal that you increase your level of stress by (1) telling others stories about your stresses and (2) telling yourself over and over how stressful life is. One of the best ways to monitor stressful situations is by keeping a written record of your reactions to specific difficult situations each day. It is helpful to record the events that tend to produce stress for you and as well your behavior in these situations. Recording your thoughts, actions, and feelings in a variety of situations will give you clues to what kind of stressors you most need to pay attention to. Once you detect patterns, you can begin to make some changes. Most books on stress management will provide you with specific hints on practical steps in this self-monitoring process.

Marshaling your resources.   After identifying a stressor, you need to draw on your resources and plan effective strategies for combat. You might make the mistake of underestimating your resources for dealing actively with stressful situations. For example, you might focus more on your deficits than on your personal strengths. It is important to remember that the aim of a stress-management program is not to eliminate stress but to cope with it in effective ways. As Hans Selye (1974), one of the pioneers in the field, noted, life without the challenge of stressful situations would be boring. The aim is to learn how to call on the many resources available to you so that you can combat unnecessary stress.

Lowering stress arousal. A number of means are available to reduce arousal that interferes with coping. For example, relaxation methods can be most useful in reducing tension. Other forms of tension reduction include play, vigorous physical exercise, and hobbies. Leisure is a good way to cope with stress. By allowing yourself to enjoy this time away from work, you will probably be in a better position to deal with stressors at work. You might find an activity such as gardening, meditating, practicing yoga, playing tennis, jogging, biking, knitting, or sitting in a park and watching ducks to be your way of relaxing.

In addition to these ways in which you can unwind and let go, you can also practice systematic relaxation training. This will take about 20 minutes a couple of times a day, but it could be most useful in your war against stress. Of course, you need to grant yourself the latitude to relax, and you must be convinced that practicing relaxation exercises is not a waste of valuable time. Relaxation training will not work unless you are willing to learn skills, practice them on a regular basis, and apply them to everyday life situations that bring on stress. The following books have some excellent guidelines for relaxation training: Charlesworth and Nathan (1984), Butler (1981), and Meichenbaum (1985).

Eliminating stressors or stressful situations. Another approach to combating stress is attacking stressors by eliminating them. This can be done by using problem-solving methods, which include assessing the problem, finding out relevant information, challenging limiting assumptions, and identifying alternative behaviors. Much has been written about problem-solving training as an approach to coping with stress. Common to most of the problem-solving methods are the following steps as outlined and discussed by Meichenbaum (1985):

- Identify the stressor as a problem to be solved.
- Set concrete and realistic goals, and identify specific steps necessary to reach these goals.
- Generate a wide range of many possible courses of action.
- Consider how others might respond if they were asked to deal with a similar stress problem.
- Evaluate the pros and cons of each of the proposed solutions, and then rank these solutions from least practical to most practical.
- Rehearse and practice new behaviors by means of imagery and behavioral rehearsal.
- Experiment with the solution that appears to be most feasible.
- Expect some setbacks and failures, but reward yourself for honest efforts.
- Reconsider the original problem in the light of your attempt at problem solving.

As a way of making the problem-solving approach more concrete and personal, picture yourself working with clients who have been sent to you by the court. You find the resistance of these involuntary clients to be stressful, since you are constantly trying to convince them that counseling might be of benefit to them. One way to solve this problem would be to find another job. If you are not willing or able to take this step, consider how you might apply problem-solving strategies. You could first of all ask "What do I find as the stressor that I want to change?" Suppose you are most stressed by meeting clients who do not want to be in your office. You are continually having your invitations for help turned down, and thus you are having to put up with feelings of rejection. Next you can identify realistic goals. Although you would prefer a caseload of clients who were motivated to change and were seeking your help, the chances are that you cannot magically transform your clients.

One goal might be to approach these clients differently, inviting them to use you as a resource but not taking full responsibility for whether they decide to take advantage of their resources for change. Next, you could challenge them when they tell you that they are being "forced to see you." You might see them for one session to tell them what they can expect from the counseling sessions and what you expect from them. As a condition of continuing the sessions, you could insist that they develop a clear contract delineating what they are willing to do as their part of the relationship. You could make a proposal to your supervisor for alternatives to seeing such clients on an individual basis. You could make appropriate referrals. After generating many possible approaches and imagining how you and others might respond in these circumstances, you could try out some new strategies with clients to test these alternatives. As a part of your job you might still be working with clients who are sent to you, but you could certainly come up with new ways of approaching these clients that are designed to cut down on the stress factor for you.

Adjusting to stress by using cognitive approaches. When certain stressors prove difficult to eliminate, successful coping involves adjusting to them in the ways that are least harmful. Cognitive restructuring is one of the most promising combative strategies. A good deal of stress results from our beliefs and stressful mental sets, including negative self-talk and catastrophic thinking. If we keep these beliefs alive and well, we are also painfully sensitive to stress. Cognitive restructuring aims at demolishing negative self-programming and learning constructive self-talk. The aim is to change the meaning that stressful situations hold for you. You can accomplish this by being less self-critical when you do not have perfect performances, identifying some positive elements in possible failure, and convincing yourself that you are not alone in facing stress.

Combining Preventive and Combative Strategies

The integrated model of coping with stress includes a combination of preventive and combative strategies. Probably the best way to cope with stress is to develop a multiple-pronged approach, rather than limiting yourself to a single strategy. As Meichenbaum (1985) has noted, stress-management programs should foster flexibility, and the techniques need to be tailored to your individual personality and unique situation. Good training programs do not promote a simple formula or a "cookbook" approach for coping with stress.

Remain open to developing a stress-management program that suits you. An effective program should be future-oriented, in that it prepares you to apply strategies to various stressful life situations as they arise. You also need to be prepared for inevitable setbacks, and it is essential to stick with your program if you hope to see results. Thus, your program should help you identify sources of possible failure and prepare for them.

One of the programs for preventing and reducing stress is stress inoculation training (SIT), as developed and refined by Meichenbaum (1977, 1985). SIT is not a single strategy for coping but combines aspects of didactic teaching, Socratic discussion, cognitive restructuring, problem solving, relaxation training, behavioral rehearsal, imagery, self-monitoring, self-instruction, self-reinforcement, and efforts at changing the environment. It is designed to help people not only resolve immediate problems but also apply what they learn to dealing effectively with future stress situations. In short, SIT is designed to build "psychological antibodies" that will increase one's resistance to stressful situations. It generally consists of 12 to 15 sessions, plus booster and follow-up sessions.

Ideally, taking a course on stress management utilizing the strategies outlined by Meichenbaum would be a good way to learn and apply specific coping skills. If you are interested in learning more about the details of SIT, we recommend that you read Meichenbaum's excellent short book, which is listed in the Suggested Readings. Taking a workshop on stress management would be another approach. If these options are not practical at this time, you could at least carefully select some self-help books, of which there are an increasing number. As with many other endeavors, however, merely reading about stress management is not enough to combat some of the stresses you face. It is essential that you regularly practice the stress-management techniques that you read about.

Cognitive Approaches to Stress Management

Our beliefs largely determine how we interpret events. Thought of in this way, events are not the cause of our stress; rather, the meaning we give to these events is what is crucial. Albert Ellis, the founder of rational-emotive therapy (RET) and the precursor of cognitive therapy, is fond of citing the following quotation by the stoic Epictetus: "Men are disturbed not by things, but by the views which they take of them." In this section we draw heavily from the writings of Ellis and other cognitive therapists, especially Aaron Beck, Gary Emery, and Donald Meichenbaum. All of these therapists have developed approaches to help people become increasingly aware of their cognitions, the dialogue that goes on inside of them, and the ways in which their thinking affects their behavior and how they feel. The cognitive approaches offer specific strategies to clients for challenging and changing self-defeating cognitions and for developing sound thinking that leads to less stressful living.

You may often engage in types of self-defeating thinking and ineffective self-talk. If you can recognize the nature of your irrational beliefs and understand how they lead to problems, you can begin to convert self-defeating cognitions into self-enhancing cognitions. In the rest of this chapter we discuss cognitive approaches that shed light on how you create much of your own stress by the beliefs you hold and the statements you make to yourself. We will also describe some cognitive strategies that can be employed to lessen the effects of stress. Our examples will be geared primarily to situations that you are likely to encounter in your work as a helping professional.

The A-B-C Theory

Ellis has developed, expanded, and revised his A-B-C theory of irrational thinking (Ellis & Bernard, 1986). This theory explains the relationship between events, beliefs, and feelings. According to Ellis, the real causes of feelings are not events but the beliefs we have about these events. A is an Activating event, B represents the Belief system, and C is the emotional Consequence. Consider the situation of applying for a new job in an agency and going through an interview. Let's imagine the worst scene. The director of the agency who interviewed you kindly tells you that she does not think you would fit well in the agency. She is not really impressed with your training and experience. You do not get this job, which you very much hoped to secure. The activating event (A) in this case is the situation of being denied this particular job. The (C) would be the emotional consequences you might experience. If you felt depressed, hurt, let down, and even devastated, the chances are that you hold what Ellis would term as "irrational beliefs" about not having been accepted. For example, your beliefs (B) about this rejection might be some combination of the following thoughts: "It is absolutely horrible that I didn't get this job, and this surely proves that I'm incompetent." "I should have gotten this job, and this rejection is unbearable." "I must succeed at every important endeavor, or I'm really worthless." "Since I failed in this interview, this is a sure sign that I will fail in any other interview I might have." "This rejection means that I'm a total failure."

Common irrational beliefs. One way to monitor stress and to cope with it is by becoming increasingly aware of the rational or irrational quality of your thinking. Below are a few statements that we often hear helping professionals utter: "I am fully responsible for my clients' outcomes." "I must be successful with every client." "If a client discontinues, it's always my fault." "I should be able to help my clients more." "I must always be available for anyone who needs me." "If a client is in pain, I should take it away." "I should know everything." "If I make a mistake, that means I'm a failure." "Referring a client means that I'm inadequate." "If a couple divorces, I was not helpful enough."

In his book *Overcoming Resistance* Ellis (1985, p. 164), lists five common irrational beliefs of therapists:

1. "I have to be successful with all my clients practically all the time."
2. "I must be an outstanding therapist, clearly better than other therapists I know or hear about."
3. "I have to be greatly respected and loved by all my clients."
4. "Clients should listen to me carefully and should always push themselves to change."
5. "I must be able to enjoy myself during therapy sessions and to use these sessions to solve my personal problems as well as to help my clients."

Lists of statements such as this could go on and on, but as you can see, most of these statements refer to feelings of inadequacy, a nagging belief that we should be more, and a chronic sense of self-doubt. To the degree to which you burden yourself with beliefs such as these, you will also be burdened with stress. Furthermore, by assuming the giant share of responsibility for your clients, you are relieving them of the responsibility to direct their own life.

At this juncture you might go back over the above irrational beliefs and underline those statements that you hear yourself making. Are there any other related statements that you tend to make, especially with regard to your role in assuming responsibility for being the "perfect" helper? What are some examples of other things that you say to yourself that often get you into trouble? What are some other beliefs you hold that tend to create stress for you?

Changing distorted and self-defeating thinking. Gary Emery (1981), a cognitive therapist, has proposed the three A's as a method of challenging and changing self-defeating thinking: *awareness, answering,* and *action.*

Awareness is an essential prerequisite for any type of behavioral change. Most cognitive therapists agree that the first step in changing your thinking is to become aware of your self-defeating thoughts. This awareness can be gained by paying attention to your symptoms. For example, you can pay attention to any mood changes. Being alert to your body can offer other clues. Noticing those times when your confidence appears to fade can be helpful. Another sign is noticing when you have trouble concentrating or making decisions. Since you are continually thinking, it is important to monitor your thoughts so that you can become aware of how your thinking influences your behavior and your feelings.

Answering your negative thinking and learning how to dispute irrational beliefs is the next step in changing self-defeating thinking into rational thinking. Below are some common examples of faulty thinking:

- *"Catastrophizing."* One type of irrational thinking involves giving the worst possible meaning to an event. You might say, for example: "I just knew something terrible would happen. Because I took a vacation, one of my clients overdosed on drugs. If I had stayed home, this wouldn't have happened.''

- *Self-blame* involves a total self-condemnation rather than criticism of a specific behavior. Thus you might say "Since my client overdosed on drugs, this proves that I'm a worthless therapist, and I deserve to suffer and be punished.''

- *Over-generalizing* involves a negative absolutistic evaluation. If you failed with a given client, for instance, you might make the mistake of over-generalizing by saying to yourself "I always fail at anything that's important.'' Or you could say: "See what happened when I decided to take my vacation. I wasn't available when someone needed me, and I let that person down.''

- *All-or-nothing thinking.* Another form of faulty thinking is seeing life in either/or categories, rather than taking into account the full continuum of possibilities. Thus, you might say to yourself: "Either I'm a success, or I'm a failure.'' "Either I'm the perfect therapist, or I'm worthless.''

- *Language errors and negative thoughts.* Our choice of words and negative thinking often produce stress for us. By becoming aware of the quality of our language we can get some idea of how our self-talk influences us. Here are some examples of negative thinking:
  - "I *must* act competently in all situations, and I must win people's approval.''
  - "I *can't stand* making mistakes. They prove I'm a total failure.''
  - "I *must* be brilliant, and I *must* perform well at all times. If I'm ever less than brilliant, this is *horrible,* and I *can't stand* it.''
  - "I *should* always put the interests of other people before my own. My mission is to help others, and I *shouldn't* be selfish.''
  - "I *ought* to be available when anybody needs me. If I'm not, this shows that I'm not a caring person and that I've probably chosen the wrong profession.''

Learning how to answer and to dispute irrational beliefs entails identifying your core negative thoughts. As you review the above list, attempt to think of the statements you might be inclined to make. In their helpful book *A New Guide to Rational Living* Ellis and Harper (1975) identify a common set of ten irrational beliefs. The first five beliefs pertain to yourself, while the next five pertain to the way things or other people *should* be:

1. I must have everyone's love and approval for just about everything I do.
2. I should be able to do everything well, and I must be perfectly competent.
3. If something bad happens, I should worry about it.
4. It is easier to avoid difficult things than to try them and thereby risk failure.
5. If I avoid responsibilities, I will enjoy life more.
6. Some people are bad and deserve to be punished.
7. When things aren't going well in my life, it is terrible.
8. If things go wrong, I am bound to feel bad, and there is really very little I can do about my feelings.

9. The things I have done in the past will determine the way I now feel and what will happen to me in the future.
10. People and things should be the way I want them to be, and there should be perfect solutions for everything.

Before going on, study the list above, and reflect on your most common irrational thoughts. Underline those that fit you. How often do you arouse stress in yourself with such thoughts? After you have identified a few core irrational beliefs, begin to answer them. Answering faulty beliefs is best done by vigorous disputation. The method of disputing irrational beliefs can be illustrated by the following passage, in which we provide an irrational belief, a disputation, and an effective rational belief.

Self-statement: "I must be approved or accepted by people I find important."
   Disputation: Why must I? Where is it written that my own approval hinges on the approval of others? Why can't I stand someone else's disapproval? If a client disapproves of me, can't I still feel like a worthwhile person and professional?
   Rational and effective belief: Although I don't enjoy disapproval, I can stand it. I don't have to be accepted by everyone in order to feel accepted by myself.

Self-statement: "I should be able to do everything well."
   Disputation: Where did I pick up this belief? Does it make any sense that I should do everything well the first time? Can I do some things poorly and still be outstanding in other areas?
   Rational and effective belief: Although I like performing well, I can accept imperfection in myself. I can tolerate mistakes. I do not have to be perfect in order to be capable. Since perfection is an unrealistic ideal, I will be "perfectly satisfied" with being a fallible human.

Self-statement: "People must treat me fairly and give me what I need."
   Disputation: Where is this law written? Why do I expect the world to treat me fairly?
   Rational and effective belief: Even though people will not always give me what I want, I can still function. Life is sometimes unfair, yet I can stand it. Simply because people treat me unfairly, it's not the end of the world.

As we have seen, awareness is the first step in self-change, followed by learning how to answer and dispute self-defeating thinking. However, merely identifying faulty beliefs and learning to say functional statements does not alone ensure change. For change to occur it is essential that you take *action.* You need to test reality and act on your new thoughts and beliefs. For example, assume that you convince yourself that your failure to get a job does not mean that you are a failure as a person. You can act on this belief by taking the risk of applying for a job that you might want. If you are afraid of getting people's disapproval, you can put yourself in situations where approval will not always be forthcoming. If you convince yourself that making a mistake as a helper is not horrible, you can allow yourself to make a mistake and not feel devastated. This action would imply that you are willing to try new things and be open to making mistakes without condemning yourself. Rather than avoiding doing new things that you have wanted to do, you might seek out some of these new ventures and take the chance of being less than perfect. It is important for you to realize that at times you will have to force yourself to act in new ways that are not comfortable for you if you hope to challenge some self-limiting assumptions. For instance, if you have been avoiding giving talks to community groups because you are afraid that you will look like a fool, it might be important to challenge yourself by giving some of these speeches in spite of your fears. The point is that your new beliefs need to be put into action, and this is the hard part in making these changes.

To complete the A-B-C model of Ellis, we look briefly at D-E-F. D is the process of actively and forcefully Disputing irrational beliefs that lead to negative emotional reactions, many of which are stressful. E consists of Effective and rational new beliefs. If you are successful in this process of disputation and in substituting constructive thinking for destructive thinking, then you have a new F, which is a *new Feeling*. Thus, instead of feeling depressed about a loss you can put it in a new perspective and feel appropriately disappointed. Instead of feeling devastated by the lack of universal approval, you can feel appropriately hurt if a significant person rejects you. By changing your beliefs you also change your feelings, which is a useful way of learning to reduce stress.

A key point of this chapter has been that people are not machines that will go on functioning and not break down. As you know, even machines wear out. If you hope to prevent stress from controlling you, you need to take an active stance in recognizing how your stresses do lead to personal depletion. You need to pay attention to how the accumulation of stress can lead to burnout, which is the subject of the following chapter. If you give of yourself continually and ignore all the signs of stress and the toll it is taking, you will eventually find that your well runs dry.

We hope you will make some decisions after reading this chapter about specific ways in which you can better manage stress in your life. You can begin by monitoring how you are affected by stress, and you can follow up by applying some of the specific preventive and combative strategies for stress management that we have discussed. We suggest that you consider the value of implementing a time-management program as a key strategy in coping with stress. The next section discusses this particular approach.

Time Management as a Strategy for Coping with Stress

So often we hear students complaining that there simply are not enough hours in the day and night to do everything they want to do. Ask yourself the degree to which you are satisfied with how you are balancing your needs for work and for leisure. How do you manage to keep up with responsibilities at school, at work, and at home? Are you able to keep up with your studies and still maintain a social life? Is life only work, or do you make any time for play? Is life only play, and do you put off work lest it get in the way of your fun? Time is the thing we have in common, for we all have the same amount of it. Yet how we manage this time to our best advantage is a very individual matter. We offer you some suggestions for ways of keeping better track of what you are doing, what you want to be doing, and what you might do differently. If you'd like further suggestions on time-management strategies, we especially recommend Rice (1987) and Charlesworth and Nathan (1984).

Before you continue reading, spend a few minutes in taking the following time-management inventory. It will help you assess the danger signals of poor time management. Read each statement, decide whether it is more true or more false as it applies to you, and rate it accordingly with a T or an F.

___ 1. I often feel confused and unsure of where I'm going.
___ 2. At the end of most days I'm amazed at how little I have accomplished.
___ 3. I have a hard time getting to important tasks and sticking with them.
___ 4. I often find myself taking on tasks because I'm the only one who can do them.
___ 5. I often feel overwhelmed because I try to do too much in too little time.
___ 6. No matter how much I do, I feel that I'm always behind and never quite caught up.
___ 7. I find that I'm working longer and longer and sometimes wonder if I'm accomplishing much.
___ 8. I frequently miss deadlines.
___ 9. I simply have too many irons in the fire.
___ 10. It is very easy for me to put off until tomorrow what I know needs to be done today.
___ 11. I'm bothered by many unscheduled interruptions when I'm trying to do important work.
___ 12. I'm aware of hurrying much of the time and often feel hassled.
___ 13. I just don't have time to attend to important things, because I get lost in dealing with one crisis after another.
___ 14. I tend to be a perfectionist, and this leaves me never feeling satisfied with what I'm accomplishing.
___ 15. I feel guilty about leaving work behind me.

See whether there are any patterns in the way you are using your time. Are you able to identify particular ways in which you are wasting time? What most gets in your way of effectively using what time you have? If at the end of a day you often find yourself wondering where your time went, you can probably benefit by doing a time study. Several times a day, stop to record in a schedule book what you have done in each half-hour period and how much time it took. At the end of each week simply look for patterns that emerge. Ask yourself questions such as "Where is most of my time going? Am I enjoying all the things I do? Is there a way that I could cut out some of the things I'm doing?" Merely identifying patterns will be an important first step in finding the areas in which you need to improve your managing of time.

After you have made this inventory of how you use your time, the next step is to find some positive way to eliminate wasting of time. Here are a few suggestions for effective and positive time management:

- Identify your priorities. What do you most want to accomplish, and what are you doing to move toward these goals? Ask yourself where you would like to be and what or who you'd like to be at different points in your future. Identifying these long-range goals includes specifying what personal changes you want to make, what kind of interpersonal relationships you'd like to develop and maintain, what activities you'd like to engage in, what projects you'd like to accomplish, and so forth.
- Break down your long-range goals into subgoals that can be accomplished in a shorter period. It might be helpful to prioritize your goals, from most important to least important.
- Realize that if you plan well today, you are likely to be more relaxed tomorrow. Allocate your time according to your priorities. Build recreation time into your schedule.
- Learn to thin your schedule out somewhat. Realize that you probably won't be able to do all that you need or want to do in any given week. Therefore, focus on what you see as most essential and prune out those activities that are cluttering your life.
- Avoid procrastination. Keeping a schedule of what you have to do and when it must be done can give you some sense of pacing yourself. If you know that waiting until the very end causes you stress and that you function poorly, you could at least experiment with getting certain assignments or tasks completed before the last minute.
- If you become aware of engaging in insignificant activities that distract you from doing the important things in your life, write down these time wasters and ways to avoid them. Then, before you engage in these activities again, pause to ask yourself if you are willing to use your time in such a manner.
- Learn to delegate. Rather than convincing yourself that you are the only one who can do certain tasks, learn to ask for help and to assign specific tasks to others. Even if some tasks do not get done as well as they might if you had done them yourself, ask yourself if this isn't a better arrangement.
- Realize that you probably need some idle time for your physical and psychological health. Tell yourself that this open time is needed to refresh your body and your psyche. Learn to avoid feeling guilty for being nonproductive occasionally.
- Consider the requests of others for you to take on new projects. Before you say yes, make sure that you really feel ready and willing to accept such a project.

- Try to do a task only once. Rather than dealing with paperwork several times, make a quick decision the first time this paper comes your way. If you can throw it away rather than filing it, do so.

Effective use of time is not something that simply happens to you. Instead, it is a skill that you acquire and refine. It is essential to write down your goals, prioritize them, and plan how to spend the time you have. At the end of each week and each month review your activities in light of your long-range and short-range goals to determine whether you are putting your time to best use. If you practice a systematic approach to time management, you will probably find that you have more time to devote to your studies, your work, your friends, and your leisure activities.

By Way of Review

- Since it is next to impossible to completely eliminate stress from your life, the crucial question is "Does stress control you, or do you control stress?"
- You do not have to be the victim of stress, for you have the capacity to recognize situations that lead to stress, and you can make decisions about how you will think, feel, and behave in response to these stressful situations.
- One of the hazards of the helping professions is that helpers are typically not very good at asking for help for themselves.
- It is helpful to sensitize yourself to both the external and the internal factors that contribute to your experience of stress.
- One of the major environmental sources of job stress is the friction that arises out of working in an organization.
- Studies of therapists' perceptions of client behaviors find the following to be the most stressful: suicidal statements, anger toward the helper, aggression and hostility, severe depression, apathy and lack of motivation, and premature termination.
- Three types of negative personal outcome are related to work stress: physical symptoms, psychological symptoms, and behavioral symptoms.
- Preventive strategies for coping with stress include avoiding or reducing stressors, altering stress-inducing behavior patterns, and acquiring coping skills.
- There are also combative strategies for coping with stress. Self-monitoring is the first step in developing an effective stress-management program.
- Perhaps one of the most useful ways of managing stress is through the use of cognitive approaches. These include becoming aware of your self-talk, learning to challenge self-critical thinking, and cognitive restructuring.
- Time is one thing we all have the same amount of. How we use our time is another matter. Perhaps one of the best ways to cope with stress is by learning time-management skills and applying them to daily life in a systematic fashion.

- There are a number of strategies for effectively managing stress. Review the many sources available that discuss these various strategies, and then design a stress-management program that is best suited to you.

What Will You Do Now?

1. Make a list of some of the factors that are most stressful in your life. Next, write down a few ideas of what you see that you can do now to minimize at least some of these sources of stress. Develop a plan of action, and try it out for at least a week. Consider making a contract with someone so that you will be accountable for doing something about reducing stress in your life.

2. Make a poster that contains the essence of a cognition that is producing stress in your life. For instance, if you tell yourself "I must be perfect in everything I try," create a poster that captures this idea. Now, make another poster that challenges this idea, such as "It's human to be imperfect, and since I'm human, it's OK for me to be imperfect!" Try acting as if you really believed your countermessage poster for at least a week, and record how you are doing in different situations.

3. If you have trouble doing everything that you want with the time you have available, consider implementing the time-management strategies that we described. Keep a written record of what you do in the coming week. At the end of the week review your activities, and ask yourself if you are spending the time you have in the ways you want.

Suggested Readings

Butler, P. E. (1981). *Talking to yourself: Learning the language of self-support.* New York: Harper & Row. The author gives a practical treatment of some self-defeating internal dialogues. She discusses self-talk related to a variety of interpersonal situations. The book is easy to read and can be used as a practical workbook.

Charlesworth, E. A., & Nathan, R. G. (1984). *Stress management: A comprehensive guide to wellness.* New York: Ballantine. This is probably one of the better self-help books in the field of stress management. It is readable, and the authors offer many recommendations for learning how to cope with stress in daily living. There are detailed descriptions of progressive relaxation and other methods of relaxing; of stressful behaviors, thoughts, and attitudes, and how to attack them; and of assertion techniques and time-management skills. There is also a good chapter on Type A and Type B behaviors.

Emery, G. (1981). *A new beginning: How you can change your life through cognitive therapy.* New York: Simon & Schuster (Touchstone). A very clear description of how cognitive therapy works, with special emphasis on changing distorted and self-defeating thinking. Methods are given for dealing with sadness, anxiety, guilt, shame, and anger. Also discussed are ways to deal with weight gain, alcohol and drug dependency, depression, the stresses of motherhood, and the stresses of aging. The author shows clearly how much of our stress is created by our thoughts and what we tell ourselves.

Lakein, A. (1974). *How to get control of your time and your life.* New York: New American Library (Signet). A useful book for those who want to learn more about time management.

Meichenbaum, D. (1985)., *Stress inoculation training*. New York: Pergamon Press. If you are interested in learning and applying the principles of SIT discussed in this chapter, this book will prove useful. The author gives specific steps for learning to reduce and prevent maladaptive stress reactions.

Rice, P. L. (1987). *Stress and health: Principles and practice for coping and wellness.* Pacific Grove, CA: Brooks/Cole. This is a comprehensive treatment of stress and its affects on our health. It is a useful textbook and is also interesting reading. Separate chapters are devoted to taking control of stress and personal health, psychological sources of stress, family stresses, work stress, methods of relaxation, and time-management and behavioral-health strategies.

Dealing with Professional Burnout

Focus of the Chapter

In the previous chapter you saw the toll that stress can take on your life. When stresses are not coped with effectively, the end result can be burnout. Too often this term is used loosely, and it is used as an excuse for laziness. Although the term has limitations, it does describe a critical problem in the helping professions. Although people in many different careers can experience burnout, helpers are especially vulnerable because of the nature of their involvement with people in need. Although there is no guarantee that you will remain immune, we hope that you can increase your awareness of the early warning signs of burnout and develop practical strategies for staving if off. The focus of this chapter is on studying the factors that contribute to burnout and on learning what you can do to prevent this condition in yourself.

The Nature of Burnout

Burnout has been described as a state of physical, emotional, and mental exhaustion that results from constant or repeated emotional pressure associated with an intense, long-term involvement with people. It is characterized by feelings of helplessness and hopelessness and by a negative view of self and negative attitudes toward work, life, and other people. Burned-out helpers recognize that they can no longer help others, for they have nothing left in themselves to give (Pines & Aronson, 1981). Freudenberger (1980, p. 17) says that to burn out is "to deplete oneself. To exhaust one's physical and mental resources. To wear oneself out by excessively striving to reach some unrealistic expectation imposed by one's self or by the values of society."

Maslach (1982b) has given a list of brief definitions of burnout, a few of which will give a sense of its nature:

- a progressive loss of energy, idealism, and purpose experienced by helping professionals as a result of their work conditions
- a state of exhaustion, irritability, and fatigue that markedly decreases a professional's effectiveness
- a syndrome of emotional exhaustion, depersonalization, and reduced personal accomplishment that can occur among members of the helping professions

In her analysis of the similarities among many definitions of burnout, Maslach (1982a) found a common core that could be used as a working definition. The dimension where there is the most agreement is that of exhaustion: an ongoing process of loss of energy, depletion, debilitation, and fatigue. There is not only physical but also emotional exhaustion, marked by a loss of feeling and concern, a loss of trust, and a loss of spirit. Secondly, there is general agreement that burnout is an internal psychological experience that encompasses feelings, attitudes, motives, and expectations. There is a negative shift in responses to others that is characterized by depersonalization, negative attitudes toward clients, a decline of idealism, and general irritability. Thirdly, there is general agreement that burnout leads to personal feelings of depression, loss of morale, feelings of isolation and a wish to withdraw, reduced productivity, and a decreased capacity to cope.

Burnout is not something that simply happens to you suddenly. Rather, it is an ongoing process with developmental stages. It might be helpful to think of burnout on a continuum, rather than in either/or terms. In the beginning of a helping career the worker might have the motivation to ''set the world afire.'' As one experiences the inevitable frustrations and stresses of being a professional helper, this flame may be dampened, and the initial ideals may give way to a cynical and hard view of the world.

Are You in Danger of Burning Out?

Before you continue reading, it is a good idea to assess how likely a candidate you are for burnout. Take the following self-inventory to determine the degree to which you have the characteristics that identify the burned-out person.*

Directions. Look back over the past six months. Have you been noticing changes in yourself or in the world around you? Think of your work, your family, and social situations. As you take the inventory, allow about 30 seconds for each answer. Then assign it a number from 1 (for no or little change) to 5 (for a great deal of change).

___ 1. Do you tire more easily? feel fatigued rather than energetic?

___ 2. Are people annoying you by telling you "You don't look so good lately"?

___ 3. Are you working harder and harder and accomplishing less and less?

___ 4. Are you increasingly cynical and disenchanted?

___ 5. Are you often invaded by a sadness you can't explain?

___ 6. Are you forgetting appointments, deadlines, personal possessions?

___ 7. Are you increasingly irritable? more short-tempered? more disappointed in the people around you?

___ 8. Are you seeing close friends and family members less frequently?

___ 9. Are you too busy to do even routine things like making phone calls, reading reports, or sending out your Christmas cards?

___ 10. Are you suffering from physical complaints (aches, pains, headaches, a lingering cold)?

___ 11. Do you feel disoriented when the activity of the day comes to a halt?

___ 12. Is joy elusive?

___ 13. Are you unable to laugh at a joke about yourself?

___ 14. Does sex seem like more trouble than it's worth?

___ 15. Do you have very little to say to people?

---

*From *Burn-Out: How to Beat the High Cost of Success*, by H. J. Freudenberger, with G. Richelson. Copyright 1980 by Doubleday & Company, New York. Reprinted by permission.

Very roughly, now, place yourself on the burnout scale that follows. Keep in mind that this is merely an approximation of where you are, useful as a guide on your way to a more satisfying life. Don't let a high total alarm you, but pay attention to it. Burnout is reversible, no matter how far along it is. The higher number signifies that the sooner you start being kinder to yourself, the better (Freudenberger, 1980, pp. 17–19).

The Burnout Scale

0–25   You're doing fine.
26–35   There are things you should be watching.
36–50   You're a candidate.
51–65   You're burning out.
over 65 You're in a dangerous place, threatening to your physical and mental well-being.

The Experience of Burnout

There is a heavy price to pay for being a professional care giver. No one is immune to the toll of taking care of other people. Not only are you physically and psychologically affected, but other people in your life also suffer when you experience burnout.

As we mentioned, burnout is not a simple phenomenon. It is useful to consider the various levels at which care givers are affected by the strains of constant interaction with people in need of help. As an example consider the case of a counselor named Daniel, who is suffering from many of the symptoms of burnout.

Physically, Daniel is fatigued most of the time. He has accepted an increased caseload and works long hours. He exercises very little because of a lack of time, does not have time to eat regularly or properly, and is so wrapped up in his work that he does not sleep well. He finds it a real chore to get up in the morning. He suffers from headaches that just will not go away as well as a range of other health problems that stem from his stressful life-style.

Intellectually, Daniel has lost his curiosity and desire to question or to learn. Although when he was in graduate school he enjoyed sharing and discussing ideas about human behavior and counseling, now he cannot be bothered by argumentation, discussion, and revision of his ideas. With all the pressures at work, he finds no time to read or to take courses to keep current. Instead, he hopes to find quick remedies to deal with the crisis situations that he faces in his daily work.

Emotionally, Daniel has spent so much time focusing on the emotional needs of others that he has failed to recognize his own needs. At one time he was able to provide nurturance for others, yet by chronically neglecting his needs for expression he has become indifferent in his professional life and also withdraws from those he loves in his personal life. He is isolated and unable to feel either pain or joy. He feels very alone at work, and he tends to blame himself for not doing well. Since he is not feeling a sense of personal accomplishment, his view of his own worth is also declining. He experiences an increasing sense of wanting to get away from demands and pressures.

Interpersonally, he has lost interest in being with others. Daniel feels "peopled out" and is gleeful when clients cancel. He sometimes "forgets" his appointments with clients and fails to show up for staff meetings. When he began his career, he had high hopes of making an impact on the lives of others. Now his ideals are tarnished, and his motivation is low. His job performance is hurting, and much of the time he is indifferent. His family is also suffering from his burnout, for he shrinks away from involvement with his wife and children. He just wants everybody to leave him alone and make no more demands on him. He feels emotionally dry and has little energy to listen to what they might want from him. Even minor requests are heard as demands that only burden him more.

Daniel has paid a steep price for ignoring the stressful circumstances that resulted in his indifference. Not only has he become an impaired professional, but he is suffering in his personal life as well. By withdrawing from his friends, family, and coworkers, he has cut off all sources of possible nourishment.

Symptoms of Burnout

We asked some former students who had become mental-health professionals about their experience with burnout. We asked them to describe the symptoms they had noticed, their methods for dealing with burnout, and their strategies for preventing this syndrome. Most of the people we talked with pointed to symptoms such as chronic tiredness, depression, strain, detachment, boredom, and a desire to retreat. One woman who was working in management and organizational development commented:

"I've felt burned out when I've filled my calendar too much and have not recognized my limitations. When I don't have the time to regroup, I begin to feel inadequate. The worse I feel, the worse I do. I finally recognize what's going on when I begin to feel tired and depressed. At those times I've dealt with it by taking charge of my schedule and pulling back. I also seek advice from my supervisor, who offers me a lot of support. When I'm burned out, I also take time off for personal time out."

When we become psychologically overloaded, we are much like a computer that is filled with too much data. Just as the computer refuses to function, we also cease effective functioning in both our professional endeavors and our personal life.

One counselor we interviewed described her feelings of being emotionally spent after becoming saturated with client concerns:

"When I get too invested in a client's life, I sometimes feel bored and depressed, and I lack the energy and motivation to do my job. I usually deal with it by taking time off to focus on taking care of myself, which I do by going to therapy, meditating, and spending time with people whom I can vent out and replenish myself with."

Another woman, who is a human-service manager and director of community planning activities, said:

"When I become overly involved in the administrative end of the agency, I tend to feel stretched. I start to feel detached and somewhat depressed. I begin to recognize burnout when I become short tempered. I usually deal with this by getting involved with the more human side of this agency. For example, I'm currently developing some new programs for one of our youth shelters. This involves spending time with teenagers, which gives me the opportunity to touch base with people again."

How Work Affects the Helper's Personal Life

In talking with mental-health providers, we find that many of them are not able to separate themselves from their work. They find it difficult to make a clear distinction between their personal life and their professional life. One provider said:

"My work takes a toll on me personally at times. In sad and difficult cases, such as working with clients who have been sexually abused, there is the danger of getting overly involved. I find that if I get a series of severe clients, then stress builds up."

Although this helper's professional life spills over negatively into his personal life at times, there are also some constructive effects of his work on him personally. Working intimately with others is a catalyst for him to look at the things he is doing in his own life. As he put it:

"My work helps me feel that I'm out there contributing and helping people. I feel that I'm doing something worthwhile and feel a sense of accomplishment. My work helps me put my own struggles in perspective. I'm able to learn a lot about myself through my involvement in the lives of others."

The myth of the wounded healer. The myth of the wounded healer sheds some light on the ways in which the helper is personally affected by the helping process. Jaffe (1986) argues that health professionals must see that they cannot simply give and remain detached from their feelings. Instead, they must look inward at their personal needs. Jaffe decries the notion that healers are not supposed to have needs, that personal feelings are not relevant, and that helpers should learn to cut themselves off from their own pain as they work with others' pain. He describes the Greek myth attributing healing powers to the wounded healer. Such healers were supposed to possess the wisdom of life and death, yet they were not able to heal their own incurable wound. According to Jaffe, helping professionals need to recognize the impact on their own life of working with suffering people. They need to become aware of their inner responses and to learn to work through their own pain in a constructive manner if they hope to avoid burnout.

Kottler (1986) argues that most therapists understand that they are jeopardizing their own emotional well-being when they intimately encounter the pain of others. Kottler observes that the client and the therapist change each other and that there are hazards to the therapist as a result of this intimate relationship:

There are tremendous risks for the therapist in living with the anguish of others, in being so close to others' torments. Sometimes we become desensitized by human emotions and experience an acute overdose of feeling; we turn ourselves off. Other times we overreact to personal incidents as a result of lingering dissonance created during sessions [p. 7].

Case example. Imagine a beginning counselor who is working in an agency, where she is asked to colead a group of adults who are in some stage of grief over a significant loss. Nancy feels that there is a real need for this work, and she is enthusiastic in accepting the coleadership role. She lost her husband through a tragic death, yet she feels that she has allowed herself to fully experience the pain of his death and has accepted the loss. Nancy works very well with the members in her group. She can be compassionate, supportive, and empathetic, and she is able to facilitate the members' working through some of their pain.

After a few weeks Nancy notices that she is no longer looking forward to going to the group. She feels somewhat depressed and finds herself becoming apathetic toward the members. What she does not realize is that even though some of her old wounds were healed, exposure to the intense pain of so many other people has reopened these wounds. Thus, the only way Nancy could survive was to numb herself from feeling the others' pain. This numbing led to her depression and her inability to work effectively with her clients. What Nancy has ignored is her vulnerability to the pain of her loss and her need to express and work through this pain as it is being reexperienced.

Simply because Nancy reexperiences her old pain does not necessarily mean that she will become ineffective in working with this type of group. Quite to the contrary, if she accepts the fact that she is still wounded and explores these feelings, she can heal her own wounds at the same time that she is facilitating the healing process in others. She can model the ongoing nature of grief work and teach the members that although the pain will never be completely erased, it can become less controlling. If at times her own pain feels overwhelming in the group, she can share it with the members. She can use her experiences as a bridge to connect with the struggles of others. Alternately, Nancy can choose to seek personal therapy. If she puts her own emotions time and time again "on hold," either in or out of the group, she is bound to become ineffectual as a helper, and if she continues this type of involvement over a long period, the chances are that she will burn out. The challenge for Nancy is to learn to pay attention to her inner experience and to use it as a road to her growth and as a way of making contact with others.

How Your Ideals Can Become Dulled

An important factor in burnout is whether your ideals are working for you or against you. According to Freudenberger (1980), those who set high goals for themselves seem to have a built-in need for recognition. As long as they feel satisfied by their efforts, their energy level remains high. But when they get stuck in routine patterns and do not see the fruits of their efforts, an uncomfortable listlessness overtakes them.

Most professional providers were initially attracted to their career in a large part because of their hope of making a significant difference in the lives of others. One sign of burnout is the dulling of these ideals and the loss of caring about others. Learning the fine balance between idealism and realism is most essential if you hope to survive as a helping professional. The idealism that is embodied in the desire to "save the world" can sometimes be transformed into feelings of cynicism. The ideals that you hold when you begin your career can be a positive force, and this idealism can also be a direct path toward burnout. Your idealism can result in brainstorming ideas that are translated into new projects. Yet if you are not careful, you can get carried away with your enthusiasm and immerse yourself in your work and projects. If your total worth as a person hinges on your projects' bearing fruit, you may experience personal devastation when your projects cease being rewarding.

The toll of devoting yourself to your profession is more pronounced if you are set on changing the system quickly and efficiently. You may believe that it is possible to revolutionize the system, only to find time and again that systems are rigid and resistant to change. Thus, when you fail to succeed in your attempts to remake the system, you are likely to experience a deep frustration, which can easily result in a "what's the use" attitude toward future goals.

If you are set on challenging people who have been in a system for a long time, you will probably run into many roadblocks. In challenging others you may alienate many staff members. Rather than setting yourself up for eventual failure, focus your energies on learning how to take constructive action within a system. This entails first knowing how systems work and understanding the reasons for the particular structure of a system. If you are unrealistically idealistic, you can fight a losing battle of trying to change others who are committed to the status quo and who will fight you on your every proposal. We will be talking about the futility of focusing on "them out there" while ignoring your own behaviors.

The problem of tarnished idealism increases as you come into contact with cynical colleagues who are threatened by your enthusiasm. A seasoned staff member may tear down your ideals and try to convince you that you, too, will harden yourself to painful reality. Your coworkers may tell you of all the things that simply won't work. It is difficult to stay creative and excited in a job environment where those around you are continually chipping away at your efforts to make a difference. If you constantly hear that your proposals for change won't work and if you are without real support for your ideas, you are likely to face psychological erosion, and you might eventually join the ranks of your soured brethren. Faced with this onslaught of negative input, many beginners begin to doubt themselves and their competence. If you are beginning as a helper, you probably already have many self-doubts, and if these doubts are reinforced, it is easier to feel disillusioned.

A young man we know, who recently graduated with a bachelor's degree in psychology, worked briefly in a residential home for adolescents. Paul was greatly disillusioned when he encountered deeply entrenched cynicism in this facility. He quickly learned that both the residents and the staff were committed to the status quo. The apathy he experienced from the staff discouraged him and led him to wonder if he wanted to pursue this field.

If you work in an environment where you receive negative bombardment, you would do well to actively seek some source of positive support and input, either in your job setting or away from it. It would be a mistake to wait for the agency to create this support for you, so ask colleagues to join you in making the time for a regular meeting of minds.

Some Causes of Burnout

There is no single cause of burnout but, rather, a combination of factors. Burnout is a complex issue that can best be understood by taking into consideration the *individual, interpersonal,* and *organizational* sources that contribute to this condition.

Individual Factors

Helpers play a role in creating their own burnout. Certain personality traits and characteristics increase the risk factor. The chances for burnout rise if the person is younger, less self-confident, impulsive, impatient, and dependent on others for approval and affection and has goals and aspirations that are out of tune with reality (Maslach, 1982a).

The need to be needed can work for and against you. There is a considerable expenditure of energy in thinking about and taking care of those who need you. If this need is great, you may find yourself a prisoner of the demands that in some way you have created for yourself based on your own needs. As you are starting out and building a practice, you may be flattered by those who are seeking your help. Indeed, it feels psychologically affirming to be sought after and needed. It is possible to become impressed with the economic rewards associated with helping people. The temptation is there not to turn away people, for both emotional and financial reasons. Some helpers have a difficult time in taking a vacation, especially when they figure the lost income. Soon these helpers forget that they, too, have needs, which are probably not being met because of their overinvolvement with others and their overcommitments. There are limits to how much you can take on without paying a price in terms of your physical, mental, and emotional health.

Freudenberger (1980) observes that what militates against helping professionals is that they are fighting a battle against the pressures of society, the needs of the people they serve, and their own personality traits. He describes the price helpers pay for their involvement with people in this way:

The work of the helping professions is taxing and tough. Rewards are often few and not highly visible. Pressures are constant. New situations calling for ingenuity as well as diligence crop up all the time. The helper has come to his profession with visions of a supportive institution peopled with wise superiors and cooperative patients, students, or clients. What he finds instead is red tape, harried administrators, intractable cases. No one has prepared him for this. No one comes forward to ameliorate his feelings of inadequacy, and this is where his own psychological make-up comes into play. If the worker has been looking for the kind of personal fulfillment he should be finding elsewhere, he will quickly begin to burn out [p.154].

Interpersonal Factors

Maslach (1982a) writes about involvement with people as a main source of burnout. She contends that the hallmark of the syndrome is a shift in the way professionals view the people they are helping. They change from feeling positive and caring to feeling negative and uncaring. Continuous contact with clients who are unappreciative, upset, and depressed often leads helpers to view all recipients in helping relationships in negative terms. Practitioners may care less, begin to make derogatory comments about their clients, ignore them, and want to move away from them. Dehumanized responses are a core ingredient of burnout.

One counselor in an agency setting notices that she is on the path toward burnout when she becomes too involved with her clients' struggles. She commented:

"Sometimes I'm unable to escape personal issues that arise when my clients' problems trigger issues similar to my own. This affects me in a positive way in that it holds me accountable within my own life and keeps me moving toward the best person I can become. Sometimes it affects me negatively when I become overly self-critical."

There is a vicious circle operating here. If you get an abundance of negative reactions from others, you will tend to become self-critical and wonder if you are making any difference to those you are supposedly helping. Being critical and unkind to yourself usually leads to being uncritical and unkind toward others.

The impact that other people have on burnout should not be overlooked. If you are a part of an institutional setting, the quality of your contacts with coworkers and supervisors is extremely important. Coworkers can be helpful in providing support for you, but if there is no climate of trust and openness in the work setting, you become more vulnerable to burnout. If these relationships are strained and the atmosphere is hostile and unsupportive, the chances of burnout are increased.

Organizational Factors

In addition to the individual and interpersonal factors, social and organizational factors also cause burnout. An organization contributes to burnout by making too many demands on workers, by reducing employees' autonomy, by providing little positive feedback for job performance, and by setting policies that put the worker in conflict. Poor management, inadequate supervision, rigid organizational policies, and excessive demands are other contributing factors. (See Chapter 7 for an account of the stresses involved in working in an organization.)

Case example.   Agencies can easily be run in dehumanizing ways, and the battle to retain your integrity is often fierce. The following interview with a social worker in a community agency in a large city gives some flavor of how endless demands can wear down one's stamina and lead to feelings of futility:

"Seeing clients is my primary interest. I must make progress notes after each client. These notes include descriptions of treatment methods, proof of measurable results, and assessment. The agency expects me to write notes after each session. We are further expected to write specifically and behaviorally. There is a press for constant justification for seeing a client. On one hand, if your client improves, there is pressure from the agency to terminate work with the client. On the other hand, if the client regresses, then treatment is typically judged as ineffective. Thus, there is the hassle with the paperwork game. What some of us write may not be what we are actually doing. In the back of my mind there is the constant stress of unfinished paperwork. The expectation of the agency is that of short-term treatment. I have to deal with edicts from above, which I often find frustrating.

"There is also the need for professional consultation. The expectation is that an interview can be completed in an hour, yet this often takes one and a half hours. I attend staff meetings, where we talk about policies. I have to deal with staff issues about clients and case conferencing at these meetings. On top of this there are many unexpected tasks that endlessly come up. There are phone calls, checking up on clients, contacts, and networking. I have to contact parents, teachers, and school counselors in cases involving children. Quality work takes time. There is so much indirect time that does not get recognized by the agency. I spend some time in peer review and in supervising case presentations. Supervising interns is part of my job, which takes much time. I am ultimately responsible for all of the clients my interns are seeing. The push is toward direct service and for seeing many clients. The more clients seen, the more money for the agency.

"Part of my work involves community outreach. I must make referrals and then check up on these referrals. This involves talking with personnel at the probation department and at schools. Although much of my time is taken up by many of these indirect services, we don't get credit for these activities. For every client seen, there is much extra work. Listening to tapes of client sessions and to interns' tapes takes time. At times, there are unexpected meetings with the auditors.

"Because of the pressure of these unanticipated audits, we must keep current with our paperwork, which is not always realistic or possible. At times I feel overwhelmed by petty policies and procedures. Once I made a mistake on a date on a written report, and I was told that this represented a 5% level of inefficiency. This resulted in being monitored by my supervisor for a month.

"There are ethical issues in submitting to the demands of a system or transgressing the demands of the system. Many of us are guilty of creative lying and stretching the truth. This involves writing reports in ways that we know they will be accepted. Working in an agency involves knowing when and how to report clients. Yet reporting always means more work. Because of the extra work and time involved in the process of making reports and following up, some workers tend to avoid reporting in certain cases where they should do so."

After reading this account you might consider how you can creatively and successfully cope with the demands that agencies will make on you. How can you do what you believe in and at the same time deal with the multiple demands of your job? What are your reactions to the social worker's personal account above?

Lack of appreciation. A major theme heard by those who are suffering from burnout is that they do not feel recognized for who they are or what they do, that they receive little positive feedback, and that they do not feel appreciation of their dedication. In such a setting they are eventually bound to lose their striving for excellence. This lack of recognition is compounded by the fact that you may have entered the helping professions because of your need for recognition and appreciation. You may be sincerely devoted to helping others, yet your efforts may seem meager at times. You will hear more often about what you are failing to do and about your deficiencies than about what you have done well. If appreciation is lacking on the job, it is difficult over a period of time to know whether what you are doing really makes a difference to anyone. This process tends to erode both your ideals and enthusiasm, which leads to demoralization.

The real challenge is to learn ways of working for your own appreciation and self-worth. Unless you want to depend on clients or colleagues to give you positive feedback and confirmation, it is imperative that you give yourself the appreciation that you might be seeking from others.

When we consulted at a state mental hospital, we found many workers who were suffering from burnout. They claimed to have difficult clients, a difficult administration, and difficult colleagues. If you find yourself in a similar situation with this combination of factors, you are in trouble. What we attempted to teach these workers at the state facility was to seek out others to talk with when they felt the acute pains of being the unappreciated helper.

Steps in the Prevention of Burnout

Just as many sources contribute to the process of burnout, so many steps can be taken to combat it. You can do much personally to lessen the chances of burning out or to restore yourself. Individual strategies alone, however, are not enough. You need to make effective use of others as a source of support, which requires that you learn certain interpersonal skills. There is also the organizational level to consider. Institutions certainly do contribute to burnout, and they can develop strategies for prevention of this problem. This section considers some of the individual, interpersonal, and organizational strategies for coping with the ongoing problem of professional burnout.

You Have Control over Yourself

We have suggested that to a large extent you create your own stress by the interpretation you give to events in your life. Although you cannot always control these events, you do have much control over how you react to them and the stance you take toward your life. If you are responsible for contributing to your physical and emotional exhaustion, you can also take action to change this condition. An important step is to realize that you are not an omnipotent being and that you cannot be the eternal giver to the universe. If you attempt this impossible dream, you ought to be prepared for the price you'll pay. Become attuned to the danger signals that you are being depleted, and take seriously your own need for nurturing and for recognition. What follows is some thoughts on what you can do to significantly lessen the chances that you will get stuck in the rut of disillusionment. We do not present these ideas dogmatically but more in the spirit of encouraging you to develop your own strategy for keeping yourself alive personally and professionally.

• Look at your goals to determine if they are working for you. Although you may have initially become a helper because you wanted to create a better world to live in, it is essential to temper your ideals with reality if you are to avoid continual frustration. Setting realistic goals means asking yourself whether they have been given to you by someone else or whether you have made them your own. It is hard to maintain enthusiasm if you are living by someone else's design.

• Look at your expectations to determine whether they are realistic. You may expect that you can be all things to all people, and you may think that it is your mission in life to always be available for anyone who needs you. These self-expectations will eventually wear you down. Even though it is hard to accept, there are clients whom you will not be able to help. Regardless of how much you have to offer to others, there is a limit to what you can give. In fact, the more capable you are, the more likely you are to be asked to take on just one more project. Eventually the weight of these projects will crush any of us.

• Recognize that you can be an active agent in your life. If you passively submit by allowing yourself to get into a rut of hopelessness and helplessness, you will feel that your destiny is out of your control.

• Learn to monitor the impact of stress, both on the job and at home. In addition to recognizing the ways that stress affects you, commit yourself to applying some of the strategies for stress management that we discussed in the previous chapter. Even though you may wish that you could eliminate the many sources of stress in your life, such a wish is not realistic. But you can learn how to think differently about the stresses you encounter in everyday life, and you can learn a wide range of techniques to lessen the negative impact of stress on you physically and psychologically.

• Find other sources of meaning besides your work. These activities and interests can help you at least temporarily escape from job stresses and keep a balance in your life.

• Examine your priorities. You can ask yourself: "Is what I am doing what I really want to be doing? If not, why am I continuing in this direction?" "What are some things I want to be doing professionally that I am not doing? Who or what is stopping me?" "Am I accepting projects that I really want to reject? If so, why is it so difficult for me to say no?" Once you have answered some of these questions for yourself in an honest way, decide what action to take. For example, if you often say yes when you really want to firmly say no, you can begin to change this behavior.

• Granted that there are some unpleasant aspects about your job that may be difficult to change, you can approach your work differently. You can rearrange your schedule to reduce your stress. If you have some exceptionally difficult clients, for example, you can avoid seeing them one after the other. You can also look for ways to bring your talents and interests to your work. You can devise ways of exchanging jobs with a colleague for a time. If you stop blaming the institution for your problems and start assuming more control of your own destiny, this shift alone can make a key difference.

• It is very easy to become overwhelmed by thinking about all of the things that you feel powerless to change. Rather than contributing to your feelings of futility, focus more on the aspects of your work that you have the power to change. Creativity grinds to a halt when most of your time is spent in thinking of all that you cannot do rather than thinking about what you are able to do, within the limits that are imposed on you.

• Learn your own limits, and learn to set limits with others. Take care to avoid overextending yourself in an agency. Others might not make this easy, so it will take considerable self-discipline to maintain your limits. This means that you will have to struggle with clients who demand things from you that you are not willing to give. The same is true for those who employ you. If you have ignored setting limits, it may be extremely difficult to change this pattern, but it is not impossible.

• Look to colleagues and friends for support. Don't try to internalize all of your concerns and deal with them alone. Colleagues who face the same realities as you on the job can provide you with new information, insights, and perspectives. In the helping professions the companionship of colleagues can be your greatest asset. And remember, you sometimes get support for yourself when you give support to others.

• Create a support group. If you wait for the system to organize a formal support group for you and your coworkers, you may have a long and frustrating wait. You can take the initiative to organize your coworkers for the purpose of listening to one another and providing help. Yet do not get caught in the trap of using these meetings as mere gripe sessions. Although it may temporarily feel good to ventilate by sharing your troubles, if you stop at this level, this process will do little good. In fact, merely listening to your colleagues blame their clients or the system for their misery is likely to increase your stress level. You will have to deal not only with your feelings of hopelessness but also with the quagmire of their depression. With your colleagues you can collectively come up with alternative ways of approaching problems and can think of new ways to find hope. You can also use this time to get to know your colleagues on a personal level, to have fun with them, to talk about light subjects unrelated to work, and to simply share whatever is on your mind and in your heart.

• Rather than waiting until you are hit with a chronic case of burnout, recognize the early signs and take remedial action quickly. Don't deceive yourself into thinking that only your colleagues will burn out while you will retain your unbounded enthusiasm forever.

• Pay attention to the nonfeeling state of burnout, which includes being chronically exhausted, detached, bored, and cynical. Take special note of your tiredness, as this is the best indicator for detecting the initial phase of burnout. Rather than making excuses for your tiredness, acknowledge how tired you feel (Freudenberger, 1980).

According to Maslach (1982a), it's never too early to be thinking of ways to prevent burnout. She suggests not waiting passively until problems arise but using solutions now. Maslach stresses that detecting the first signs of burnout is critical, for the condition can be dealt with more effectively in the initial stages. During the formative stages the symptoms are not so severe, the individual is still committed and caring, and there is more receptivity to change. In the course of many interviews as part of her research on burnout, Maslach heard a constant refrain of "Why didn't anyone tell me that this was what I was in for?" Over and over she found that helpers were ignorant and ill-prepared to cope with the emotional stresses of being a helping professional. They simply had not been made aware of the potential difficulties involved in working with people.

In asking several people in the helping professions about the steps they take to prevent burnout, we came up with a few strategies:

• "To prevent burnout, I try to exercise daily, take personal time out with friends, go to personal therapy, and talk with coworkers and supervisors."
• "I plan my schedule carefully and make sure not to overextend myself. I take time off for vacations."
• "I take time out for myself to have fun. I do things like reading junk novels, shopping, spending time with my family, and going on vacations, and I always pat myself on the back for all my accomplishments."
• "I learn to say no and set limitations for myself. I try to allow as much time for play as I do for work, and I always try to leave my job at work."
• "I try to manage my time well. I reward myself with little presents. I take time off to go for a bike ride, go out for dinner, or take a bubble bath."

- "I don't bring work home with me. I try to leave my paperwork at school. I also take days off to relax when I need them."
- "I prevent burnout by doing a variety of things such as teaching, taking personal time out, writing, spending time with colleagues doing workshops, and spending lazy time off by being nonproductive."

A couple, both social workers, shared their thoughts on the challenges of remaining personally and professionally alive as they work in community agencies. They have to remind themselves continually not to become overwhelmed by the myriad of demands, not to lose sight of why they are in the agency, and not to get lost by being a cog in the production line. They have managed to temper their idealism by accepting that they cannot do everything they wanted to do. They are continuing to learn to cut down rather than taking on more and more. To prevent getting caught in a comfortable rut, they are creative in finding ways to vary their activities. They work with children and adults, colead groups, supervise interns, teach, and give inservice presentations. They attempt to develop a perspective when the agency gets petty, which they do partly by keeping a sense of humor. They both assess their priorities and maintain limits. To be sure, this is not a simple matter, but instead involves a commitment to self-assessment and openness to change.

Our Personal Experiences with Burnout

We would like to share with you our own struggles with burnout and talk about what we do to keep ourselves fresh. First of all, even though we are aware of the dangers of burnout, we are not immune to it. At different times throughout our professional lives we have lost a sense of enthusiasm, become cynical, felt depressed, and wanted to withdraw and get away from it all. One of the realizations that both of us have had is that the answer does not lie merely in cutting out activities that we don't enjoy. Much of what we do professionally we like very much, and we have to remind ourselves that we cannot accept all the attractive projects that we may be interested in. The psychological and financial rewards, however high and tempting, do not always compensate for the emotional and physical depletion that results from an overscheduled professional life. At one time, for example, we scheduled as many as six weeklong residential groups a year, all of which were held at our home. Although these groups were professionally rewarding, it took a great deal of energy to lead them, and it necessitated rearranging our personal life. Now we limit ourselves to two of these weeklong groups, both of which we do in the summer when we have fewer demands from our regular jobs. In another instance we became aware that too many of our "vacations" were coupled with professional commitments such as giving a workshop or attending a convention. Although we see this mixture as a good balance, we nevertheless realized that we missed "real vacations" that were separate from any professional commitments. For the most part, traveling and vacations have been a welcomed pause that refreshes.

One way in which we attempt to prevent burnout is to pay attention to the early signals that we are overextending ourselves, and we involve ourselves in diverse projects. We engage in a variety of professional tasks, such as teaching, consulting, doing groups and workshops, and writing books. Besides offering our services to others, we recognize our need for input from others in the field, and we attend workshops for our own personal and professional development. Being aware of the demands that our profession puts on us, we are highly conscious of living a healthy life-style. Therefore, we pay attention to our nutritional habits, and no matter how busy we are, we make the time that we need for adequate rest and regular exercise. As part of our life-style, we made the decision to live in a remote mountain community. The reality of this remoteness and our busy schedules kept us, at times, from making time for our friends and colleagues. We had to realize that we could easily separate ourselves too much from relationships that were much needed and a source of joy and support for us. Thus, we make extra efforts to schedule blocks of time with our friends. We feel blessed in having many good colleagues, friends, and two daughters, and we take the time needed to maintain and to nourish these valued relationships.

By Way of Review

- Learning to recognize and cope with the reality of professional burnout is essential for your survival as a helper. Intense involvement with people over a period of time can lead to physical and psychological exhaustion.
- Burnout is not something that suddenly happens to you. Rather, there are stages in the burnout process. Recognizing the early signs is an important step toward prevention.
- There is a heavy price to pay for being a professional care giver. No one is immune from the cost of caring for others.
- Being a professional care giver often reopens your own psychological wounds. If you are not willing to work on your unfinished business, you might consider whether you want to accompany clients into the journey of dealing with their past wounds.
- Most helpers enter their profession with a high degree of idealism. Later, these ideals are sometimes tempered with realism. The danger is that idealism can be transformed into cynicism, which is a step away from burnout.
- There is no single cause of burnout; rather, there are individual, interpersonal, and organizational factors that lead to it. Understanding these factors can help you learn how to prevent or cope with burnout.
- Burnout is often the result of the many demands placed on you by an agency. It is important to learn specific ways of surviving with dignity in an agency setting.
- If you work in an environment where there is a great deal of negativity, it is good to seek sources of positive support, both on your job and at home.

- Just as there are many sources of burnout, there are multiple ways to prevent and combat it. Individual, interpersonal, and organizational strategies can be devised.

What Will You Do Now?

1. Find a person in the helping profession who is willing to be interviewed about burnout. Focus your discussion with this person on what he or she does to keep alive personally and professionally. Questions to consider are "What do you find to be the major source of burnout?" "What do you do to prevent burnout?"

2. Think about how you are when you are at work and when you are on vacation. Ask someone who knows you in both situations to describe you in these situations. Does this person see you as the same in both contexts, or different? Use this exercise as a way of thinking about the ways in which your work affects your personal life.

3. Identify a few of the signs warning that you are not taking care of yourself or that you are close to burnout. For example, you might not be getting adequate sleep, or you might be ignoring exercise, or you might be experiencing a variety of physical symptoms. Now, develop a plan of action that will encourage you to work on at least one of these sources of burnout. Are you willing to assume responsibility for eliminating something that you are doing that is contributing to your level of fatigue?

Suggested Readings

Freudenberger, H. J., with Richelson, G. (1980). *Burn-out: The high cost of high achievement.* New York: Bantam Books. This is a highly readable, excellent source that describes the phenomenon of burnout, shows its connection with work, provides many case examples, deals with curing the problem, and provides strategies for combating it.

Maslach, C. (1982a). *Burnout: The cost of caring.* Englewood Cliffs, NJ: Prentice-Hall (Spectrum). This is a well-researched yet readable account of the burnout syndrome as it applies to professional care givers. Both the causes and effects of burnout are clearly described. The author deals with the sources of burnout on an individual, interpersonal, and institutional level, and she describes ways of coping with burnout on all of these levels.

Pines, A. M., & Aronson, E., with Kafry, D. (1981). *Burnout: From tedium to personal growth.* New York: Free Press. The authors do a good job of describing the path toward burnout, with a particular focus on the causes among helping professionals. They present organizational coping strategies, social-support systems, and interpersonal coping strategies as ways of effectively dealing with the problem.

CHAPTER   9

Ethical Dilemmas

Focus of the Chapter

Regardless of what helping profession you decide on, you will be faced with learning to make difficult ethical decisions. As will become clear in this chapter, part of becoming a professional involves being able to apply ethical codes to practical situations. The aim of the chapter is to introduce you to an array of current ethical concerns that helpers encounter.

Ethics: A Hot Topic

There has been an increased interest in ethical matters in recent years. The professional journals are a forum for this expanded discussion, a number of new books have been written on ethical and professional concerns, and separate courses are now being required in most graduate programs. Although we don't want to be cynical about the motivations for the rising interest in ethics, we suspect that this trend is grounded on an attempt to avoid malpractice actions. How to lessen the chances of a malpractice suit is one topic of this chapter.

The chapter will not provide you with an in-depth knowledge of ethical issues. But we hope it will stimulate you to read some of the books listed in the Suggested Readings. We encourage you to take an ethics course or, at the very least, to attend professional conferences and workshops dealing with ethical, legal, and professional concerns.

Inventory of Ethical Issues

What are some of your major concerns about ethical practices? Perhaps at this point you have not even raised this question. Our hope is not that you learn an answer to all the many ethical problems that will confront you but that you broaden your awareness of the significant issues at stake. This inventory is designed to help you focus on potential ethical concerns. Read each statement, and apply this code in responding: 4 = this issue concerns me very much; 3 = this issue concerns me somewhat; 2 = this issue concerns me very little; 1 = this issue does not concern me at all.

___ 1. I'm not sure how I would respond to a client who asked me for a date or wanted some other social involvement with me.

___ 2. I'm uncertain how I would deal with a client who expressed an interest in a sexual relationship with me.

___ 3. It would be hard for me to refer a client to another professional, even if I felt this was in the client's best interest.

___ 4. It would be difficult for me to decide when I had to break confidentiality.

___ 5. I would have trouble terminating a client even if it were clear that the client was no longer benefiting.

___ 6. I feel uncertain how to go about resolving ethical dilemmas.

___ 7. I often doubt whether I know enough or possess the skills needed to effectively help others.

___   8.   If a client was unwilling to accept my referral, I might continue the relationship even if I felt unqualified to work with the client.

___   9.   I am likely to promote dependency on the part of my clients by being too ready to offer advice or too quick to find solutions to their problems.

___   10. I am not at all certain what I might do if I felt that one of my clients posed a danger either to self or to others.

___   11. At times I'm concerned about my ability to keep relationships with my clients professional.

___   12. I don't think my training has prepared me to deal with sexual attractions in the helping relationship.

___   13. I think I know what I should do and probably would do if I were to become aware of unethical behavior on the part of my colleagues.

___   14. I'm more likely to focus on unethical behavior on my colleagues' part than I am to focus on my own unethical behavior.

___   15. I'm concerned about the possibility of becoming involved in a malpractice suit as a result of something I do or don't do as a helper.

Now that you have finished this inventory, spend a few minutes reflecting on any ethical concerns that you have at this time. This reflection can help you read the chapter more actively and formulate ethical questions.

Ethical Decision Making

Ethical practice involves far more than merely knowing and following professional groups' codes of ethics. In dealing with ethical dilemmas, you will rarely find clear-cut answers. Most of the problems are complex and thus defy simple solution. The process of making ethical decisions involves acquiring a tolerance for dealing with gray areas and for coping with ambiguity. Although knowing the ethical standards of your profession is important, this knowledge alone is not sufficient. Ethical codes are not dogmas but guidelines to assist you in making the best possible decisions for the benefit of your clients and yourself. Ethical standards vary among agencies. It is essential that you become aware of the specific ethical guidelines of the agency in which you are working.

In our teaching we find that students often begin an ethics course with the expectation of getting concrete answers to some of the questions raised in their fieldwork. They do not expect to have to engage in personal and professional self-exploration to find the best course of action. At times, readers of our ethics book (Corey, Corey, & Callanan, 1988) comment that it raises many more questions than it answers. We tell them that the book's purpose is to challenge them to develop the resources to deal intelligently with ethical dilemmas.

Case example.   Susan became aware of unethical practices in a community agency where she was participating as an intern. She and other interns were expected to take on some difficult clients. She realized that doing so would mean that she was clearly practicing beyond the boundaries of her competence. To make the situation worse, supervision at the agency left much to be desired. Her superior was not willing to offer regular supervision and was often "too busy" to keep appointments to talk about her cases. In her fieldwork seminar on campus she learned that supervisors are ethically and legally responsible for what interns do. She had some trouble in knowing what to do. She did not want to change placements in the middle of the semester, and yet she was struggling with the appropriateness of confronting her supervisor about the situation. Unclear about how to proceed, Susan made an appointment with her fieldwork professor on campus, who shared responsibility with the agency supervisor.

In consultation with her professor Susan explored a number of alternatives. She might approach her agency supervisor herself and be more assertive in getting an appointment. Another option could be a meeting of Susan, her agency supervisor, and her professor to explore the situation. It might be decided that this particular agency was inappropriate for students. What was important was that Susan knew she could ask for and get help in dealing with her problem. Sometimes students who are in similar predicaments arrive too quickly at the conclusion that they will merely tolerate things as they are rather than stirring up a hornet's nest and also making themselves uncomfortable in the process.

At the beginning of the course Susan thought that clear answers were available for the variety of situations that would surface. By the end of the semester she was learning to appreciate that codes and standards provide general guidelines but that she would have to apply these guidelines to specific cases. She also learned the value of initiating the consultation process in ethical decision making.

Another example involves interpreting the ethical guideline that the client's welfare should be the primary consideration in the therapeutic relationship. Consider the case of a client who is talking about his struggles in an alcoholic family. As the therapist listens, her own pain over having alcoholic parents is triggered. She wonders whether she should tell her client about her personal reactions. Will her disclosure meet her own needs or the needs of her client? How is the therapist to judge whether the disclosure would help or hinder the client in working through places where he is stuck?

Responsible practice requires that you base your actions on informed, sound, and responsible judgment. For us, this means that you must be willing to consult with colleagues, keep yourself current in your knowledge and skills, and engage in a continuing process of self-examination. Thinking about ethical issues and learning to make wise decisions is an evolutionary process that requires an always open attitude.

Dealing with Your Competence as a Helper

Virtually all of the professional codes spell out that you should not practice beyond the limits of your competence. In thinking about this matter, you may go from one extreme to the other. At one extreme you may be plagued with self-doubts, fearing that you will never have enough knowledge or skills to effectively help people. At the other extreme you may be overly confident, thinking that you can tackle any problem a client presents.

Learn to assess your ability to work with a range of clients. If you followed the practice of referring all clients with whom you had difficulty, you might have very few left! It is a good idea to think about the reasons you'd be inclined to suggest a referral. In cases where you have limited experience, it is especially important to be open to consulting another professional. We hope that you will always be willing to say to a client "I don't know what to do, but I know where we can get some help." Beginning helpers sometimes believe that they must have all the answers, and they hesitate to let their clients know that they might not know how to best proceed. Although we would not expect you to know everything, we certainly expect that you can learn much under supervision.

Imagine that you are an intern at a community mental-health center. This is your first experience in this type of setting. One of your first clients presents himself with much confusion about his sexual identity. He is unclear about how to proceed. Should he follow through on his homosexual inclinations or remain in his marriage? You feel overwhelmed, you are very uncomfortable with his choice, and you don't know quite how to handle this situation. What might you say or do?

The following are a few approaches you might take:

- You could deny your discomfort and not express any of your feelings or reactions.
- You could share your negative reactions about homosexuality and actively attempt to persuade the client to live a different life-style.
- You might let your client know that you feel both uncomfortable and overwhelmed but that you would like to challenge yourself by working with him. You could also tell him that you will seek supervision to help you avoid imposing your values on him.
- You could tell this client that you are very new in this work, that you are uncertain about how to proceed, and that you would like to refer him.

Competence Issues in Marital and Family Therapy

Interns are frequently asked to work with a population with which they have had little formal training. For example, a supervisor might expect an intern to work with a family or counsel a couple. Out of shyness or lack of assertiveness some interns agree to work with a family yet do so feeling very unprepared. They may let themselves be talked into the assignment on the grounds that the best way for them to learn is to jump in and swim.

If you find yourself in a predicament such as this, we hope that you will not submit to the pressure from your supervisor to exceed the limits of your competence. As a student or an intern you are not immune to a lawsuit. If you were to accept a family for treatment and provided counseling without adequate supervision, the family could sue you on the basis that you did not provide them with competent services.

If you expect to engage in any marital and family therapy, you need to have the minimal educational requirements for this work. These include specific courses in marriage and family counseling as well as training and supervision in working with couples and families. Merely knowing something about family dynamics is not sufficient. It is in the supervised practicum and internship that your academic knowledge is translated into practical terms. We are not implying that you are unethical if you practice as a learner. There is no way for you to gain experience and to acquire skills without actual practice. What is essential is that you gain this experience at the same time that you are under supervision and are receiving feedback.

Competence Issues in Group Work

If you work as an intern in an agency or in a position as a professional health provider, you are likely to find that a supervisor or a director of the agency would like you to design a group. Groups for various populations appear to be gaining in popularity, and many institutions now use a variety of them as the primary therapeutic approach. You are faced with an ethical dilemma if a supervisor asks you to design or lead a group when you have not had the proper professional training in group work. In talking with both students and professionals, we find that they have often not had even minimal training in group work. The only group experiences that some of them have been exposed to are activities as a part of a required group course. This group experience is often led by students, and sometimes there is very little supervision or direction given to the group participants or the leaders.

There are many ways in which you can obtain the training and supervision needed for group work. At the very least you should have a course in group process. You should also have opportunities to lead a group under supervision and to learn from this practice. The Association for Specialists in Group Work has developed *Professional Standards for Training of Group Counselors* (ASGW, 1983). The association takes the position that qualified group leaders must acquire specialized knowledge, demonstrate a mastery of certain skills, and have supervised experiences in group work. Supervision is required, for example, and feedback is expected. Trainees critique group tapes, observe group counseling sessions, colead groups with supervision, and practice as a group leader with on-the-job supervision.

We recommend at least three experiences as adjuncts to a training program for group workers. First, we endorse personal therapy so that trainees are better able to perceive any countertransference feelings and can use their personal attributes effectively in groups. This therapy can continue while trainees are leading groups. Beginning group leaders often find emotional issues arising that can be dealt with in such therapy. Second, we highly recommend participation as a member in some kind of therapeutic group, such as group counseling, group therapy, or a personal-growth group. Some of the benefits of participation include experiencing the power of a group, learning what self-disclosure is about, experiencing the difficulty of being honest with others, and gaining an emotional sense of group experience. Third, by participating in a training and supervision group one can develop the skills needed for effective intervention. Leaders can bring into their supervision group problems they are encountering with members, and they can be exposed to various viewpoints.

Professional codes and legislative mandates alone will not ensure ethical and professional practice in group work. We think that students need to be presented with typical dilemmas that they are likely to face as group leaders. We have found that an effective way to teach ethical decision making to group leaders is to present them with case vignettes of problems that occur in groups and to lead a discussion of these issues.

This section is designed to help you to decide what you might do if you were asked to lead a group and were aware that you did not possess the knowledge or skills to do so. If you are interested in further information on this topic, we suggest that you consult ASGW (1980, 1983) or the ethics chapter in Corey and Corey (1987). These sources will give you more help in formulating your guidelines on this topic.

Knowing When and How to Make Referrals

The ethical standards of most professional organizations stipulate that making referrals is one of the main responsibilities of the professional helper. How do you know when and how to refer? Why would you want to refer? What kind of referral might be the most appropriate? What if there are few referral resources available? As we've mentioned, it is crucial for you to refer clients to other resources when working with them is beyond your ability or when personal factors are likely to interfere with a productive working relationship. If a client is not making progress with you, it might be well to consider a referral.

Referral resources are sometimes limited. This is particularly true in some less populated areas where mental-health facilities are scant. One helper told us: "I realize that I may not be much to some of my clients, but then again, I'm all they have! The nearest referral agency is over a hundred miles away, so what are they to do?" In order to make good referrals, it is necessary that you first know of the possibilities that might be best for your clients.

Ethical standards usually imply that it is improper to continue a professional relationship if it is clear that a client is not benefiting. The tricky problem is to assess whether the client is really being helped. What if you are convinced that a client is not making significant gains, yet she assures you that she is growing from this experience?

Case example.   You have been seeing a client for some time. She is very consistent, yet she typically reports that she has really nothing to discuss. You have confronted her on her unwillingness to invest much of herself in the counseling sessions. The client agrees yet continues to return. Finally, you suggest termination, because in your opinion she is not benefiting from the relationship. The client is quite resistant to your suggestion, despite her lack of involvement in the sessions. How would you handle this resistance?

Client Rights

What should you know about the rights of your clients? How can you teach your clients about their rights and responsibilities from the outset of the helping relationship? Clients are often unaware that they have rights. For most clients asking for formal or professional help is a new experience, so they are unclear about what is expected of them and what they should expect from the helper. The ethical codes of most professional organizations require that clients be given adequate information to make informed choices about entering and continuing in the therapeutic relationship. We will focus first on the client's right to informed consent, because of its central importance.

Informed Consent

Perhaps the best way to safeguard the rights of clients is to develop procedures to help them make informed choices. Getting their informed consent involves a delicate balance between telling them too little and overwhelming them with too much information too soon. Although most professionals agree on the ethical duty to provide clients with relevant information about the helping process, there is not much consensus about what should be revealed and in what manner. In deciding what you would most want to tell a client, consider the following questions:

- What services are you willing to provide?
- What do you expect of your client? What can your client expect of you?
- What are the risks and benefits of your approaches and techniques?
- What is the approximate length of treatment?
- Are there any alternatives to the approaches you might suggest?
- What do you want to tell your client about yourself?
- What are the financial considerations?
- What are the limitations of confidentiality?
- Are you likely to consult with a supervisor or other colleagues about the case?

Although some mental-health workers use written informed-consent procedures, you will need to decide which approach works best for you and your clients. We suggest that you develop comprehensive written statements that you give to clients at the first session so that they can take the materials home and read them before the next session. In this way they have a basis for asking questions, and valuable time is saved. After all, when clients finally make an appointment, they are often anxious to get help on some pressing problem. Too much information and talking about the process can dampen the client's inclination to return for further sessions.

We have found that one of the best ways of building trust with clients is by being open and above board with them from the onset. It is not a good idea to have hidden agendas for clients. By taking a stance of providing your clients with adequate information, you are also increasing the chances that they will become active participants and carry their share of the responsibilities in the helping relationship.

Confidentiality

Although your clients have every right to expect that their relationship with you will remain confidential, there are limits to your responsibility to them. Since your obligation to safeguard your clients' disclosures is not absolute, you need to develop a sense of professional ethics for determining when confidentiality must be broken.

There are many ethical and legal ramifications of confidentiality. Although this is a highly complex subject and deserves considerable discussion, our treatment is limited to some major points for you to consider. The ethics of confidentiality rests on the assumption that the client/counselor relationship is a deeply personal one and that clients have a right to expect that what they reveal will be kept private. If trust is to be established, then clients need some assurance that they will be protected from unauthorized disclosures. As a helper, therefore, you must discuss with your clients the circumstances that might affect the confidential relationship.

The laws of your state spell out special circumstances under which confidentiality must be compromised. One general guideline is that you must reveal information when there is a clear and imminent danger that clients will bring harm to others or themselves. In cases such as incest and child abuse there are mandatory reporting laws. If clients are suicidal, you cannot merely ignore this situation, even if they request that you not report it. Human-services professionals are vulnerable to lawsuits if they improperly handle confidentiality issues, so it behooves you to know the laws, to follow them, and to be aware of the ethical principles of your profession. Most of the professional organizations can provide you with information leading to assistance in dealing with some thorny ethical dilemmas. We list a variety of these organizations in Appendix D.

Miller and Thelen (1986) assessed the public's knowledge and beliefs about the confidentiality of therapeutic communications. Their survey revealed some surprising results, for the majority of the respondents (69%) believed that everything discussed with a professional helper would be held strictly confidential. Further, even more of the respondents (74%) thought that there should be no exceptions to maintaining confidential disclosures. The vast majority of respondents (96%) wanted information about confidentiality. Many of them (46%) wanted to be told of the exceptions to confidentiality before the first session, whereas some (29%) preferred discussions at various points during the helping process. The authors pointed out a huge gap between what clients expected and standard professional practice with regard to maintaining confidentiality. These findings add weight to the argument for making sure that clients know about the nature, purpose, and restrictions of confidentiality from the outset of treatment.

As a way to sharpen your thinking about issues surrounding confidentiality, think about the following cases.

Case example.   Two young girls are brought to a community agency by their aunt, who has gained custody of them in the last few months. One girl, age 11, is quite verbal, but the other, 13, is not. As they begin to talk and you ask about their history, they tell you of aunts and uncles who attempted to touch one of them and of an aunt who severely beat them. The 11-year-old tells of a suicide attempt by her sister after one such beating. If you were working with these girls, what course of action would you take, and why? Would you have available the telephone number of the Child Protective Service for the area in which you are working?

Case example.   A student intern works with pupils in an elementary school. She says to the children in a group "Everything you say in here will stay in here." Then a boy reveals a detailed plan to run away from home. The counselor, who has not talked about the exceptions to confidentiality with the children, does not know what to do. If she reports the boy, he may feel betrayed. If she fails to report him, she may face a malpractice action for failure to notify the parents. What might you suggest to her if she came to you for advice in this situation?

Case example.   You are a counselor intern in a local agency. You are part of a training group of students that meets weekly to discuss cases. One day, while you are having lunch in a local restaurant with some of the students, they begin to discuss their cases in detail, mentioning names and details of the clients loudly enough for others in the restaurant to overhear. What would you do in this situation?

It is tempting to talk about your clients and their stories, especially since others are usually curious about what you are doing. It may give you a sense of importance to be able to tell "juicy anecdotes." You may talk more than you should because of feeling overwhelmed with sagas of clients and the need to unburden yourself. As a professional helper you must learn how to talk about clients and how to report without breaking confidentiality. Even though your clients should know that confidentiality cannot be guaranteed absolutely, they should have your sincere assurance that you will respect their privacy and that you will avoid talking about them, except when it is professionally necessary to do so.

Confidentiality involving clients with AIDS.   As we discussed in Chapter 5, helpers will be increasingly confronted with ethical and professional problems in working with clients who have the AIDS virus. In the professional literature and in the ethical codes of various professional organizations, the limits of confidentiality have not been defined in the case of AIDS clients who continue to be sexually active without informing their partner(s). What are the responsibilities of counselors to preserve the life of these partners?

Gray and Harding (1988) have proposed guidelines for counselors who deal with AIDS clients. On learning that a client has the AIDS virus, Gray and Harding suggest, counselors should ask the client to inform his or her current sexual partners. They endorse a process of helping these clients assume responsibility for informing their partners. This process includes educating, consulting, and actively supporting clients in this situation. Gray and Harding emphasize that for this process to be effective and therapeutic for the client, it is first necessary to establish a supportive and trusting counseling relationship. If this process of education, consultation, and active support does not persuade AIDS clients to inform their sexual partners, Gray and Harding suggest, the following steps should be taken by the counselor:

• In order to protect the helping relationship, counselors should first inform the clients of their intention to breach confidentiality.
• Counselors who work with clients who have identified sexual partners should directly inform the partners.
• Counselors who work with clients who have anonymous sexual partners should inform the state public health officer.

Kain (1988) has concerns about the consequences of mandatory breaching of confidentiality. He contends that Gray and Harding's proposed guidelines might well result in more harm than good. If a client is not telling his or her sexual partner about AIDS infection, Kain wonders why not and recommends a working through of the issues of rejection, abandonment, loneliness, homophobia, and infidelity.

Posey (1988) has facilitated a support group for people with AIDS, people with AIDS-related complex, and people who test positive for the AIDS virus. She sees confidentiality as a matter of responsibility, and she raises the question "Who is responsible for protecting whom?" She adds further suggestions to those provided by Gray and Harding: (1) Helpers can refer a client to a support group if one is available; (2) helpers can explore any reluctance to inform sexual partners or others at risk; and (3) helpers can offer to work with significant others, such as partners, family members, and friends.

The issues surrounding the limits of confidentiality with clients who have the AIDS virus pose new challenges for all those in the helping professions. Some questions that are raised include "Who is the client—the individual, the uninformed sexual partner(s), the family, or society?" "What are the responsibilities of helpers when education and appeals to reason fail with AIDS clients?" "Will the practice of reporting people with AIDS, especially those who have anonymous partners, threaten those people who most need educating?" "Should informing public-health and mental-health personnel be a mandatory practice, or should it be used as a last resort?" "How can the rights of the client with AIDS and the rights of others best be safeguarded?" Although clear answers to these questions may be difficult to identify, reading and discussions with colleagues can be practical steps in getting a clearer perspective on these issues.

Confidentiality in marital and family therapy. If you are working with couples or families, confidentiality takes on a special meaning. There are therapists who contend that whatever information they get from one family member should never be divulged to the other members. By contrast, some therapists have a policy of refusing to keep any information private within the family. Their assumption is that secrets are counterproductive in the attempt to help family members be open with one another. These therapists encourage bringing all secrets out into the open. It is essential that you be clear in your own mind about how you will deal with disclosures obtained from family members and that you let your clients know your policy before they enter a relationship with you.

Case example. Owen is involved in individual therapy and later has his wife, Flora, attend some of the sessions so they can receive marriage counseling. In an individual session Owen discloses that he became involved in a gay relationship a few months previously. He doesn't want his wife to know, for fear that she will divorce him. In a later session in which the therapist is seeing the couple, Flora complains that she feels neglected and wonders if her husband is really committed to working on their marriage. She says that she is willing to continue marital counseling as long as she is assured that he wants to stay in the marriage and devote his efforts to working through their difficulties. The therapist knows about this gay relationship that is causing Owen a great deal of difficulty. The therapist decides to say nothing about it in the joint session and maintains that it is the husband's decision whether to mention it.

- What do you think of the therapist's ethical decision in this situation?
- If you were involved in a somewhat similar situation, what might you do differently?
- Assume that Owen confided that he was concerned that he had contracted AIDS and was very worried. What course of action might you take? Are you concerned about the ethics of his withholding this information from Flora? Can a case be made for the duty to warn and protect an innocent party?

Confidentiality in group counseling. If you ever lead a group, you will have to consider some special ethical, legal, and professional aspects of confidentiality. In a group setting, as is true for individual counseling, you must disclose the limitations of confidentiality. You must also make it clear that you cannot guarantee confidentiality, because so many more people are privy to information shared in the group. Even if you continually emphasize to the members how essential it is to maintain confidentiality, there is still the possibility that some of them will talk inappropriately to others about what has been shared in the group. Leaders need to encourage members to bring up any of their reservations about possible breaches of confidentiality. If members see it as their responsibility to talk about these concerns, this topic can be openly explored in the group.

Assume that members of a group you were coleading brought up their reluctance to participate because they were concerned about the need for a firm commitment to keep in the group whatever was discussed. How would you deal with their concerns?

Your Obligation to Warn and Protect

Put yourself into this situation: A new client visits you at a college counseling center. He says he was severely abused by his father as a child and is now extremely angry. He is making threats to kill his father and tells you he has a gun. How do you proceed?

In light of recent court cases mental-health professionals are becoming increasingly conscious of a double duty: to protect other people from potentially dangerous clients and to protect clients from themselves. The responsibility to protect the public from potentially violent clients entails liability for civil damages when professionals neglect this duty by failing to diagnose or predict dangerousness, failing to warn potential victims of violent behavior, failing to commit dangerous individuals, and prematurely discharging dangerous clients from a hospital.

There is also the duty to protect clients who are likely to harm themselves. Many therapists inform their clients that they have an ethical and legal responsibility to break confidentiality when they have good reason to suspect suicidal behavior. Even if clients take the position that they are free to do with their life what they want, therapists do have a legal duty to protect them. The problem is to determine when a client is serious about committing suicide.

Cases have been made both for and against suicide prevention. Fujimura and her associates (1985) contend that most suicides could be prevented if those who work with suicidal clients could learn to recognize, evaluate, and intervene effectively in crisis situations. Many clients who are in crisis may feel temporary hopelessness, yet if they can be given help in learning to cope with the immediate problem, their potential for suicide can be greatly reduced. It is generally held that once mental-health professionals determine that a significant risk does exist, appropriate action is necessary. Practitioners who fail to act in such a way as to prevent suicide can be held liable.

Szasz (1986) argues the case against suicide prevention. He presents the thesis that suicide is an act of a moral agent who is ultimately responsible. Therefore he opposes coercive methods of preventing suicide, such as forced hospitalization. He further contends that by attempting to prevent suicide, practitioners basically ally themselves with the police power of the state and resort to coercion. Clients are thus deprived of assuming responsibility for their own actions. Szasz agrees that helpers have an ethical and legal obligation to provide help to those clients who seek this professional assistance for their suicidal tendencies. For those clients who do not ask for this help or who actively reject it, however, he takes the position that professionals have a duty to either persuade them to accept help or to leave them alone.

Case example. A client is depressed and talks about putting an end to everything. He tells you that he is only bringing this topic up because he trusts you, and he insists that you not mention the conversation to anyone. He wants to talk about how desperate he feels, and he wants you to understand him and ultimately to accept whatever decision he makes. What would you say to him?

Keeping Relationships with Clients Professional

You may be tempted to form social relationships with clients who admire you excessively and who invite you to develop a friendship. This lure can be especially strong if you like your client and if you have a limited circle of friends. It is easy to make the mistake of becoming socially involved with clients, for you may not have had the experience of setting limits. You may also be afraid to deal with your clients' potential feelings of rejection if you tell them that a friendship is not possible.

The codes of ethics caution against forming dual relationships with clients, which are defined as any relationships that might interfere with the effective maintenance of the professional relationship. Some examples of dual relationships are accepting clients who are family members or friends, engaging in sexual intimacies with clients, bartering of services, or any other combination of roles where objectivity will be difficult to maintain. Certainly, attempting to balance a professional and a personal relationship with a client is a tricky business. As a counselor you may not be inclined to challenge clients, lest you endanger the friendship. You may experience difficulty in separating yourself from your clients, as would be the case if you found yourself overidentifying with them and doing more work for them than they are doing. Even if you are able to maintain your objectivity, provide an optimal balance between confrontation and support, and still be a therapeutic agent, your clients may have trouble maintaining a friendship with you. They may be extra cautious in what they reveal out of fear of displeasing you. If they value the personal relationship with you, they are likely to censor their disclosures so that they do not threaten the friendship. They, too, may have difficulty in keeping the two relationships separate. One factor to consider is that no matter how you look at this issue, the relationship is bound to be unequal. The client/friend pays you for your time and attention. Even if you don't charge a fee, the relationship is still unequal, since you are likely to be doing more of the listening, giving, and challenging. In an equal friendship both partners are giving and receiving.

Friendships between professionals and their clients do occur. Although we have stated our concerns about these practices, we do not condemn them. The questions we ask of ourselves are "Does the friendship get in the way of effectively working with the client or student?" "Does the friendship get in the client's or student's way of working with us?" "Am I retaining enough objectivity to determine any possible negative effects?" We also have concerns about professional helpers who rely on their circle of clients to make social and personal contacts. If these helpers make most of their social acquaintances with people whom they professionally serve, we wonder if they are relying on their role to meet their needs.

Case example. A client whom you have been seeing for some time asks you if you'd be willing to meet for lunch. When you ask about the reason for the out-of-office meeting, your client tells you that he(she) would like to get to know you better in an informal setting and would like to treat you to lunch as an expression of appreciation for the help you have provided. To make matters a bit more difficult, one of your client's personal issues is the fear of being rejected. The client tells you that he(she) is taking a chance and a risk by asking you for lunch. How would you handle this situation? Would it make a difference whether the client was of the same or the opposite sex? Would your own feelings toward your client influence your decision?

Fostering Client Dependence as an Ethical Issue

Most professional codes warn about creating a dependent relationship with clients. Although your clients may temporarily become dependent on you at some point in the counseling process, an ethical issue arises if you foster their dependency and actually prevent their growth. You might ask yourself these questions as a way of determining the degree to which you encourage either dependent or independent behavior:

- Do I have a hard time terminating a case? Do I have trouble in "losing" a client? Am I concerned about a reduction in my income?
- Might I need some clients more than they need me? Do I have a need to be needed? On some level do I feel a sense of power when clients express dependency on me?
- Do I challenge clients to do for themselves what they are able to do? Am I unwilling to provide clients with quick resolutions or easy answers, even when they press me for such solutions?
- To what degree do I encourage clients to look within themselves for their own answers?
- Do I keep the counseling process mysterious as a way of maintaining power, or do I do as much as possible to teach my clients what the therapeutic process is about?

Some counselors foster dependence in their clients as a way of feeling important. They convince themselves that they are all-wise and that they can direct a client's life. They may feed off the dependent needs of clients in order to derive a sense of significance. When clients play a helpless role and beg for answers, they all-too-quickly respond with problem-solving solutions. Such actions may not be helpful to clients in the long run, for they are being reinforced for their lack of willingness to support themselves. It seems to us that your main job as a helper is to eventually put yourself out of business, which is done by encouraging clients to rely on their own resources rather than yours. By reinforcing the dependency of your clients, you are telling them that you do not trust that they can help themselves or that they can function independently from you.

Dealing with Sexual Attractions

Some helpers feel guilty over an attraction toward a client, and they feel uncomfortable if they sense that a client is attracted to them. We do not think that helpers should be distressed over experiencing sexual attractions to clients. Such attractions do not mean that they are guilty of therapeutic errors or that they are perverse. It is important, however, that they acknowledge their feelings and avoid acting obsessively or acting out by developing inappropriate sexual intimacies with their clients.

Case example. A single male colleague of yours tells you that he is having trouble with one of his female clients, whom he is very much attracted to. He finds himself willing to run overtime in the sessions, and if she were not a client, he would like to ask her out for a date. He feels somewhat guilty about his feelings. He is wondering if he should terminate the professional relationship and begin a personal one. He has shared with his client that he is sexually attracted to her, and she admits finding him attractive. Your colleague comes to you for your suggestions on how he should proceed. What do you think you would say to him? What do you think you would do if you found yourself in a similar situation?

In one study researchers found clear evidence that attraction to clients is prevalent among both male and female therapists (Pope, Keith-Spiegel, & Tabachnick, 1986). Although most of the respondents reported having had the experience of being sexually attracted to clients, the vast majority reported that they had never seriously considered actual sexual involvement with a client. Some of the reasons they gave for refraining from acting out their attractions to clients related to their professional values and their concern for the welfare of the client. The authors of this study concluded that a discussion of sexual attraction should be a part of the educational and training programs of therapists. They suggested that professional preparation programs would do well to provide a safe environment in which trainees could acknowledge and discuss the range of their feelings.

Sexual Misconduct

Research indicates that sexual misconduct is one of the major causes for malpractice actions against mental-health providers. Those who have written about the practice of sexual intimacy between therapists and clients generally report that such misconduct is more widespread than is commonly believed. The frequency of these unethical practices is alarming. Brodsky (1986) maintains that reports of sexual intimacies and sexual harassment have been increasing. Furthermore, in the last few years the greatest single category of complaints to the ethics committee of the American Psychological Association involves sexual intimacy. Judgments against therapists, dismissal of professors, revocation of licenses, and large civil damage awards are no longer unusual.

The fact that sexual misconduct is as common as it is may be an indication of the susceptibility of the helping profession to such unethical conduct. As you read this, you may think that you would never become involved in sexual misconduct with any of your clients. The chances are that those practitioners who have engaged in sexual intimacies with clients made the same assumption. Realize that you are not immune to becoming sexually involved with those you help. Knowledge of the possibility of this involvement will at least allow you to be on the alert to your own needs and motivations and how they could get in the way of being therapeutic.

As a care giver you are likely to receive respect and adulation and to be perceived as someone who can do no wrong. You may be compared by your clients to their significant others, and many times you will rank higher. Your clients are usually with you a short time, and they probably are getting the best side of you. Their picture of you is distorted because they do not live with you. This unconditional admiration can become very seductive. You may learn to like their reactions to you too much. You can get in trouble as a helper if you cease to keep the feelings your clients express to you in proper perspective.

As a beginning helper you are especially vulnerable to believing everything positive that your clients tell you about yourself. Thus, if clients tell you how sexually attractive you are, how understanding you are, and how different you are from anyone else they have met, it may be very difficult to resist believing what they tell you. Without self-awareness and honesty you may direct the sessions toward meeting your needs and may eventually become sexually indiscreet.

Rather than consider sexual misconduct only in terms of sexual intercourse between client and therapist, it is helpful to consider a range of sexual contacts. Coleman and Schaefer (1986) write that sexual abuse of clients by therapists can best be viewed along a continuum consisting of psychological, covert, and overt abuse. In psychological abuse, clients are forced into the position of taking care of the helper's needs. This is especially the case when helpers inappropriately self-disclose and work with their own problems during the client's session. Clients sometimes find themselves taking care of the emotional needs of the helper. In covert abuse, the helper's boundary confusion with the client becomes more pronounced. The helper may intrude further into the client's intimacy boundaries through sexual gazes, seductiveness through dress and gestures, sexual hugs, and over-attention to the client's appearance. At the far end of the continuum are overt forms of sexual misconduct such as fondling and sexual intercourse. Although overt abuse is clearly unethical and unprofessional—and illegal in many states—some helpers fail to see the unethical nature of more subtle sexual violations. For example, some helpers may steer their clients toward a discussion of their sexual feelings toward the helper. By dwelling on possible sexual attractions, the helper may satisfy his or her own needs for affection and attention while the client's needs go unmet.

All of the professional organizations have some specific statement that condemns sexual intimacies in the client/therapist relationship. In addition to specifically prohibiting erotic contact in the helping relationship, most codes of ethics warn against any activities on the helper's part that could lead to the risk of exploitation. If a client/helper relationship develops into a sexual one, most professional codes require a termination of the relationship and a referral to another professional. The reasons that erotic contact is unethical center on the abuse of power that helpers have by virtue of their professional role. Since clients are talking about very personal aspects of their life and making themselves highly vulnerable to the helper, it is easy to betray this trust by exploiting clients for one's own personal motives. Erotic contact is also unethical because it fosters dependency and makes objectivity on the part of the helper impossible.

Perhaps the most important argument against sexual involvement with clients is that most clients report harm as a result of such practices. They typically become very resentful and angry at having been sexually exploited and abandoned. They approached counseling because of problems they hoped to deal with. Now they not only still have most of these problems but also are typically stuck with unresolved feelings relating to the traumatic experience with their helper.

How sexual intimacy harms clients.   Most writers on the subect of sexual intimacy in the helping relationship contend that when sexual intercourse begins, the therapeutic value of the relationship ends. When sex is involved in the professional relationship, the helper loses objectivity and control of the helping process. Sexual contact is especially disruptive if it begins early in the relationship and if it is initiated by the therapist (Bouhoutsos, Holroyd, Lerman, Forer, & Greenberg, 1983). Ninety percent of 559 surveyed clients who had become sexually involved with their therapist appeared to have been negatively affected. This harm included mistrust of opposite-sex relationships, hospitalization in some cases, and even suicide in other cases. Many clients reported a deterioration of their sexual relationship with their primary partner. Coleman and Schaefer (1986) describe other negative outcomes such as depression, emotional disturbances, substance abuse, and impaired social adjustment.

Sex between professors or supervisors and students.   As is the case with erotic contact between therapists and clients, sex in the supervisory relationship or in the professor/student relationship can result in an abuse of power because of the role differences. There is also the reality of poor modeling for students for their future relationships with their clients. An anonymous survey of 464 female clinical psychologists revealed that sexual contact was quite prevalent between graduate students and supervisors or educators. The overall rate was 17%; among recent doctoral student graduates it was 22%; and among students divorcing or separating during graduate training the rate was 34% (Glaser & Thorpe, 1986).

In an earlier survey the results were similar, with 16.5% of female respondents reporting such sexual contact. Also, of the respondents who had received their degree within the previous 6 years, 25% had experienced sexual contact with their psychology educators (Pope, Levenson, & Schover, 1979).

In the study by Glaser and Thorpe (1986) the judgments of the majority of the respondents were very negative; over 95% of them evaluated such contact as unethical, coercive, and harmful to the working relationship to a considerable degree. Sexual advances were reported by 31% and were judged by most to be overwhelmingly negative. Almost all of the respondents judged sexual contact between an educator and a student during a working relationship to be highly unethical.

The core ethical implication pertains to the difference in power or status between the teacher and the student. The student is in an extremely vulnerable position. Faced with a faculty member who makes a sexual proposition, the student may be intimidated and thus accept the offer (Pope, Schover, & Levenson, 1980). Students and interns recognize that their decision to reject a sexual proposition might well have a negative effect on their current performance.

In summary, the Glaser and Thorpe survey indicated that 20% to 25% of female psychology graduate students had had sexual relationships with psychology educators, most often during a working relationship. Although these intimate relationships were evaluated by many respondents as coercive and exploitive, half of the respondents who had experienced sexual contact during a working relationship perceived no professional ethical problem at the time of the relationship. Several studies indicate that the preponderance of sexual relationships involve men in the more powerful social role and women in the less powerful role.

Recognizing Unethical Behavior in Yourself

We encourage you to apply the general principles being discussed in this chapter to your own behavior, rather than placing yourself in a judgmental position toward others. It is easier to see the shortcomings of others and to judge their behavior than to develop the attitude of honest self-examination in looking at your own behavior. You can control your own professional behavior far easier than you can that of your colleagues, so the proper focus is to honestly look at what you are doing. There is a tendency to think in terms of gross ethical violations while overlooking the more subtle ways of being unethical. Consider for a moment some of the following behaviors, and ask yourself the degree to which you could picture yourself in each situation.

- A client calls you frequently and pleads that he is in great need of your direction. He is afraid to make decisions lest he "mess up my life even more than it is." Might you be flattered by being needed? Could you see yourself fostering his dependency out of your need to be needed?

- A client who is in private therapy with you is ambivalent about continuing counseling sessions. She wonders whether it is time to terminate and "try it alone." Things are rather tight financially for you right now, and several other clients have recently terminated. Would you be inclined to support her decision to terminate? Might you be inclined to encourage her to continue, partly out of financial motives?
- A client whom you find attractive tells you how accepting, kind, gentle, understanding, and strong you are. This client expresses a desire to hear more about your life. Might you take the focus off the client and engage in self-disclosure for your own needs? Could you see yourself getting carried away with personal conversations that are really not relevant to the therapeutic purpose of your relationship?

The beliefs and behaviors of therapists. A study by Pope, Tabachnick, and Keith-Spiegel (1987) provides a useful reference point for identifying unethical behavior in yourself. These authors designed a questionnaire to assess the beliefs and behaviors of therapists. The 465 psychologists who responded to this survey were members of the Division of Psychotherapy of the American Psychological Association. Below are some specific behaviors that were surveyed, along with the percentage of those who stated that the behavior had *never* occurred in their practice and the percentage who stated that this behavior was *unquestionably unethical*:

Therapist behavior	*Never engaged in behavior*	*Consider behavior unethical*
Becoming social friends with a former client	42.1%	6.4%
Providing therapy to one of your friends	70.4	47.6
Hugging a client	13.4	4.6
Terminating therapy if a client cannot pay	32.6	12.1
Seeing a minor client without parental consent	65.8	23.5
Telling a client "I'm sexually attracted to you"	78.5	51.5
Working when too distressed to be effective	38.8	46.7
Raising fees during the course of therapy	27.6	8.3
Breaking confidentiality if a client is suicidal	16.2	2.0
Inviting clients to a party or social event	82.9	50.0
Crying in the presence of a client	42.5	0.7

Therapist behavior	Never engaged in behavior	Consider behavior unethical
Accepting a client's decision to commit suicide	73.9%	45.2%
Providing therapy to your student or supervisee	63.8	45.8
Becoming sexually involved with a former client	88.2	50.2
Lending money to a client	73.7	40.1
Providing therapy to one of your employees	79.6	55.0
Kissing a client	70.8	48.0
Engaging in erotic activity with a client	97.1	95.0
Engaging in sex with a clinical supervisee	95.0	85.1
Getting paid to refer clients to someone	98.0	88.4
Going into business with a client	95.6	78.5
Being sexually attracted to a client	9.2	11.2
Discussing a client (by name) with friends	91.2	94.5
Engaging in sexual fantasy about a client	27.0	18.9
Directly soliciting a person to be a client	89.3	67.5

On the basis of questionnaire responses, it appears that the psychologists' behavior was generally in accordance with their ethical beliefs. The results show that some behaviors were relatively rare, such as engaging in sexual contact with clients, engaging in sexual intimacy with clinical supervisees, becoming involved in business practices with clients, getting paid to refer clients to someone, inappropriately breaching client confidentiality, performing therapy under the influence of alcohol, and discussing clients by name with friends. Some areas involved difficult ethical judgments, including accepting goods in place of payment, avoiding certain clients for fear of being sued, engaging in sexual fantasy about a client, and being sexually attracted to a client.

The authors of this study concluded that the integrity of the profession of psychology is based to a large extent on the ability of individuals within the profession to regulate their own behavior. They add that the ability to engage in effective and ethical regulation is contingent on our willingness to study our own behavior and beliefs about that behavior. As you look over the survey responses, reflect on your views pertaining to these behaviors. We hope that rather than being quick to detect the unethical behavior of others, you will focus more on your own behaviors and beliefs about ethical practice. We also highly recommend that you read the entire article (Pope, Tabachnick, and Keith-Spiegel, 1987).

Unethical Behavior by Your Colleagues

Even though you do focus on being your own judge, there are times when you may encounter colleagues who are behaving in unethical and unprofessional ways. Professional codes of conduct generally state that in such cases the most prudent action is to approach the colleague and share your concerns directly in an attempt to rectify the situation. If this step fails, you are then expected to make use of procedures established by your professional organization, such as reporting the colleague.

Reflect for a few minutes, on being in each of the following situations. Attempt to formulate what you would do in each case:

- A colleague frequently talks about his clients in inappropriate ways in places where others are able to hear him. The colleague says that joking about his clients is his way of "letting off steam" and preventing himself from taking life too seriously.
- A couple of female clients have told you that they were sexually seduced by another counselor at the agency where you work. In their counseling sessions with you they are dealing with their anger over having been taken advantage of by this counselor.
- A colleague has several times initiated social contacts with her clients. She thinks that this practice is acceptable, because she sees her clients as consenting adults. Furthermore, she contends that time spent socializing with these clients gives her insights into issues that she can productively work with in the therapy sessions.
- You see that one of your colleagues is practicing beyond what you think is the scope of his competence and training. This person is unwilling to seek additional training and is also not receiving adequate supervision. He maintains that the best way to learn to work with unfamiliar problems that clients present is simply to "jump in and learn by doing."

Certainly, dealing with the unethical behavior of colleagues demands a measure of courage. If these people are in a position of power, you are obviously vulnerable. Even in the case of peers, confrontations may not be pleasant. The other person may react defensively and tell you to mind your own business.

In one study of graduate students in psychology the students were asked what they *should* do and what they *would* do in a hypothetical situation in which a friend or colleague had violated an ethical code (Bernard & Jara, 1986). The general finding was that although most of these students were aware of the proper ethical procedure, they admitted that they would not choose to follow this course of action. The authors contend that the problem in training professionals to have an ethical sense rests not with the mere communication of ethical principles but, rather, with motivating them to apply what they know when they face difficult situations.

Malpractice in the Helping Professions

Malpractice is generally defined as the failure to render proper service, through ignorance or negligence, resulting in injury or loss to the client. Professional negligence consists of departing from the usual standard of practice or not exercising due care. For malpractice litigation to occur, these three conditions must be present: (1) you must have a duty to the client, (2) you must have acted in a negligent or improper manner, and (3) there must be a causal relationship between that negligence and the damage claimed by the client.

Grounds for Malpractice Actions

The two areas that have probably received the greatest attention in the literature as grounds for malpractice are violations of confidentiality and sexual misconduct. (Both of these topics have been discussed in earlier sections of this chapter.) A review of articles dealing with frequent causes of malpractice actions against people in the helping professions shows the following as other key factors leading to a suit:

• abandoning a client
• the failure to respect the client's integrity and privacy
• the improper death of a client
• the failure to supervise properly
• the failure to refer a client when the case warrants it
• the failure to warn and protect others from a dangerous client
• improper methods of collecting fees
• misrepresenting one's professional training and skills
• improper diagnosis and utilization of assessment techniques
• breaching of a contract with a client
• the failure to provide for informed consent
• the failure to have exercised reasonable care in cases of suicide

There are other grounds for malpractice charges, but the intent here is simply to show some of the actions that often lead to malpractice suits.

If you are a student, you may think that you have no worries about being sued for malpractice. Unfortunately, student practitioners are vulnerable to such action. At this time in your professional development you might well give serious consideration to ways in which you can lessen your chances of having to go through the stressful experience of being sued for failing to practice in a professional manner. The reality of today is that even if you abide by the ethical codes of your profession and even if you practice within the boundaries of the law, you can still become embroiled in a malpractice action.

Case example. One of your teenage clients might eventually commit suicide, regardless of how prudent your interventions have been. It is possible that the parents could fault you for not having known more and done more to prevent this final action. Although you do not have to prove that you are a superior or perfect being, you do have to demonstrate that you possess and exercise the knowledge and skill required for the services you offer. The questions that you might ask yourself are "Do I have to be able to predict a possible suicide? Assuming that I am able to spot a suicidal client, will I always know the best course of action to take?" You must be able to demonstrate that you acted in good faith, that you have been willing to seek supervision and consultation when needed, and that you have practiced within your competence. It is also essential that you can produce documentation to support your claims.

Ways to Prevent Malpractice Suits

We hope it is becoming clear that you would be wise to know your limitations in working with clients, to accept them, and to act only within the scope of your competence. Although making the best decision in every case is not always possible, we hope that you will never hesitate to seek consultation, regardless of your professional experience. Consultation with colleagues often sheds light on a subject by providing a perspective that you have not thought of. Even if you are able to make wise decisions, it is validating to get support for your position from other professionals. If you are involved in litigation, it will be helpful to be able to demonstrate that your interventions were in accord with the standard of care exercised by other practitioners. On the other hand, if you employ exotic therapeutic techniques with little rationale behind them, you are likely to find yourself the loser in a civil action. Contending that you were following your instincts and doing what "felt right" is not likely to get you very far if you are asked to defend your therapeutic practices.

If you want a guarantee that you will not be sued for professional negligence, you probably should think about another career. Although there are no absolute protections in the mental-health professions, there are some practical ways in which to protect yourself from malpractice suits. In addition to the ways we have mentioned, here are some further guidelines:

- Make use of informed-consent procedures. Do not attempt to mystify the helping process. Professional honesty and openness with clients will go a long way in establishing genuine trust.
- Consider ways to define contracts with your clients that clearly structure the helping relationship. What are your clients coming to you for? How can you best help them obtain their goals?
- Since you can be sued for abandonment, take steps to provide coverage for emergencies when you are going away.
- Always consult with colleagues when you are in doubt. Since the legal standard is based on the practices of fellow professionals, the more consensus you have, the less likely you are to have a judgment against you.

- Be aware of the limits of confidentiality, and clearly communicate these to your clients. Obtain written consent from your clients when it becomes necessary to make disclosures.
- Clearly define financial considerations at the outset of a professional relationship.
- Do not get involved in bartering goods or services for your professional services. Exchanging of services is likely to lead to resentment on both your part and your client's.
- Keep adequate records, and write them in such a manner that you would be willing to let a client read them.
- Learn about landmark court decisions, and be aware of those rulings when you are required to warn and protect others.
- Know the laws of your state and the policies of your agency. Practice in accordance with these guidelines.
- Learn how to assess and intervene in cases in which clients pose a danger to themselves and others. Knowing the danger signs of suicide is the first step toward prevention.

By Way of Review

- One of the trends in the helping professions is an increased interest in ethical and professional practice. This trend stems, at least in part, from increased malpractice actions against mental-health practitioners.
- Ethical decision making is a continuing process. Issues that you look at as a student can be examined from another perspective as you gain experience in your professional speciality.
- Ethical issues rarely have clear-cut answers. Ethical dilemmas, by their very nature, involve the application of professional judgment on your part. It is essential that you be familiar with the professional codes of ethics. However, knowledge of ethical standards is not sufficient in solving ethical problems.
- Ultimately, you will have to make many difficult decisions as a practitioner. Responsible practice entails basing your actions on informed, sound, and responsible judgment. Be open to consulting with colleagues and supervisors throughout your professional career.
- Most of the professional codes explicitly state that it is unethical to practice outside the boundaries of your competence. It is important to learn what clients you can best work with and to understand when referral is appropriate.
- Either as an intern or on your job, you may be asked to take on clients or to provide therapeutic strategies that are beyond the scope of your training and experience. Learn to be assertive in staying within your limits.
- One way to increase your competence is by seeking supervision whenever it is called for and by remaining open throughout your professional career to learning new skills and techniques. Remember that continuing education is necessary to keep abreast of current developments in your field.

- Many clients have not even thought about their rights or responsibilities. As a helper you can do much to safeguard your clients by developing informed-consent procedures to help them make wise choices.
- Confidentiality is the cornerstone of the helping relationship. Although clients have a right to expect that what they talk about with you in the professional relationship will remain private, there are times when you will have to breach confidentiality. Clients have a right to know from the outset of the relationship the specific grounds for divulging confidences. It is essential that you know and follow the laws pertaining to confidentiality.
- Confidentiality takes on special meaning if you work with couples, families, or groups.
- At times you will have a professional and legal obligation to warn and to protect clients. It is essential that you know your duties in this area.
- It helps to keep your relationships with your clients on a professional, rather than a personal, basis. Mixing social relationships with professional relationships often works against the best interests of both the client and the helper.
- Your job is to teach clients how to help themselves and thus decrease their need to continue seeing you. Encouraging dependence of your clients is both unethical and untherapeutic.
- Sexual attractions are a normal part of helping relationships. It is important to learn how to recognize these attractions and how to deal with them in a therapeutic manner.
- Sexual misconduct is the leading cause of malpractice actions against mental-health providers. Sexual intimacies between helpers and clients are unethical for a number of reasons. One of the main reasons is that they entail an abuse of power and trust.
- Although it is important to know how to deal with unethical behavior on the part of your colleagues, it is even more important to recognize your own potential unethical behaviors. These unethical acts are often subtle. It is important to maintain a stance of honest self-exploration to ensure ethical behavior.
- Malpractice actions are on the increase. Not only are mental-health professionals being sued with increasing frequency, but as a student you are also vulnerable. It is essential, therefore, that you understand what can lead to being sued and learn practical ways to lessen the chances of this happening.

What Will You Do Now?

1. Find at least one person in the helping professions whom you can talk to about ethical issues in practice. Focus on the major ethical problem that this person has faced. How does this helper deal with this ethical concern? Refer to the ethical standards in Appendixes A, B, and C and see if any guidelines apply to this situation.

2. Visit a community agency (such as a Child Protective Service) and ask about ethical and legal situations that are being reported. What are some key ethical concerns that this agency has to cope with? Are the staff members concerned about malpractice issues? How does the current malpractice crisis influence what they do in their agency?

3. Think about a particular ethical dilemma that you have experienced in one of your field placements. How did you deal with the situation? If you could replay the situation, would you do anything differently? Review the ethical standards for some guidance on this ethical dilemma.

Suggested Readings

American Psychological Association (1987). *Casebook on ethical principles of psychologists.* Washington, DC: Author. This 1987 revision contains a wide variety of cases involving ethical issues. These cases cover areas such as responsibility, competence, moral and legal standards, public statements, confidentiality, welfare of the consumer, professional relationships, assessment techniques, research with human participants, and care and use of animals. This is excellent material for reflection and discussion, and each case includes an adjudication.

American Psychological Association. *Professional psychology: Research and practice.* The articles in this journal provide a good way to keep abreast of recent developments of interest to mental-health practitioners. This publication frequently features articles dealing with ethical and professional issues, ethnic minority issues, the relationship between research and practice, and innovative therapy approaches. The journal is published bimonthly at a rate of $40 for nonmembers. Write to Subscription Section, APA, 1400 North Uhle Street, Arlington, VA 22201.

Corey, G., Corey, M., & Callanan, P. (1988). *Issues and ethics in the helping professions* (3rd ed.). Pacific Grove, CA: Brooks/Cole. The book deals at length with the topics introduced in this chapter and with issues such as the counselor as a person, values, professional competence, training and supervision, client rights, confidentiality, the duty to warn and protect, the client/therapist relationship, unethical behavior, malpractice issues, ethical concerns in multicultural counseling, the counselor in the community and the system, ethics in marital and family therapy, and ethical and professional issues in group work. Each chapter offers a number of case examples and activities designed to promote a way of thinking about applying ethical principles to practical situations.

Flores, A. (Ed). (1988). *Professional ideals.* Belmont, CA: Wadsworth. This book examines professionalism and professional ethics. Its purpose is to provide a conceptual framework for thinking about what it means to be a "professional" from the moral point of view. The essays focus on the primary ideals and virtues implicit in professionalism as a way of life.

Keith-Spiegel, P., & Koocher, G. (1985). *Ethics in psychology: Standards and cases.* New York: Random House. This is a comprehensive treatment of professional standards and cases, geared to the ethical principles of the American Psychological Association. Issues covered include ethical decision making, ethics committees, confidentiality and privacy, psychological testing, money matters, advertising, dual relationships with clients, relationships with colleagues, scholarly publishing and teaching, research issues, and ethical dilemmas in special work settings. The case studies described throughout the book are quite effective in stimulating thought and discussion.

Loewenberg, F., & Dolgoff, R. (1985). *Ethical decisions for social work practice* (2nd ed.). Itasca, IL: F. E. Peacock. This useful resource deals with values and ethics in social work. Some topics include societal ethics and professional ethics, foundations for ethical decisions, specific ethical dilemmas in practice, guidelines for making ethical decisions, and codes of ethics. The book contains many case examples that are helpful in applying ethical codes to a variety of problem situations.

Van Hoose, W. H., & Kottler, J. A. (1985). *Ethical and legal issues in counseling and psychotherapy* (2nd ed.). San Francisco: Jossey-Bass. A useful treatment of a range of ethical issues, including perspectives on ethical practice, incompetent and unethical behavior, marketing therapeutic services, therapy and the law, professional and legal regulation, ethics in group work, value problems in therapy, and diagnosis and assessment.

Concluding Comments

The process of becoming a helper is intrinsically related to the process of becoming a person. In this book we have emphasized the importance of looking at your life and of understanding your motivations. Although it is not essential for helpers to be problem-free, we have stressed the importance of modeling on the part of helpers. We hope you'll reflect on whether what you do in your own life is what you encourage for your clients. If you urge your clients to take the risks that growth entails, it is essential that you do this in your own life. Your clients are not likely to believe you if they sense a discrepancy between what you do and what you say.

To remain in the helping professions, you must meet your own needs, but never at the expense of your clients. While the profession at times may seem difficult and draining, it can also be exciting, challenging, and very rewarding.

References
and Reading List

Alberti, R. E., & Emmons, M. L. (1986). *Your perfect right: A guide to assertive behavior* (5th ed.). San Luis Obispo, CA: Impact Publishers.

American Association for Counseling and Development. (1981). *Ethical standards* (rev. ed.). Alexandria, VA: Author.

American Association for Marriage and Family Therapy. (1985). *Code of ethical principles for marriage and family therapists.* Washington, DC: Author.

American Psychiatric Association. (1986). *The principles of medical ethics, with annotations especially applicable to psychiatry.* Washington, DC: Author.

American Psychological Association. (1981). *Ethical principles of psychologists* (rev. ed.). Washington, DC: Author.

American Psychological Association. (1985). *White paper on duty to protect.* Washington, DC: Author.

American Psychological Association. (1987). *Casebook on ethical principles of psychologists.* Washington, DC: Author.

American School Counselor Association. (1984). *Ethical standards for school counselors.* Alexandria, VA: Author.

Association for Specialists in Group Work. (1980). *Ethical guidelines for group leaders.* Alexandria, VA: Author.

Association for Specialists in Group Work. (1983). *Professional standards for training of group counselors.* Alexandria, VA: Author.

Attneave, C. L. (1985). Practical counseling with American Indian and Alaska native clients. In P. Pedersen (Ed.), *Handbook of cross-cultural counseling and therapy* (pp. 135–140). Westport, CT: Greenwood Press.

Austin, M. J. (1978). *Professionals and paraprofessionals.* New York: Human Sciences Press.

Axelson, J. A. (1985). *Counseling and development in a multicultural society.* Pacific Grove, CA: Brooks/Cole.

Baird, K. A., & Rupert, P. A. (1987). Clinical management of confidentiality: A survey of psychologists in seven states. *Professional Psychology: Research and Practice, 18*(4), 347–352.

Basow, S. A. (1986). *Gender stereotypes: Traditions and alternatives* (2nd. ed.). Pacific Grove, CA: Brooks/Cole.

Beck, A. T. (1976). *Cognitive therapy and the emotional disorders.* New York: New American Library.

Benjamin, A. (1987). *The helping interview: With case illustrations.* Boston: Houghton Mifflin.

Bernard, J. L., & Jara, C. S. (1986). The failure of clinical psychology graduate students to apply understood ethical principles. *Professional Psychology: Research and Practice, 17*(4), 313–315.

Black, C. (1981). *It will never happen to me!* New York: Ballantine.

Borders, L. D., & Leddick, G. R. (1987). *Handbook of counseling supervision.* Alexandria, VA: Association for Counselor Education and Supervision.

Bouhoutsos, J., Holroyd, J., Lerman, H., Forer, B. R., & Greenberg, M. (1983). Sexual intimacy between psychotherapists and patients. *Professional Psychology: Research and Practice, 14*(2), 185–196.

Brammer, L. M. (1985). Nonformal support in cross-cultural counseling and therapy. In P. Pedersen (Ed.), *Handbook of cross-cultural counseling and therapy* (pp. 87–92). Westport, CT: Greenwood Press.

Brammer, L. M. (1988). *The helping relationship: Process and skills* (4th ed.). Englewood Cliffs, NJ: Prentice-Hall.

Brodsky, A. M. (1986). The distressed psychologist: Sexual intimacies and exploitation. In R. R. Kilburg, P. E. Nathan, & R. W. Thoreson (Eds.), *Professionals in distress: Issues, syndromes, and solutions in psychology* (pp. 153–172). Washington, DC: American Psychological Association.

Bugental, J. F. T. (1987). *The art of the psychotherapist.* New York: Norton.

Butler, P. E. (1981). *Talking to yourself: Learning the language of self-support.* San Francisco: Harper & Row.

Carifio, M. S., & Hess, A. K. (1987). Who is the ideal supervisor? *Professional psychology: Research and practice, 18*(3), 244–250.

Carkhuff, R. R. (1983). *The art of helping* (5th ed.). Amherst, MA: Human Resource Development Press.

Caileff, S. E. (1986). Ethical issues in counseling gender, race, and culturally distinct groups. *Journal of Counseling and Development, 63*(6), 362–364.

Cerney, M. S. (1985). Countertransference revisited. *Journal of Counseling and Development, 63*(6), 362–364.

Charlesworth, E. A., & Nathan, R. G. (1984). *Stress management: A comprehensive guide to wellness.* New York: Random House (Ballantine).

Cherniss, C. (1980). *Professional burnout in human service organizations.* New York: Praeger.

Cherniss, C., & Dantzig, S. A. (1986). Preventing and managing job-related stress. In R. R. Kilburg, P. E. Nathan, & R. W. Thoreson (Eds.), *Professionals in distress: Issues, syndromes, and solutions in psychology* (pp. 255–274). Washington, DC: American Psychological Association.

Coleman, E., & Schaefer, S. (1986). Boundaries of sex and intimacy between client and counselor. *Journal of Counseling and Development, 64*(5), 341–344.

Combs, A. W. (1986). What makes a good helper? A person-centered approach. *Person-Centered Review, 1*(1), 51–61.

Corey, G. (1985). *Theory and practice of group counseling* (2nd ed.) and *Manual.* Pacific Grove, CA: Brooks/Cole.

Corey, G. (1986a). *Case approach to counseling and psychotherapy* (2nd ed.). Pacific Grove, CA: Brooks/Cole.

Corey, G. (1986b). *Theory and practice of counseling and psychotherapy* (3rd ed.) and *Manual.* Pacific Grove, CA: Brooks/Cole.

Corey, G., with Corey, M. (1986). *I never knew I had a choice* (3rd ed.). Pacific Grove, CA: Brooks/Cole.

Corey, G., Corey, M., & Callanan, P. (1988). *Issues and ethics in the helping professions* (3rd. ed.). Pacific Grove, CA: Brooks/Cole.

Corey, G., Corey, M., Callanan, P., & Russell, J. M. (1988). *Group techniques* (rev. ed.). Pacific Grove, CA: Brooks/Cole.

Corey, M., & Corey, G. (1987). *Groups: Process and practice* (3rd ed.). Pacific Grove, CA: Brooks/Cole.

Cormier, S., & Hackney, H. (1987). *The professional counselor: A process guide to helping.* Englewood Cliffs, NJ: Prentice-Hall.

Cormier, W. H., & Cormier, L. S. (1985). *Interviewing strategies for helpers: Fundamental skills and cognitive behavioral interventions* (2nd ed.). Pacific Grove, CA: Brooks/Cole.

Deutsch, C. J. (1984). Self-reported sources of stress among psychotherapists. *Professional Psychology: Research and Practice, 15*(6), 833–845.

Deutsch, C. J. (1985). A survey of therapists' personal problems and treatment. *Professional Psychology: Research and Practice, 16*(2), 305–315.

Devore, W. (1985). Developing ethnic sensitivity for the counseling process: A social-work perspective. In P. Pedersen (Ed.), *Handbook of cross-cultural counseling and therapy* (pp. 93–98). Westport, CT: Greenwood Press.

Eberlein, L. (1987). Introducing ethics to beginning psychologists: A problem-solving approach. *Professional Psychology: Research and Practice, 18*(4), 353–359.

Edelwich, J., with Brodsky, A. (1980). *Burn-out: Stages of disillusionment in the helping professions.* New York: Human Sciences Press.

Edelwich, J., with Brodsky, A. (1982). *Sexual dilemmas for the helping professional.* New York: Brunner/Mazel.

Egan, G. (1986). *The skilled helper: A systematic approach to effective helping* (3rd ed.). Pacific Grove, CA: Brooks/Cole.

Ellis, A. (1985). *Overcoming resistance: Rational-emotive therapy with difficult clients.* New York: Springer.

Ellis, A. (1986). Rational-emotive therapy approaches to overcoming resistance. In A. Ellis & R. Grieger (Eds.), *Handbook of rational-emotive therapy* (Vol. 2), (pp. 246–274). New York: Springer.

Ellis, A. (1987). The impossibility of achieving consistently good mental health. *American Psychologist, 4*(4), 364–375.

Ellis, A., & Bernard, M. E. (1986). What is rational-emotive therapy (RET)? In A. Ellis & R. Grieger (Eds.), *Handbook of rational-emotive therapy* (Vol. 2), (pp. 3–30). New York: Springer.

Ellis, A., & Harper, R. A. (1975). *A new guide to rational living.* North Hollywood, CA: Wilshire Books.

Emery, G. (1981). *A new beginning: How you can change your life through cognitive therapy.* New York: Simon & Schuster (Touchstone).

Erikson, E. (1963). *Childhood and society* (2nd ed.). New York: Norton.

Erikson, E. (1982). *The life cycle completed.* New York: Norton.

Farber, B. A. (1983a). Psychotherapists' perceptions of stressful patient behavior. *Professional Psychology: Research and Practice, 14*(5), 697–705.

Farber, B. A. (1983b). *Stress and burnout in the human service professions.* New York: Pergamon Press.

Farber, B. A., & Heifetz, L. J. (1982). The process and dimensions of burnout in psychotherapists. *Professional Psychology, 13*(2), 293–301.

Flores, A. (1988). *Professional ideals.* Belmont, CA: Wadsworth.

Freudenberger, H. J., with Richelson, G. (1980). *Burn-out: How to beat the high cost of success.* New York: Bantam Books.

Friedman, M., & Rosenman, R. H. (1974). *Type A behavior and your heart.* New York: Knopf.

Fujimura, L. E., Weis, D. M., & Cochran, J. R. (1985). Suicide: Dynamics and implications for counseling. *Journal of Counseling and Development, 63*(10), 612–615.

Glaser, R. D., & Thorpe, J. S. (1986). Unethical intimacy: A survey of sexual contact and advances between psychology educators and female graduate students. *American Psychologist, 41*(1), 42–51.

Glasser, W. (1984). *Take effective control of your life.* New York: Harper & Row.

Graham, D. L. R., Rawlings, E. I., Halpern, H. S., & Hermes, J. (1984). Therapists' need for training in counseling lesbians and gay men. *Professional Psychology: Research and Practice, 15*(4), 482–496.

Gray, L. A., & Harding, A. K. (1988). Confidentiality limits with clients who have the AIDS virus. *Journal of Counseling and Development, 66*(5), 219–223.

Grimm, L. G., & Yarnold, P. R. (1984). Performance standards and the Type A behavior pattern. *Cognitive Therapy and Research, 8,* 59–66.

Gustafson, K. E., & McNamara, J. R. (1987). Confidentiality with minor clients: Issues and guidelines for therapists. *Professional Psychology: Research and Practice, 18*(5), 503–508.

Guy, J. D., & Liaboe, G. P. (1986). The impact of conducting psychotherapy upon the interpersonal relationships of the psychotherapist. *Professional Psychology: Research and Practice, 17*(2), 111–114.

Guy, J. D., & Liaboe, G. P. (undated). *Personal therapy for the experienced psychotherapist: A discussion of its usefulness and utilization.* Unpublished paper.

Haaga, D. A., & Davison, G. C. (1986). Cognitive change methods. In F. H. Kanfer & A. P. Goldstein (Eds.), *Helping people change* (3rd ed.) (pp. 236–282). New York: Pergamon Press.

Hackney, H., & Cormier, L. S. (1988). *Counseling strategies and interventions* (3rd ed.). Englewood Cliffs, NJ: Prentice-Hall.

Hagen, C. M., & Pennington, K. L. (1987). Students react to experiential learning. *Michigan Journal of Counseling and Development, 18*(1), 50–51.

Hall, J. E. (1987). Gender-related ethical dilemmas and ethics education. *Professional Psychology: Research and Practice, 18*(6), 573–579.

Hare-Mustin, R. T. (1980). Family therapy may be dangerous to your health. *Professional Psychology, 11*(6), 935–938.

Hart, G. M. (1978). *Values clarification for counselors.* Springfield, IL: Charles C Thomas.

Hess, A. K. (1987). Psychotherapy supervision: Stages, Buber, and a theory of relationship. *Professional Psychology: Research and Practice, 18*(3), 251–259.

Hillenberg, J. B., & DiLorenzo, T. M. (1987). Stress management training in health psychology practice: Critical clinical issues. *Professional Psychology: Research and Practice, 18*(4), 402–404.

Ho, D. Y. F. (1985). Cultural values and professional issues in clinical psychology: Implication from the Hong Kong experience. *American Psychologist, 40*(11),1212–1218.

Holloway, E. L., & Roehlke, H. J. (1987). Internship: The applied training of a counseling psychologist. *The Counseling Psychologist, 15*(2), 205–260.

Huhn, R. P., Zimpfer, D. B., Waltman, D. E., & Williamson, S. K. (1985). A survey of programs of professional preparation for group counseling. *The Journal for Specialists in Group Work, 10*(3), 124–133.

Hutchins, D. E., & Cole, C. G. (1986). *Helping relationships and strategies.* Pacific Grove, CA: Brooks/Cole.

Ivey, A. E. (1988). *Intentional interviewing and counseling* (2nd ed.). Pacific Grove, CA: Brooks/Cole.

Jaffe, D. T. (1986). The inner strains of healing work: Therapy and self-renewal for health care professionals. In C. D. Scott & J. Hawk (Eds.), *Heal thyself: The health of health care professionals.* New York: Brunner/Mazel.

Kain, C. D. (1988). To breach or not to breach: Is that the question? A response to Gray and Harding. *Journal of Counseling and Development, 66*(5), 224–225.

Kanfer, F. H., & Gaelick, L. (1986). Self management methods. In F. H. Kanfer & A. P. Goldstein (Eds.), *Helping people change* (3rd ed.) (pp. 283–345). New York: Pergamon Press.

Kanfer, F. H., & Goldstein, A. P. (Eds.). (1986). *Helping people change* (3rd ed.). New York: Pergamon Press.

Keith-Spiegel, P., & Koocher, G. (1985). *Ethics in psychology: Standards and cases.* New York: Random House.

Kilburg, R. R. (1986). The distressed professional: The nature of the problem. In R. R. Kilburg, P. E. Nathan, & R. W. Thoreson (Eds.), *Professionals in distress: Issues, syndromes, and solutions in psychology* (pp. 13–26). Washington, DC: American Psychological Association.

Kilburg, R. R., Nathan, P. E., & Thoreson, R. W. (Eds.). (1986). *Professionals in distress:*

Issues, syndromes, and solutions in psychology. Washington, DC: American Psychological Association.

Kottler, J. A. (1986). *On being a therapist.* San Francisco: Jossey-Bass.

Lakein, A. (1974). *How to get control of your time and your life.* New York: New American Library (Signet).

Laliotis, D. A., & Grayson, J. H. (1985). Psychologist heal thyself: What is available for the impaired psychologist. *American Psychologist, 40*(1), 84-96.

Levine, C. (1987). *Taking sides: Clashing views on controversial bioethical issues* (2nd ed.). Guilford, CT: Dushkin Publishing Group.

Levinson, D. J. (1978). *The seasons of a man's life.* New York: Knopf.

Loewenberg, F., & Dolgoff, R. (1985). *Ethical decisions for social work practice* (2nd ed.). Itasca, IL: F. E. Peacock.

Lorion, R. P., & Parron, D. L. (1985). Countering the countertransference: A strategy for treating the untreatable. In P. Pedersen (Ed.), *Handbook of cross-cultural counseling and therapy* (pp. 79-86). Westport, CT: Greenwood Press.

Lovallo, W. R., & Pishkin, V. (1980). A psychophysiological comparison of Type A and B men exposed to failure and uncontrollable noise. *Psychophysiology, 17*, 29-36.

Lum, D. (1986). *Social work practice and people of color: A process-stage approach.* Pacific Grove, CA: Brooks/Cole.

Mabe, A. R., & Rollin, S. A. (1986). The role of a code of ethical standards in counseling. *Journal of Counseling and Development, 64*(5), 294-297.

Margolin, G. (1982). Ethical and legal considerations in marital and family therapy. *American Psychologist, 37*(3), 788-801.

Maslach, C. (1982a). *Burnout: The cost of caring.* Englewood Cliffs, NJ: Prentice-Hall (Spectrum).

Maslach, C. (1982b). Understanding burnout: Definitional issues in analyzing a complex phenomenon. In W. S. Paine (Ed.), *Job stress and burnout: Research, theory, and intervention perspectives* (pp. 29-40). Beverly Hills, CA: Russell Sage Foundation.

Maslach, C. (1986). Stress, burnout, and alcoholism. In R. R. Kilburg, P. E. Nathan, & R. W. Thoreson (Eds.), *Professionals in distress: Issues, syndromes, and solutions in psychology* (pp. 53-76). Washington, DC: American Psychological Association.

Matheny, K. B., Aycock, D. W., Pugh, J. L., Curlette, W. L., & Cannella, K. A. S. (1986). Stress coping: A qualitative and quantitative synthesis with implications for treatment. *The Counseling Psychologist, 14*(4), 499-549.

Meichenbaum, D. (1977). *Cognitive behavior modification: An integrative approach.* New York: Plenum.

Meichenbaum, D. (1985). *Stress inoculation training.* New York: Pergamon Press.

Meichenbaum, D. (1986). Cognitive behavior modification. In F. H. Kanfer & A. P. Goldstein (Eds.), *Helping people change* (3rd ed.) (pp. 346-380). New York: Pergamon Press.

Miller, D. J., & Thelen, M. H . (1986). Knowledge and beliefs about confidentiality in psychotherapy. *Professional Psychology: Research and Practice, 17*(1), 15-19.

Mokuau, N. (1987). Social workers' perceptions of counseling effectiveness for Asian-American clients. *Social Work, 32*(4), 331-335.

Moses, A. E., & Hawkins, R. O. (1982). *Counseling lesbian women and gay men: A life issues approach.* St. Louis: C. B. Mosby.

Moursund, J. (1985). *The process of counseling and therapy.* Englewood Cliffs, NJ: Prentice-Hall.

Munson, C. E. (1987). Sex roles and power relationships in supervision. *Professional Psychology: Research and Practice, 18*(3), 236-243.

National Association of Social Workers. (1979). *Code of ethics.* Silver Spring, MD: Author.

National Board for Certified Counselors. (1987). *Code of ethics.* Alexandria, VA: Author.

National Federation of Societies for Clinical Social Work. (1985). *Code of ethics.* Silver Spring, MD: Author.

Nishio, K. & Bilmes, M. (1987). Psychotherapy with Southeast Asian American Clients. *Professional Psychology: Research and Practice, 18*(4), 342–346.

Nye, R. D. (1986). *Three psychologies: Perspectives from Freud, Skinner, and Rogers* (3rd ed.). Pacific Grove, CA: Brooks/Cole.

Olson, S. K., Downing, N. E., Heppner, P. P., & Pinkney, J. (1986). Is there life after graduate school? Coping with the transition to postdoctoral employment. *Professional Psychology: Research and Practice, 17*(5), 415–419.

Patterson, C. H. (1985). *The therapeutic relationship: Foundations for an eclectic psychotherapy.* Pacific Grove, CA: Brooks/Cole.

Patterson, C. H. (in press). Values in counseling and psychotherapy. *Counseling and Values.*

Peck, M. S. (1978). *The road less traveled: A new psychology of love, traditional values and spiritual growth.* New York: Simon & Schuster (Touchstone).

Pedersen, P. (Ed.). (1985). *Handbook of cross-cultural counseling and therapy.* Westport, CT: Greenwood Press.

Pedersen, P. B. (1986). *Are the APA ethical principles culturally encapsulated?* Unpublished manuscript, Syracuse University, Syracuse, NY.

Pfifferling, J. H. (1986). Cultural antecedents promoting professional impairment. In C. D. Scott & J. Hawk (Eds.), *Heal thyself: The health of health care professionals.* New York: Brunner/Mazel.

Pines, A., & Aronson, E., with Kafry, D. (1981). *Burnout: From tedium to personal growth.* New York: Free Press.

Pines, A. M. (1986). Who is to blame for helpers' burnout? Environmental impact. In C. D. Scott & J. Hawk (Eds.), *Heal thyself: The health of health care professionals.* New York: Brunner/Mazel.

Ponzo, Z. (1985). The counselor and physical attractiveness. *Journal of Counseling and Development, 63*(8), 482–485.

Pope, K. S. (1987). Preventing therapist-patient sexual intimacy: Therapy for a therapist at risk. *Professional Psychology: Research and Practice, 18*(6), 624–628.

Pope, K. S., & Bouhoutsos, J. C. (1986). *Sexual intimacy between therapists and patients.* New York: Praeger.

Pope, K. S., Keith-Spiegel, P., & Tabachnick, B. G. (1986). Sexual attraction to clients: The human therapist and the (sometimes) inhuman training system. *American Psychologist, 41*(2), 147–158.

Pope, K. S., Levenson, H., & Schover, L. R. (1979). Sexual intimacy in psychology training: Results and implications of a national survey. *American Psychologist, 34*(8), 682–689.

Pope, K. S., Schover, L. R., & Levenson, H. (1980). Sexual behavior between clinical supervisors and trainees: Implications for professional standards. *Professional Psychology, 10*, 157–162.

Pope, K. S., Tabachnick, B. G., & Keith-Spiegel, P. (1987). Ethics of practice: The beliefs and behaviors of psychologists as therapists. *American Psychologist, 42*(11), 993–1006.

Posey, E. C. (1988). Confidentiality in an AIDS support group. *Journal of Counseling and Development, 66*(5), 226–227.

Price, A., Omizo, M., & Hammett, V. (1986). Counseling clients with AIDS. *Journal of Counseling and Development, 65*(2), 96–97.

Quackenbos, S., Privette, G., & Klentz, B. (1986). Psychotherapy and religion: Rapprochement or antithesis? *Journal of Counseling and Development, 65*(2), 82–85.

Remley, T. P., Benshoff, J. M., & Mowbray, C. A. (1987, September). Postgraduate peer supervision: A proposed model for peer supervision. *Counselor Education and Supervision,* pp. 53–59.

Rice, P.L. (1987). *Stress and health: Principles and practice for coping and wellness.* Pacific Grove, CA: Brooks/Cole.

Rogers, C. (1961). *On becoming a person.* Boston: Houghton Mifflin.

Rogers, C. (1980). *A way of being.* Palo Alto, CA: Houghton Mifflin.

Rogers, C. (1983). *Freedom to learn for the 80's.* Columbus, OH: Charles E. Merrill.

Rosenman, R. H., et al. (1964). A predictive study of coronary heart disease. The Western Collaborative Group Study. *Journal of the American Medical Association, 189,* 15–22.

Rubanowitz, D. E. (1987). Public attitudes toward psychotherapist-client confidentiality. *Professional Psychology: Research and Practice, 18*(6), 613–618.

Saeki, C., & Borow, H. (1985). Counseling and psychotherapy: East and West. In P. Pedersen (Ed.), *Handbook of cross-cultural counseling and therapy* (pp. 223–229). Westport, CT: Greenwood Press.

Saper, B. (1987). Humor in psychotherapy: Is it good or bad for the client? *Professional Psychology: Research and Practice, 18*(4), 360–367.

Scarato, A. M., & Sigall, B. A. (1979). Multiple role women. *The Counseling Psychologist, 8*(1), 26–27.

Schultz, D. (1986). *Theories of personality* (3rd ed.). Pacific Grove, CA: Brooks/Cole.

Scott, C. D., & Hawk, J. (Eds.). (1986). *Heal thyself: The health of health care professionals.* New York: Brunner/Mazel.

Sell, J. M., Gottlieb, M. C., & Schoenfeld, L. (1986). Ethical considerations of social/romantic relationships with present and former clients. *Professional Psychology: Research and Practice, 17*(6), 504–508.

Selye, H. (1974). *Stress without distress.* New York: Lippincott.

Stoltenberg, C. D., & Delworth, U. (1987). *Supervising counselors and therapists: A developmental approach.* San Francisco: Jossey-Bass.

Sue, D. W. (1981a). *Counseling the culturally different: Theory and practice.* New York: Wiley.

Sue, D. W. (1981b). *Position paper on cross-cultural counseling competencies.* Education and Training Committee report delivered to Division 17, APA Executive Committee.

Sue, D. W., Bernier, J. E., Durran, A., Feinberg, L., Pedersen, P., Smith, E. J., & Nuttall, E. V. (1982). Position paper: Cross-cultural counseling competencies. *The Counseling Psychologist, 10*(2), 45–52.

Sue, D. W., & Sue, D. (1985). Asian-American and Pacific islanders. In P. Pedersen (Ed.), *Handbook of cross-cultural counseling and therapy* (pp. 141–146). Westport, CT: Greenwood Press.

Szasz, T. (1986). The case against suicide prevention. *American Psychologist, 41*(7), 806–812.

Thiers, N. (1987). AIDS: Counselors called to the front lines. *Guidepost: American Association for Counseling and Development, 30*(4).

Van Doornen, L. J. P. (1980). The coronary risk personality: Psychological and psychophysiological aspects. *Psychotherapy and Psychosomatics, 34,* 204–215.

Van Hoose, W. H., & Kottler, J. A. (1985). *Ethical and legal issues in counseling and psychotherapy* (2nd ed.). San Francisco: Jossey-Bass.

Watkins, C. E. (1983). Transference phenomena in the counseling situation. *Personnel and Guidance Journal, 62*(4), 206–210.

Watkins, C. E. (1985). Countertransference: Its impact on the counseling situation. *Journal of Counseling and Development, 63*(6), 356–359.

Watson, D. L., & Tharp, R. G. (1985). *Self-directed behavior: Self-modification for personal adjustment* (4th ed.). Pacific Grove, CA: Brooks/Cole.

Wolfgang, A. (1985). The function and importance of nonverbal behavior in intercultural counseling. In P. Pedersen (Ed.), *Handbook of cross-cultural counseling and therapy.* Westport, CT: Greenwood Press.

Woodman, N. J., & Lenna, H. R. (1980). *Counseling with gay men and women.* San Francisco: Jossey-Bass.

Woodside, M. R. (1987). Peer supervision: Improving the field experience. *Human Service Education, 8*(1), 14–20.

Woody, R. (1984). Professional responsibilities and liabilities. In R. Woody (Ed.), *The law and the practice of human services*. San Francisco: Jossey-Bass.

Woody, R. H., & Associates. (1984). *The law and the practice of human services*. San Francisco: Jossey-Bass.

Wright, R. H. (1981). What to do until the malpractice lawyer comes: A survivor's manual. *American Psychologist, 36*(12), 1535–1541.

Ziegler, J. L., & Kanas, N. (1986). Coping with stress during internship. In C. D. Scott & J. Hawk (Eds.), *Heal thyself: The health of health care professionals*. New York: Brunner/Mazel.

Code of Ethics
National Board for Certified Counselors

(Approved on July 1, 1982; amended on February 21, 1987.)

PREAMBLE

The National Board for Certified Counselors (NBCC) is an educational, scientific, and professional organization dedicated to the enhancement of the worth, dignity, potential and uniqueness of each individual and, thus, to the service of society. This code of ethics enables the NBCC to clarify the nature of ethical responsibilities for present and future certified counselors.

Section A: General

1. Certified counselors influence the development of the profession by continuous efforts to improve professional practices, services, and research. Professional growth is continuous throughout the certified counselor's career and is exemplified by the development of a philosophy that explains why and how a certified counselor functions in the helping relationship. Certified counselors must gather data on their effectiveness and be guided by their findings.

2. Certified counselors have a responsibility to the clients they are serving and to the institutions within which the services are being performed. Certified counselors also strive to assist the respective agency, organization, or institution in providing the highest caliber of professional services. The acceptance of employment in an institution implies that the certified counselor is in agreement with the general policies and principles of the institution. Therefore, the professional activities of the certified counselor are in accord with the objectives of the institution. If, despite concerted efforts, the certified counselor cannot reach agreement with the employer as to acceptable standards of conduct that allow for changes in institutional policy that are conducive to the positive growth and development of clients, then terminating the affiliation should be seriously considered.

3. Ethical behavior among professional associates (i.e., both certified and non-certified counselors) must be expected at all times. When accessible information raises doubts as to the ethical behavior of professional

colleagues, whether certified counselors or not, the certified counselor must take action to attempt to rectify this condition. Such action uses the respective institution's channels first and then uses procedures established by the NBCC.

4 . Certified counselors neither claim nor imply professional qualifications which exceed those possessed, and are responsible for correcting any misrepresentations of these qualifications by others.

5 . Certified counselors must refuse a private fee or other remuneration for consultation or counseling with persons who are entitled to these services through the certified counselor's employing institution or agency. The policies of some agencies may make explicit provisions for staff members to engage in private practice with agency clients. However, should agency clients desire private counseling or consulting services, they must be apprised of other options available to them. Certified counselors must not divert to their private practices legitimate clients in their primary agencies or of the institutes with which they are affiliated.

6 . In establishing fees for professional counseling services, certified counselors must consider the financial status of clients and the respective locality. In the event that the established fee status is inappropriate for a client, assistance must be provided in finding comparable services of acceptable cost.

7 . Certified counselors seek only those positions in the delivery of professional services for which they are professionally qualified.

8 . Certified counselors recognize their limitations and provide services or only use techniques for which they are qualified by training and/or experience. Certified counselors recognize the need, and seek continuing education, to assure competent services.

9 . Certified counselors are aware of the intimacy in the counseling relationship, maintain respect for the client, and avoid engaging in activities that seek to meet their personal needs at the expense of the client.

10. Certified counselors do not condone or engage in sexual harassment, which is defined as deliberate or repeated comments, gestures, or physical contacts of a sexual nature.

11. Certified counselors avoid bringing their personal or professional issues into the counseling relationship. Through an awareness of the impact of stereotyping and discrimination (i.e., biases based on age, disability, ethnicity, gender, race, religion, or sexual preference), certified counselors guard the individual rights and personal dignity of the client in the counseling relationship.

12. Certified counselors are accountable at all times for their behavior. They must be aware that all actions and behaviors of the counselor reflect on professional integrity and, when inappropriate, can damage the public trust in the counseling profession. To protect public confidence in the counseling profession, certified counselors avoid public behavior that is clearly in violation of accepted moral and legal standards.

13. Certified counselors have a social responsibility because their recommendations and professional actions may alter the lives of others. Certified counselors remain fully cognizant of their impact and are alert to personal, social, organizational, financial, or political situations or pressures which might lead to misuse of their influence.

14. Products or services provided by certified counselors by means of classroom instruction, public lectures, demonstrations, written articles, radio or television programs or other types of media must meet the criteria cited in Sections A through F of these Standards.

Section B: Counseling Relationship

1. The primary obligation of certified counselors is to respect the integrity and promote the welfare of a client, regardless of whether the client is assisted individually or in a group relationship. In a group setting, the certified counselor is also responsible for taking reasonable precautions to protect individuals from physical and/or psychological trauma resulting from interaction within the group.

2. The counseling relationship and information resulting from it remains confidential, consistent with the legal obligations of the certified counselor. In a group counseling setting, the certified counselor sets a norm of confidentiality regarding all group participants' disclosures.

3. Certified counselors know and take into account the traditions and practices of other professional groups with whom they work and cooperate fully with such groups. If a person is receiving similar services from another professional, certified counselors do not offer their own services directly to such a person. If a certified counselor is contacted by a person who is already receiving similar services from another professional, the certified counselor carefully considers that professional relationship and proceeds with caution and sensitivity to the therapeutic issues as well as the client's welfare. Certified counselors discuss these issues with clients so as to minimize the risk of confusion and conflict.

4. When a client's condition indicates that there is a clear and imminent danger to the client or others, the certified counselor must take reasonable personal action or inform responsible authorities. Consultation with other professionals must be used where possible. The assumption of responsibility for the client's behavior must be taken only after careful deliberation, and the client must be involved in the resumption of responsibility as quickly as possible.

5. Records of the counseling relationship, including interview notes, test data, correspondence, audio or visual tape recordings, electronic data storage, and other documents are to be considered professional information for use in counseling. They should not be considered a part of the records of the institution or agency in which the counselor is employed unless specified by state statute or regulation. Revelation to others of counseling material must occur only upon the expressed consent of the client; certified counselors must make provisions for maintaining confidentiality in the storage and disposal of records. Certified counselors providing information to the public or to subordinates, peers, or supervisors have a responsibility to ensure that the content is general; unidentified client information should be accurate and unbiased, and should consist of objective, factual data.

6. Certified counselors must ensure that data maintained in electronic storage are secure. The data must be limited to information that is appropriate and necessary for the services being provided and accessible only to appropriate staff members involved in the provision of services by using the best computer security methods available. Certified counselors must also ensure that the electronically stored data are destroyed when the information is no longer of value in providing services.

7. Data derived from a counseling relationship for use in counselor training or research shall be confined to content that can be disguised to ensure full protection of the identity of the subject/client and shall be obtained with informed consent.

8. Certified counselors must inform clients before or at the time the counseling relationship commences, of the purposes, goals, techniques,

rules and procedures, and limitations that may affect the relationship.

9. All methods of treatment by certified counselors must be clearly indicated to prospective recipients and safety precautions must be taken in their use.

10. Certified counselors who have an administrative, supervisory and/or evaluative relationship with individuals seeking counseling services must not serve as the counselor and should refer the individuals to other professionals. Exceptions are made only in instances where an individual's situation warrants counseling intervention and another alternative is unavailable. Dual relationships with clients that might impair the certified counselor's objectivity and professional judgment must be avoided and/or the counseling relationship terminated through referral to another competent professional.

11. When certified counselors determine an inability to be of professional assistance to a potential or existing client, they must, respectively, not initiate the counseling relationship or immediately terminate the relationship. In either event, the certified counselor must suggest appropriate alternatives. Certified counselors must be knowledgeable about referral resources so that a satisfactory referral can be initiated. In the event that the client declines a suggested referral, the certified counselor is not obligated to continue the relationship.

12. Certified counselors may choose to consult with any other professionally competent person about a client and must notify clients of this right. Certified counselors must avoid placing a consultant in a conflict-of-interest situation that would preclude the consultant's being a proper party to the certified counselor's efforts to help the client.

13. Certified counselors who counsel clients from cultures different from

their own must gain knowledge, personal awareness, and sensitivity pertinent to the client populations served and must incorporate culturally relevant techniques into their practice.

14. When certified counselors are engaged in intensive, short-term therapy, they must ensure that professional counseling assistance is available to the client(s) during and following the counseling.

15. Certified counselors must screen prospective group counseling participants, especially when the emphasis is on self-understanding and growth through self-disclosure. Certified counselors must maintain an awareness of each group participant's welfare throughout the group process.

16. When electronic data and systems are used as a component of counseling services, certified counselors must ensure that the computer application, and any information it contains, is appropriate for the respective needs of clients and is non-discriminatory. Certified counselors must ensure that they themselves have acquired a facilitation level of knowledge with any system they use including hands-on application, search experience, and understanding of the uses of all aspects of the computer-based system. In selecting and/or maintaining computer-based systems that contain career information, counselors must ensure that the system provides current, accurate, and locally relevant information. Certified counselors must also ensure that clients are intellectually, emotionally, and physically compatible to using the computer application and understand its purpose and operation. Client use of a computer application must be evaluated to correct possible problems and assess subsequent needs.

17. Certified counselors who develop self-help/stand-alone computer software for use by the general

public, must first ensure that it is initially designed to function in a stand-alone manner, as opposed to modifying software that was originally designed to require support from a counselor. Secondly, the software must include program statements that provide the user with intended outcomes, suggestions for using the software, descriptions of inappropriately used applications, and descriptions of when and how counseling services might be beneficial. Finally, the manual must include the qualifications of the developer, the development process, validation data, and operating procedures.

Section C: Measurement and Evaluation

1. Certified counselors must provide specific orientation or information to an examinee prior to and following the administration of assessment instruments or techniques so that the results may be placed in proper perspective with other relevant factors. The purpose of testing and the explicit use of the results must be made known to an examinee prior to testing.
2. In selecting assessment instruments or techniques for use in a given situation or with a particular client, certified counselors must evaluate carefully the instrument's specific theoretical bases and characteristics, validity, reliability and appropriateness. Certified counselors are professionally responsible for using invalidated information carefully.
3. When making statements to the public about assessment instruments or techniques, certified counselors must provide accurate information and avoid false claims or misconceptions concerning the meaning of psychometric terms. Special efforts are often required to avoid unwarranted connotations of terms such as IQ and grade-equivalent scores.

4. Because many types of assessment techniques exist, certified counselors must recognize the limits of their competence and perform only those functions for which they have received appropriate training.
5. Certified counselors must note when tests are not administered under standard conditions or when unusual behavior or irregularities occur during a testing session, and the results must be designated as invalid or of questionable validity. Unsupervised or inadequately supervised assessments, such as mail-in tests, are considered unethical. However, the use of standardized instruments that are designed to be self-administered and self-scored, such as interest inventories, is appropriate.
6. Because prior coaching or dissemination of test materials can invalidate test results, certified counselors are professionally obligated to maintain test security. In addition, conditions that produce most favorable test results must be made known to an examinee (e.g., penalty for guessing).
7. Certified counselors must consider psychometric limitations when selecting and using an instrument, and must be cognizant of the limitations when interpreting the results. When tests are used to classify clients, certified counselors must ensure that periodic review and/or retesting are made to prevent client stereotyping.
8. An examinee's welfare, explicit prior understanding, and agreement are the factors used when determining who receives the test results. Certified counselors must see that appropriate interpretation accompanies any release of individual or group test data (e.g., limitations of instrument and norms).
9. Certified counselors must ensure that computer-generated test administration and scoring programs function properly thereby providing clients with accurate test results.

10. Certified counselors, who are responsible for making decisions based on assessment results, must have appropriate training and skills based on educational and psychological measurement, validation criteria, test research, and guidelines for test development and use.
11. Certified counselors must be cautious when interpreting the results of instruments that possess insufficient technical data, and must explicitly state to examinees the specific purposes for the use of such instruments.
12. Certified counselors must proceed with caution when attempting to evaluate and interpret performances of minority group members or other persons who are not represented in the norm group on which the instrument was standardized.
13. Certified counselors who develop computer-based test interpretations to support the assessment process, must ensure that the validity of the interpretations is established prior to the commercial distribution of the computer application.
14. Certified counselors recognize that test results may become obsolete, and avoid the misuse of obsolete data.
15. Certified counselors must avoid the appropriation, reproduction, or modification of published tests or parts thereof without acknowledgment and permission from the publisher.

Section D: Research and Publication

1. Certified counselors will adhere to relevant guidelines on research with human subjects. These include the:
   a. Ethical Principles in the Conduct of Research with Human Participants, Washington, D.C.: American Psychological Association Inc., 1982.
   b. Code of Federal Regulations, Title 45, Subtitle A, Part 46, as currently issued.
   c. Ethical Principles of Psychologists, American Psychological Association, Principle #9: Research with Human Participants.
   d. Buckley Amendment.
   e. current federal regulations and various state rights privacy acts.

2. In planning research activities involving human subjects, certified counselors must be aware of and responsive to all pertinent ethical principles and ensure that the research problem, design, and execution are in full compliance with the principles.
3. The ultimate responsibility for ethical research lies with the principal researcher, though others involved in the research activities are ethically obligated and responsible for their own actions.
4. Certified counselors who conduct research with human subjects are responsible for the subjects' welfare throughout the experiment and must take all reasonable precautions to avoid causing injurious psychological, physical, or social effects on their subjects.
5. Certified counselors who conduct research must abide by the following basic elements of informed consent:

   a. a fair explanation of the procedures to be followed, including an identification of those which are experimental
   b. a description of the attendant discomforts and risks
   c. a description of the benefits to be expected
   d. a disclosure of appropriate alternative procedures that would be advantageous for subjects
   e. an offer to answer any inquiries concerning the procedures
   f. an instruction that subjects are free to withdraw their consent and to discontinue participation in the project or activity at any time

6. When reporting research results, explicit mention must be made of all the variables and conditions known to the investigator that may have affected the outcome of the study or the interpretation of the data.

7. Certified counselors who conduct and report research investigations must do so in a manner that minimizes the possibility that the results will be misleading.

8. Certified counselors are obligated to make available sufficient original research data to qualified others who may wish to replicate the study.

9. Certified counselors who supply data, aid in the research of another person, report research results, or make original data available, must take due care to disguise the identity of respective subjects in the absence of specific authorization from the subjects to do otherwise.

10. When conducting and reporting research, certified counselors must be familiar with, and give recognition to, previous work on the topic, must observe all copyright laws, and must follow the principles of giving full credit to those to whom credit is due.

11. Certified counselors must give due credit through joint authorship, acknowledgment, footnote statements, or other appropriate means to those who have contributed significantly to the research and/or publication, in accordance with such contributions.

12. Certified counselors should communicate to other counselors the results of any research judged to be of professional value. Results that reflect unfavorably on institutions, programs, services, or vested interests must not be withheld.

13. Certified counselors who agree to cooperate with another individual in research and/or publication must incur an obligation to cooperate as promised in terms of punctuality of performance and with full regard to the completeness and accuracy of the information required.

14. Certified counselors must not submit the same manuscript, or one essentially similar in content, for simultaneous publication consideration by two or more journals. In addition, manuscripts that are published in whole or substantial part in another journal or published work should not be submitted for publication without acknowledgment and permission from the previous publication.

Section E: Consulting

Consultation refers to a voluntary relationship between a professional helper and help-needing individual, group, or social unit in which the consultant is providing help to the client(s) in defining and solving a work-related problem or potential work-related problem with a client or client system.

1. Certified counselors, acting as consultants, must have a high degree of self awareness of their own values, knowledge, skills, limitations, and needs in entering a helping relationship that involves human and/or organizational change. The focus of the consulting relationship must be on the issues to be resolved and not on the person(s) presenting the problem.

2. In the consulting relationship, the certified counselor and client must understand and agree upon the problem definition, subsequent goals, and predicted consequences of interventions selected.

3. Certified counselors must be reasonably certain that they, or the organization represented, have the necessary competencies and resources for giving the kind of help that is needed or that may develop later, and that appropriate referral resources are available to the consultant.

4. Certified counselors in a consulting relationship must encourage and cultivate client adaptability and growth toward self-direction. Certified counselors must maintain this

role consistently and not become a decision maker for clients or create a future dependency on the consultant.

5. Certified counselors conscientiously adhere to the NBCC Code of Ethics when announcing consultant availability for services.

Section F: Private Practice

1. Certified counselors should assist the profession by facilitating the availability of counseling services in private as well as public settings.
2. In advertising services as a private practitioner, certified counselors must advertise in a manner that accurately informs the public of the professional services, expertise, and techniques of counseling available.
3. Certified counselors who assume an executive leadership role in a private practice organization do not permit their names to be used in professional notices during periods of time when they are not actively engaged in the private practice of counseling.
4. Certified counselors may list their highest relevant degree, type and level of certification and/or license, address, telephone number, office hours, type and/or description of services, and other relevant information. Listed information must not contain false, inaccurate, misleading, partial, out-of-context, or otherwise deceptive material or statements.
5. Certified counselors who are involved in a partnership/corporation with other certified counselors and/or other professionals, must clearly specify the separate specialties of each member of the partnership or corporation, in compliance with the regulations of the locality.
6. Certified counselors have an obligation to withdraw from a private practice counseling relationship if it violates the Code of Ethics, the

mental or physical condition of the certified counselor renders it difficult to carry out an effective professional relationship, or the counseling relationship is no longer productive for the client.

Appendix: Certification Examination

1. Applicants for the NBCC Counselor Certification Examination must have fulfilled all current eligibility requirements, and are responsible for the accuracy and validity of all information and/or materials provided by themselves or by others for fulfillment of eligibility criteria.
2. Participation in the NBCC Counselor Certification Examination by any person under the auspices of eligibility ascribed to another person (i.e., applicant) is prohibited. Applicants are responsible for ensuring that no other person participates in the NBCC Counselor Certification Examination through use of the eligibility specifically assigned to the applicant.
3. Participants in the NBCC Counselor Certification Examination must refrain from the use of behaviors and/or materials which would afford them unfair advantage for performance on the Examination. These behaviors and/or materials include, but are not limited to, any form of copying of responses from another participant's answer sheet, use of unauthorized notes or other informational materials, or communication with other participants during the Examination.
4. Participants in the NBCC Counselor Certification Examination must, at the end of the regularly scheduled Examination period, return all Examination materials to the test administrator.
5. After completing the NBCC Counselor Certification Examination, participants must not disclose, in either verbal or written form, items which appeared on the Examination form.

ACKNOWLEDGMENT

Reference documents, statements, and sources for the development of the NBCC Code of Ethics were as follows:

The Ethical Standards of the American Association for Counseling and Development, Responsible Uses for Standardized Testing (AMECD), codes of ethics of the American Psychological Association, National Academy of Certified Clincal Mental Health Counselors, and the National Career Development Association, Handbook of Standards for Computer-Based Career Information Systems (ASCI) and Guidelines for the Use of Computer-Based Information and Guidance Systems (ASCI).

Code of Ethics
National Federation of Societies
for Clinical Social Work

PREAMBLE

Ethical principles affecting the practice of clinical social work are rooted in the basic values of society and the social work profession. The principal objective of the profession of clinical social work is to enhance the dignity and well-being of each individual who seeks its services. It does so through use of clinical social work theory and treatment methods, including psychotherapy.

The following represents codified ethical principles which serve as a standard for clinical social workers as psychotherapists and in their various other professional roles, relationships, and responsibilities. The clinical social worker is expected to take into consideration all the principles in this code that have a bearing upon any situation in which ethical judgment is to be exercised, and to select a course of action consistent with the spirit as well as the letter of the code.

Members of State Societies for Clinical Social Work adhere to these principles. When clinical social workers' conduct is alleged to deviate from these standards, they agree to abide by the recom-mendations arrived at by State Society disciplinary panels.

It is recognized that the practice of clinical social work is complex and varied and does not lend itself to limitation by a set of rules which will particularize all of its functions. The primary goal of this code is not to restrict the practice of clinical social workers, but to offer general principles to guide their conduct and to inspire their will to act according to ethical principles in all of their professional functions.

I. General Responsibilities of Clinical Social Workers

Clinical social workers maintain high standards of the profession in all of their professional roles. Clinical social workers value professional competence, objectivity and integrity. They consistently examine, use, and attempt to expand the knowledge upon which practice is based, working to ensure that their services are used appropriately and accepting responsibility for the consequences of their work.

a . As psychotherapy practitioners, clinical social workers bear a heavy responsibility because their recommendations and professional actions may alter the lives of others. The social worker's primary responsibility is to the client. However, when the interest of the individual patient or client conflicts with the welfare of his family or of the community at large, the clinical social worker weighs the consequences of any action and arrives at a judgment based on all considerations.

b. As employees of institutions or agencies, clinical social workers are responsible for remaining alert to and attempting to moderate institutional pressures and/or policies that conflict with the standards of their profession. If such conflict arises, clinical social workers' primary responsibility is to uphold the ethical standards of their profession.

c. As teachers, clinical social workers are responsible for careful preparation so that their instruction maintains high standards of scholarship and objectivity.

d. Clinical social workers practice only within their sphere of competence. They accurately represent their abilities, education, training, and experience. They avail themselves of opportunities for continuing professional education to maintain and enhance their competence. When indicated, they seek consultation from colleagues or other appropriate professionals.

e. Clinical social workers do not exploit their professional relationships sexually, financially, or for any other personal advantage. They maintain this standard of conduct toward all who may be professionally associated with them, such as clients, colleagues, supervisees, employees, students, and research participants.

f. Clinical social workers refrain from undertaking any professional activity in which their personal problems or conflicts might lead to the inadequate provision of service. If involved in such a situation, they seek appropriate professional assistance to help them determine whether

they should suspend, terminate, or limit the scope of their professional involvement.

II. Responsibility to Clients

The clinical social worker's primary responsibility is to the client. Clinical social workers respect the integrity, protect the welfare, and maximize the self-determination of the clients with whom they work.

a. Clinical social workers inform clients of the extent and nature of services available to them as well as the limits, rights, opportunities, and obligations associated with service which might affect the client's decision to enter into or continue the relationship.

b. Clinical social workers enter and/or continue professional relationships based on their ability to meet the needs of the client appropriately. The clinical social worker terminates service to clients, and professional relationships with them, when such service and relationships are no longer required or no longer serve the clients' best interests. The clinical social worker who anticipates the interruption or termination of service to clients gives reasonable notification and provides for transfer, referral or continuation of service in relation to the clients' needs and preferences. Clinical social workers do not withdraw services precipitously except under extraordinary circumstances, giving careful consideration to all factors in the situation and taking care to minimize possible adverse effects.

c. Clinical social workers use care to prevent the intrusion of their own personal needs into relationships with clients. They recognize that the private and personal nature of the therapeutic relationship may unrealistically intensify clients' feelings toward them, thus increasing their obligation to maintain professional objectivity. Therefore, specifically:

1. Clinical social workers avoid entering treatment relationships in which their professional judgment will be compromised by prior association with or knowledge of a client. Examples might include treatment of one's family members, close friends, associates, employees, or others whose welfare could be jeopardized by such a dual relationship.
2. Clinical social workers do not engage in or condone sexual activities with clients.
3. Clinical social workers do not initiate, and should avoid when possible, personal relationships or dual roles with current clients, or with any former clients whose feelings toward them may still be derived from or influenced by the former professional relationship.

d. The clinical social worker takes care to ensure an appropriate setting for practice to protect both the client and the social worker from actual or imputed mental and/or physical harm. If the clinical social worker judges that there is a threat to safety, reasonable steps are taken to prevent the client from causing harm to self or others.

e. When the clinical social worker must act on behalf of a client, the action should always safeguard the interests and concerns of that client. When another person has been authorized to act on behalf of a client, the clinical social worker should deal with that person with the client's best interests in mind.

III. Relationships with Colleagues

Clinical social workers act with integrity in their relationships with colleagues and members of other professions. They know and take into account the traditions, practices, and areas of competence of other professionals and cooperate with them fully for the welfare of clients.

a. The clinical social worker treats with respect and represents accurately the views, qualifications, and findings of colleagues, and, when expressing judgment on these matters, does so fairly and through appropriate channels.

b. Clinical social workers know that a client's health and safety may depend on their receiving appropriate service from members of other professional disciplines. They are responsible for maintaining knowledge of, and appropriately utilizing, the expertise of such professionals on the client's behalf.

c. In referring clients to allied professionals, clinical social workers ensure that those to whom they refer clients are recognized members of their own disciplines and are competent to carry out the professional services required.

d. If a clinical social worker's services are sought by an individual who is already receiving similar services from another professional, consideration for the client's welfare shall be paramount. It requires the clinical social worker to proceed with great caution, carefully considering both the existing professional relationship and the therapeutic issues involved.

e. As supervisors or employers, clinical social workers accept their responsibility to provide competent professional guidance to colleagues, employees, and students. They foster working conditions that ensure fairness, privacy, and protection from physical or mental harm. They evaluate fairly and with consideration the performance of those under their supervision, and share evaluations with supervisees. They do not abuse the power inherent in their position.

f. Clinical social workers take appropriate measures to discourage, prevent, expose, and correct unethical or incompetent behavior by colleagues, but take equally appropriate steps to assist and defend colleagues unjustly charged with such conduct. They do not encourage the unsupervised practice of social work by those who fail to meet accepted standards of training and experience (i.e., a master's degree in social work from a school of social work accredited by the Council on Social Work Education, or a doctoral degree in social work, that included a sequence of clinically oriented course work and supervised clinical field placement, plus at least 2 years or its part-time equivalent of postmaster's or doctoral fulltime supervision in direct-service clinical experience in a clinical setting. Standards for Health Care Providers in Clinical Social Work, National Federation of Societies for Clinical Social Work, 1974.)

IV. Remuneration

Fees set by clinical social workers are in accord with professional standards that protect the client and the profession.

a. In establishing rates for professional services, clinical social workers take into account both the ability of the client to pay and the charges made by other professionals engaged in comparable work. Financial arrangements are explicitly established and agreed upon by both the clinical social worker and the client.
b. Clinical social workers do not give or receive any fee or other consideration to or from a third party for the referral of a client.
c. Clinical social workers employed by an agency or clinic and also engaged in private practice conform to agency regulations regarding their dual role.

V. Confidentiality

The safeguarding of the client's right to privacy is a basic responsibility of the clinical social worker. Clinical social workers have a primary obligation to maintain the confidentiality of material that has been transmitted to them in any of their professional roles, including the identity of the client.

a. Clinical social workers reveal con-

fidential information to others only with the informed consent of the client, except in those circumstances in which not to do so would violate the law or would result in clear and imminent danger to the client or to others. Unless specifically contraindicated by such situations, clients should be informed in advance of any limitations of confidentiality, and informed and written consent should be obtained from the client before confidential information is revealed. Such consent includes telling the client about the purpose for which information is obtained and how it may be used.
b. When confidential information is used for the purposes of professional education, research, consultation, etc., every effort will be made to conceal the true identity of the client. Such presentations will be limited to material necessary for the professional purpose, and this material will be shared only with other responsible individuals.
c. Special care needs to be taken regarding confidentiality when the client is a vulnerable adult or minor child. In disclosing information to parents, guardians, the court, or others, the clinical social worker acts to protect the best interest of the primary client. Clinical social workers uphold their obligation to observe applicable law, including state mandates to report actual or potential abuse.
d. In keeping client records, clinical social workers remain aware of the limits of confidentiality and of the conditions under which they may be required to reveal recorded information. Accordingly, they maintain records adequate to ensure proper diagnosis and treatment, but take precautions to minimize the exposure of the client to any harm that might result from improper disclosure. Clients are permitted to examine their records if they request access. Clinical social workers make provisions for maintaining confidentiality in the storage and disposal of

these records, whether written or on audio or visual tape.

VI. Societal and Legal Standards

Clinical social workers show sensible regard for the social codes and ethical expectations in their communities, recognizing that violations of accepted societal, ethical, and legal standards on their part may compromise the fulfillment of their professional responsibilities or reduce public trust in the profession.

a. Clinical social workers do not, in any of their capacities, practice, condone, facilitate, or collaborate with any form of discrimination on the basis of race, sex, sexual orientation, age, religion, socioeconomic status, or national origin.
b. Clinical social workers practice their profession in compliance with legal standards. They do not participate in arrangements undermining the law. However, when they believe laws affecting clients or their practice are in conflict with the principles and standards of the profession, clinical social workers make known the conflict and work toward change that will benefit the public interest.
c. Clinical social workers recognize a responsibility to participate in activities contributing toward improved social conditions within their community.

VII. Pursuit of Research and Scholarly Activities

In planning, conducting, and reporting a study, the investigator has the responsibility to make a careful evaluation of its ethical acceptability, taking into account the following additional principles for research with human subjects. To the extent that this appraisal, weighing scientific and humane values, suggests a compromise of any principle, the investigator incurs an increasingly serious obligation to seek advice and to observe stringent safeguards to protect the rights of the research participants.

a. In conducting research in institutions or organizations, clinical social workers obtain appropriate authority to carry out such research. Host organizations are given proper credit for their contributions.
b. Ethically acceptable research begins with the establishment of a clear and fair agreement between the investigator and the research participant that clarifies the responsibilities of each. The investigator has the obligation to honor all promises and commitments included in that agreement.
c. Responsibility for the establishment and maintenance of acceptable ethical practice in research always remains with the investigator. The investigator is also responsible for the ethical treatment of research participants by collaborators, assistants, students, and employees, all of whom, however, incur parallel obligations.
d. Ethical practice requires the investigator to inform the participant of all features of the research that might reasonably be expected to influence willingness to participate, and to explain all other aspects of the research about which the participant inquires. Failure to make full disclosure imposes additional force to the investigator's abiding responsibility to protect the welfare and dignity of the research participant. After the data are collected, the investigator provides the participant with information about the nature of the study in order to remove any misconceptions that may have arisen.
e. The ethical investigator protects participants from physical and mental discomfort, harm, and danger. If a risk of such consequences exists, the investigator is required to inform the participant of that fact, secure consent before proceeding, and take all possible measures to minimize distress. A research procedure must not be used if it is likely to cause serious or lasting harm to a participant.
f. The methodological requirements of the study may necessitate conceal-

ment, deception, or minimal risk. In such cases the investigator is required to justify the use of these techniques and to ensure, as soon as possible, the participant's understanding of the reasons and sufficient justification for the procedure in question.

g. Ethical practice requires the investigator to respect the individual's freedom to decline to participate in or withdraw from research, and to so inform prospective participants. The obligation to protect this freedom requires special vigilance when the investigator is in a position of power over the participant, as, for example, when the participant is a student, client, employee, or otherwise is in a dual relationship with the investigator. It is unethical to penalize a participant in any way for withdrawing from or refusing to participate in a research project.

h. Information obtained about the individual research participants during the course of an investigation is confidential unless otherwise agreed in advance. When the possibility that others may obtain access to such information exists, to protect confidentiality, the participants will be informed that it is part of the procedure to obtain informed consent.

i. Investigations of human participants using drugs are conducted only in conjunction with licensed physicians.

j. Research findings must be presented accurately and completely, with full discussion of both their usefulness and their limitations. Clinical social workers are responsible for attempting to prevent any distortion or misuse of their findings.

k. Clinical social workers take credit only for work actually done in scholarly and research endeavors and give appropriate credit to the contributions of others.

VIII. Public Statements

Public statements, announcements of services, and promotional activities of

clinical social workers serve the purpose of providing sufficient information to aid consumers in making informed judgments and choices. Clinical social workers state accurately, objectively, and without misrepresentation their professional qualifications, affiliations, and functions as well as those of the institutions or organizations with which they or their statements may be associated. They should correct the misrepresentations of others with respect to these matters.

a. In announcing availability for professional services, a clinical social worker may use his or her name; highest relevant academic degree from an accredited institution; specialized postgraduate training; date, type, and level of certification or licensure; address and telephone number; office hours; type of service provided; appropriate fee information; foreign languages spoken; and policy with regard to third-party payments.

b. Brochures or catalogs bearing a clinical social worker's name announcing any services offered shall describe the services accurately, but shall not claim or imply superior personal or professional competence.

c. Advertising communicated to the public by audio-visual means must be pre-recorded and approved for broadcasting by the clinical social worker.

d. Clinical social workers provide diagnostic and therapeutic services only in the context of a professional relationship. Such services are not given by means of public lectures or demonstrations, newspaper or magazine articles, radio or television programs, or anything of a similar nature. Professional use of the media or other public forum is appropriate when the purpose is to educate the public about professional matters regarding which the clinical social worker has special knowledge or expertise.

e. Clinical social workers do not offer to perform any services beyond the scope permitted by law or beyond the scope of their competence. They do not engage in any form of advertising which is false, fraudulent, deceptive, or misleading. They do not solicit or use recommendations or testimonials from clients, nor do they use their relationships with clients to promote commercial enterprises of any kind.

f. Clinical social workers respect the rights and reputation of any professional organization with which they are affiliated. They shall not falsely imply sponsorship or certification by such an organization. When making public statements, the clinical social worker will make clear which are personal opinions and which are authorized statements on behalf of the organization.

APPENDIX C

Ethical Standards
American Association for Counseling and Development

(Approved by AACD Governing Council, March 1988.)

PREAMBLE

The Association is an educational, scientific, and professional organization whose members are dedicated to the enhancement of the worth, dignity, potential, and uniqueness of each individual and thus to the service of society.

The Association recognizes that the role definitions and work settings of its members include a wide variety of academic disciplines, levels of academic preparation, and agency services. This diversity reflects the breadth of the Association's interest and influence. It also poses challenging complexities in efforts to set standards for the performance of members, desired requisite preparation or practice, and supporting social, legal, and ethical controls.

The specification of ethical standards enables the Association to clarify to present and future members and to those served by members the nature of ethical responsibilities held in common by its members.

The existence of such standards serves to stimulate greater concern by members for their own professional functioning and for the conduct of fellow professionals such as counselors, guidance and student personnel workers, and others in the helping professions. As the ethical code of the Association, this document establishes principles that define the ethical behavior of Association members. Additional ethical guidelines developed by the Association's Divisions for their specialty areas may further define a member's ethical behavior.

Section A: General

1. The member influences the development of the profession by continuous efforts to improve professional practices, teaching, services, and research. Professional growth is continuous throughout the member's career and is exemplified by the development of a philosophy that explains why and how a member functions in the helping relationship. Members must gather data on their effectiveness and be guided by the findings. Members recognize the need for continuing education to ensure competent service.

2. The member has a responsibility both to the individual who is

served and to the institution within which the service is performed to maintain high standards of professional conduct. The member strives to maintain the highest levels of professional services offered to the individuals to be served. The member also strives to assist the agency, organization, or institution in providing the highest caliber of professional services. The acceptance of employment in an institution implies that the member is in agreement with the general policies and principles of the institution. Therefore the professional activities of the member are also in accord with the objectives of the institution. If, despite concerted efforts, the member cannot reach agreement with the employer as to acceptable standards of conduct that allow for changes in institutional policy conducive to the positive growth and development of clients, then terminating the affiliation should be seriously considered.

3. Ethical behavior among professional associates, both members and nonmembers, must be expected at all times. When information is possessed that raises doubt as to the ethical behavior of professional colleagues, whether Association members or not, the member must take action to attempt to rectify such a condition. Such action shall use the institution's channels first and then use procedures established by the Association.

4. The member neither claims nor implies professional qualifications exceeding those possessed and is responsible for correcting any misrepresentations of these qualifications by others.

5. In establishing fees for professional counseling services, members must consider the financial status of clients and locality. In the event that the established fee structure is inappropriate for a client, assistance must be provided in finding comparable services of acceptable cost.

6. When members provide information to the public or to subordinates, peers, or supervisors, they have a responsibility to ensure that the content is general, unidentified client information that is accurate, unbiased, and consists of objective, factual data.

7. Members recognize their boundaries of competence and provide only those services and use only those techniques for which they are qualified by training or experience. Members should only accept those positions for which they are professionally qualified.

8. In the counseling relationship, the counselor is aware of the intimacy of the relationship and maintains respect for the client and avoids engaging in activities that seek to meet the counselor's personal needs at the expense of that client.

9. Members do not condone or engage in sexual harassment which is defined as deliberate or repeated comments, gestures, or physical contacts of a sexual nature.

10. The member avoids bringing personal issues into the counseling relationship, especially if the potential for harm is present. Through awareness of the negative impact of both racial and sexual stereotyping and discrimination, the counselor guards the individual rights and personal dignity of the client in the counseling relationship.

11. Products or services provided by the member by means of classroom instruction, public lectures, demonstrations, written articles, radio or television programs, or other types of media must meet the criteria cited in these Standards.

Section B: Counseling Relationship

This section refers to practices and procedures of individual and/or group counseling relationships.

The member must recognize the need for client freedom of choice. Under those circumstances where this is not possible, the member must apprise clients of restrictions that may limit their freedom of choice.

1. The member's primary obligation is to respect the integrity and promote the welfare of the client(s), whether the client(s) is (are) assisted individually or in a group relationship. In a group setting, the member is also responsible for taking reasonable precautions to protect individuals from physical and/or psychological trauma resulting from interaction within the group.
2. Members make provisions for maintaining confidentiality in the storage and disposal of records and follow an established record retention and disposition policy. The counseling relationship and information resulting therefrom must be kept confidential, consistent with the obligations of the member as a professional person. In a group counseling setting, the counselor must set a norm of confidentiality regarding all group participants' disclosures.
3. If an individual is already in a counseling relationship with another professional person, the member does not enter into a counseling relationship without first contacting and receiving the approval of that other professional. If the member discovers that the client is in another counseling relationship after the counseling relationship begins, the member must gain the consent of the other professional or terminate the relationship, unless the client elects to terminate the other relationship.
4. When the client's condition indicates that there is clear and imminent danger to the client or others, the member must take reasonable personal action or inform responsible authorities. Consultation with other professionals must be used where possible. The assumption of responsibility for the client's(s') behavior must be taken only after careful deliberation. The client

must be involved in the resumption of responsibility as quickly as possible.

5. Records of the counseling relationship, including interview notes, test data, correspondence, tape recordings, electronic data storage, and other documents are to be considered professional information for use in counseling, and they should not be considered a part of the records of the institution or agency in which the counselor is employed unless specified by state statute or regulation. Revelation to others of counseling material must occur only upon the expressed consent of the client.
6. In view of the extensive data storage and processing capacities of the computer, the member must ensure that data maintained on a computer is: (a) limited to information that is appropriate and necessary for the services being provided; (b) destroyed after it is determined that the information is no longer of any value in providing services; and (c) restricted in terms of access to appropriate staff members involved in the provision of services by using the best computer security methods available.
7. Use of data derived from a counseling relationship for purposes of counselor training or research shall be confined to content that can be disguised to ensure full protection of the identity of the subject client.
8. The member must inform the client of the purposes, goals, techniques, rules of procedure, and limitations that may affect the relationship at or before the time that the counseling relationship is entered. When working with minors or persons who are unable to give consent, the member protects these clients' best interests.
9. In view of common misconceptions related to the perceived inherent validity of computer generated data and narrative reports, the member must ensure that the client is provided with information as part of

the counseling relationship that adequately explains the limitations of computer technology.

10. The member must screen prospective group participants, especially when the emphasis is on self-understanding and growth through self-disclosure. The member must maintain an awareness of the group participants' compatibility throughout the life of the group.

11. The member may choose to consult with any other professionally competent person about a client. In choosing a consultant, the member must avoid placing the consultant in a conflict of interest situation that would preclude the consultant's being a proper party to the member's efforts to help the client.

12. If the member determines an inability to be of professional assistance to the client, the member must either avoid initiating the counseling relationship or immediately terminate that relationship. In either event, the member must suggest appropriate alternatives. (The member must be knowledgeable about referral resources so that a satisfactory referral can be initiated.) In the event the client declines the suggested referral, the member is not obligated to continue the relationship.

13. When the member has other relationships, particularly of an administrative, supervisory, and/or evaluative nature with an individual seeking counseling services, the member must not serve as the counselor but should refer the individual to another professional. Only in instances where such an alternative is unavailable and where the individual's situation warrants counseling intervention should the member enter into and/or maintain a counseling relationship. Dual relationships with clients that might impair the member's objectivity and professional judgment (e.g., as with close friends or relatives) must be avoided and/or the counseling relationship terminated

through referral to another competent professional.

14. The member will avoid any type of sexual intimacies with clients. Sexual relationships with clients are unethical.

15. All experimental methods of treatment must be clearly indicated to prospective recipients, and safety precautions are to be adhered to by the member.

16. When computer applications are used as a component of counseling services, the member must ensure that: (a) the client is intellectually, emotionally, and physically capable of using the computer application; (b) the computer application is appropriate for the needs of the client; (c) the client understands the purpose and operation of the computer application; and (d) that a follow-up of client use of a computer application is provided to both correct possible problems (misconceptions or inappropriate use) and assess subsequent needs.

17. When the member is engaged in short-term group treatment/training programs (e.g., marathons and other encounter-type or growth groups), the member ensures that there is professional assistance available during and following the group experience.

18. Should the member be engaged in a work setting that calls for any variation from the above statements, the member is obligated to consult with other professionals whenever possible to consider justifiable alternatives.

19. The member must ensure that members of various ethnic, racial, religious, disability, and socioeconomic groups have equal access to computer applications used to support counseling services and that the content of available computer applications does not discriminate against the groups described above.

20. When computer applications are developed by the member for use by the general public as self-help/

stand-alone computer software, the member must ensure that: (a) self-help computer applications are designed from the beginning to function in a stand-alone manner, as opposed to modifying software that was originally designed to require support from a counselor; (b) self-help computer applications will include within the program statements regarding intended user outcomes, suggestions for using the software, a description of the conditions under which self-help computer applications might not be appropriate, and a description of when and how counseling services might be beneficial; and (c) the manual for such applications will include the qualifications of the developer, the development process, validation data, and operating procedures.

Section C: Measurement and Evaluation

The primary purpose of educational and psychological testing is to provide descriptive measures that are objective and interpretable in either comparable or absolute terms. The member must recognize the need to interpret the statements that follow as applying to the whole range of appraisal techniques including test and nontest data. Test results constitute only one of a variety of pertinent sources of information for personnel, guidance, and counseling decisions.

1. The member must provide specific orientation or information to the examinee(s) prior to and following the test administration so that the results of testing may be placed in proper perspective with other relevant factors. In so doing, the member must recognize the effects of socioeconomic, ethnic, and cultural factors on test scores. It is the member's professional responsibility to use additional unvalidated information carefully in modifying interpretation of the test results.

2. In selecting tests for use in a given situation or with a particular client, the member must consider carefully the specific validity, reliability, and appropriateness of the test(s). General validity, reliability, and related issues may be questioned legally as well as ethically when tests are used for vocational and educational selection, placement, or counseling.

3. When making any statements to the public about tests and testing, the member must give accurate information and avoid false claims or misconceptions. Special efforts are often required to avoid unwarranted connotations of such terms as IQ and grade equivalent scores.

4. Different tests demand different levels of competence for administration, scoring, and interpretation. Members must recognize the limits of their competence and perform only those functions for which they are prepared. In particular, members using computer-based test interpretations must be trained in the construct being measured and the specific instrument being used prior to using this type of computer application.

5. In situations where a computer is used for test administration and scoring, the member is responsible for ensuring that administration and scoring programs function properly to provide clients with accurate test results.

6. Tests must be administered under the same conditions that were established in their standardization. When tests are not administered under standard conditions or when unusual behavior or irregularities occur during the testing session, those conditions must be noted and the results designated as invalid or of questionable validity. Unsupervised or inadequately supervised test-taking, such as the use of tests through the mails, is considered unethical. On the other hand, the use of instruments that are so designed or standardized to be self-

administered and self-scored, such as interest inventories, is to be encouraged.

7. The meaningfulness of test results used in personnel, guidance, and counseling functions generally depends on the examinee's unfamiliarity with the specific items on the test. Any prior coaching or dissemination of the test materials can invalidate test results. Therefore, test security is one of the professional obligations of the member. Conditions that produce most favorable test results must be made known to the examinee.

8. The purpose of testing and the explicit use of the results must be made known to the examinee prior to testing. The counselor must ensure that instrument limitations are not exceeded and that periodic review and/or retesting are made to prevent client stereotyping.

9. The examinee's welfare and explicit prior understanding must be the criteria for determining the recipients of the test results. The member must see that specific interpretation accompanies any release of individual or group test data. The interpretation of test data must be related to the examinee's particular concerns.

10. Members responsible for making decisions based on test results have an understanding of educational and psychological measurement, validation criteria, and test research.

11. The member must be cautious when interpreting the results of research instruments possessing insufficient technical data. The specific purposes for the use of such instruments must be stated explicitly to examinees.

12. The member must proceed with caution when attempting to evaluate and interpret the performance of minority group members or other persons who are not represented in the norm group on which the instrument was standardized.

13. When computer-based test interpretations are developed by the member to support the assessment process, the member must ensure that the validity of such interpretations is established prior to the commercial distribution of such a computer application.

14. The member recognizes that test results may become obsolete. The member will avoid and prevent the misuse of obsolete test results.

15. The member must guard against the appropriation, reproduction, or modification of published tests or parts thereof without acknowledgment and permission from the previous publisher.

Section D: Research and Publication

1. Guidelines on research with human subjects shall be adhered to, such as:
   a. Ethical Principles in the Conduct of Research with Human Participants, Washington, D.C.: American Psychological Association, Inc., 1982.
   b. Code of Federal Regulations, Title 45, Subtitle A, Part 46, as currently issued.
   c. *Ethical Principles of Psychologists*, American Psychological Association, Principle #9: Research with Human Participants.
   d. Family Educational Rights and Privacy Act (the "Buckley Amendment").
   e. Current federal regulations and various state rights privacy acts.

2. In planning any research activity dealing with human subjects, the member must be aware of and responsive to all pertinent ethical principles and ensure that the research problem, design, and execution are in full compliance with them.

3. Responsibility for ethical research practice lies with the principal researcher, while others involved in the research activities share ethical obligation and full responsibility for their own actions.

4. In research with human subjects, researchers are responsible for the subjects' welfare throughout the experiment, and they must take all reasonable precautions to avoid causing injurious psychological, physical, or social effects on their subjects.

5. All research subjects must be informed of the purpose of the study except when withholding information or providing misinformation to them is essential to the investigation. In such research the member must be responsible for corrective action as soon as possible following completion of the research.

6. Participation in research must be voluntary. Involuntary participation is appropriate only when it can be demonstrated that participation will have no harmful effects on subjects and is essential to the investigation.

7. When reporting research results, explicit mention must be made of all variables and conditions known to the investigator that might affect the outcome of the investigation or the interpretation of the data.

8. The member must be responsible for conducting and reporting investigations in a manner that minimizes the possibility that results will be misleading.

9. The member has an obligation to make available sufficient original research data to qualified others who may wish to replicate the study.

10. When supplying data, aiding in the research of another person, reporting research results, or in making original data available, due care must be taken to disguise the identity of the subjects in the absence of specific authorization from such subjects to do otherwise.

11. When conducting and reporting research, the member must be familiar with and give recognition to previous work on the topic, as well as to observe all copyright laws and follow the principles of giving full credit to all to whom credit is due.

12. The member must give due credit through joint authorship, acknowledgment, footnote statements, or other appropriate means to those who have contributed significantly to the research and/or publication, in accordance with such contributions.

13. The member must communicate to other members the results of any research judged to be of professional or scientific value. Results reflecting unfavorably on institutions, programs, services, or vested interests must not be withheld for such reasons.

14. If members agree to cooperate with another individual in research and/or publication, they incur an obligation to cooperate as promised in terms of punctuality of performance and with full regard to the completeness and accuracy of the information required.

15. Ethical practice requires that authors not submit the same manuscript or one essentially similar in content for simultaneous publication consideration by two or more journals. In addition, manuscripts published in whole or in substantial part in another journal or published work should not be submitted for publication without acknowledgment and permission from the previous publication.

Section E: Consulting

Consultation refers to a voluntary relationship between a professional helper and help-needing individual, group, or social unit in which the consultant is providing help to the client(s) in defining and solving a work-related problem or potential problem with a client or client system.

1. The member acting as consultant must have a high degree of self-awareness of his/her own values, knowledge, skills, limitations, and needs in entering a helping relationship that involves human and/or organizational change and that the focus of the relationship be on the

issues to be resolved and not on the person(s) presenting the problem.

2. There must be understanding and agreement between member and client for the problem definition, change of goals, and prediction of consequences of interventions selected.

3. The member must be reasonably certain that she/he or the organization represented has the necessary competencies and resources for giving the kind of help that is needed now or may be needed later and that appropriate referral resources are available to the consultant.

4. The consulting relationship must be one in which client adaptability and growth toward self-direction are encouraged and cultivated. The member must maintain this role consistently and not become a decision maker for the client or create a future dependency on the consultant.

5. When announcing consultant availability for services, the member conscientiously adheres to the Association's Ethical Standards.

6. The member must refuse a private fee or other remuneration for consultation with persons who are entitled to these services through the member's employing institution or agency. The policies of a particular agency may make explicit provisions for private practice with agency clients by members of its staff. In such instances, the clients must be apprised of other options open to them should they seek private counseling services.

Section F: Private Practice

1. The member should assist the profession by facilitating the availability of counseling services in private as well as public settings.

2. In advertising services as a private practitioner, the member must advertise the services in a manner that accurately informs the public of professional services, expertise, and techniques of counseling available. A member who assumes an executive leadership role in the organization shall not permit his/her name to be used in professional notices during periods when he/she is not actively engaged in the private practice of counseling.

3. The member may list the following: highest relevant degree, type and level of certification and/or license, address, telephone number, office hours, type and/or description of services, and other relevant information. Such information must not contain false, inaccurate, misleading, partial, out-of-context, or deceptive material or statements.

4. Members do not present their affiliation with any organization in such a way that would imply inaccurate sponsorship or certification by that organization.

5. Members may join in partnership/corporation with other members and/or other professionals provided that each member of the partnership or corporation makes clear the separate specialties by name in compliance with the regulations of the locality.

6. A member has an obligation to withdraw from a counseling relationship if it is believed that employment will result in violation of the Ethical Standards. If the mental or physical condition of the member renders it difficult to carry out an effective professional relationship or if the member is discharged by the client because the counseling relationship is no longer productive for the client, then the member is obligated to terminate the counseling relationship.

7. A member must adhere to the regulations for private practice of the locality where the services are offered.

8. It is unethical to use one's institutional affiliation to recruit clients for one's private practice.

Section G: Personnel Administration

It is recognized that most members are employed in public or quasi-public institutions. The functioning of a member within an institution must contribute to the goals of the institution and vice versa if either is to accomplish their respective goals or objectives. It is therefore essential that the member and the institution function in ways to: (a) make the institution's goals explicit and public; (b) make the member's contribution to institutional goals specific; and (c) foster mutual accountability for goal achievement.

To accomplish these objectives, it is recognized that the member and the employer must share responsibilities in the formulation and implementation of personnel policies.

1. Members must define and describe the parameters and levels of their professional competency.
2. Members must establish interpersonal relations and working agreements with supervisors and subordinates regarding counseling or clinical relationships, confidentiality, distinction between public and private material, maintenance and dissemination of recorded information, work load, and accountability. Working agreements in each instance must be specified and made known to those concerned.
3. Members must alert their employers to conditions that may be potentially disruptive or damaging.
4. Members must inform employers of conditions that may limit their effectiveness.
5. Members must submit regularly to professional review and evaluation.
6. Members must be responsible for in-service development of self and/or staff.
7. Members must inform their staff of goals and programs.
8. Members must provide personnel practices that guarantee and enhance the rights and welfare of each recipient of their service.
9. Members must select competent persons and assign responsibilities compatible with their skills and experiences.
10. The member, at the onset of a counseling relationship, will inform the

client of the member's intended use of supervisors regarding the disclosure of information concerning this case. The member will clearly inform the client of the limits of confidentiality in the relationship.
11. Members, as either employers or employees, do not engage in or condone practices that are inhumane, illegal, or unjustifiable (such as considerations based on sex, handicap, age, race) in hiring, promotion, or training.

Section H: Preparation Standards

Members who are responsible for training others must be guided by the preparation standards of the Association and relevant Division(s). The member who functions in the capacity of trainer assumes unique ethical responsibilities that frequently go beyond that of the member who does not function in a training capacity. These ethical responsibilities are outlined as follows:

1. Members must orient students to program expectations, basic skills development, and employment prospects prior to admission to the program.
2. Members in charge of learning experiences must establish programs that integrate academic study and supervised practice.
3. Members must establish a program directed toward developing students' skills, knowledge, and self-understanding, stated whenever possible in competency or performance terms.
4. Members must identify the levels of competencies of their students in compliance with relevant Division standards. These competencies must accommodate the paraprofessional as well as the professional.
5. Members, through continual student evaluation and appraisal, must be aware of the personal limitations of the learner that might impede future performance. The instructor must not only assist the learner in securing remedial assistance but also screen from the program those

individuals who are unable to provide competent services.

6. Members must provide a program that includes training in research commensurate with levels of role functioning. Paraprofessional and technician-level personnel must be trained as consumers of research. In addition, personnel must learn how to evaluate their own and their program's effectiveness. Graduate training, especially at the doctoral level, would include preparation for original research by the member.

7. Members must make students aware of the ethical responsibilities and standards of the profession.

8. Preparatory programs must encourage students to value the ideals of service to individuals and to society. In this regard, direct financial remuneration or lack thereof must not influence the quality of service rendered. Monetary considerations must not be allowed to overshadow professional and humanitarian needs.

9. Members responsible for educational programs must be skilled as teachers and practitioners.

10. Members must present thoroughly varied theoretical positions so that students may make comparisons and have the opportunity to select a position.

11. Members must develop clear policies within their educational institutions regarding field placement and the roles of the student and the instructor in such placement.

12. Members must ensure that forms of learning focusing on self-understanding or growth are voluntary, or if required as part of the educational program, are made known to prospective students prior to entering the program. When the educational program offers a growth experience with an emphasis on self-disclosure or other relatively intimate or personal involvement, the member must have no administrative, supervisory, or evaluating authority regarding the participant.

13. The member will at all times provide students with clear and equally acceptable alternatives for self-understanding or growth experiences. The member will assure students that they have a right to accept these alternatives without prejudice or penalty.

14. Members must conduct an educational program in keeping with the current relevant guidelines of the Association.

A Guide to
Professional Organizations

It is a good idea while you are a student to begin your identification with state, regional, and national professional associations. To assist you in learning about student memberships, we are listing five major national professional organizations, along with a summary of student membership benefits, if applicable. We suggest that you contact your local, state, and regional organizations and get involved in their activities, especially conventions and conferences.

American Association for Counseling and Development

The AACD has 56 state branches and four regional branch assemblies. Students qualify for a special annual membership rate of $32 and for half-rate membership in any of the 14 divisions. AACD membership provides many benefits, including a subscription to the *Journal of Counseling and Development,* eligibility for professional liability insurance programs, legal defense services, and professional development through workshops and conventions. For further information, write to:

American Association for
 Counseling and Development
5999 Stevenson Avenue
Alexandria, VA 22304
(703) 823-9800

American Association for Marriage and Family Therapy

The AAMFT has a student membership category. You must obtain an official application, including the names of at least two Clinical Members from whom the AAMFT can request official endorsements. You also need a statement signed by the coordinator or director of a graduate program in marital and family therapy in a regionally accredited educational institution, verifying your current enrollment. Student membership may be held until receipt of a qualifying graduate degree, or for a maximum of five years. Members receive the *Journal of Marital and Family Therapy,* which is published four times a year, and a subscription to six issues yearly of *Family Therapy News.* For applications and further information, write to:

American Association for
 Marital and Family Therapy
1717 K Street NW #407
Washington, DC 20006
(202) 429-1825

National Association of Social Workers

NASW membership is restricted to those who have graduated from an accredited social-work program.

For information on membership categories and benefits, write to:

National Association of Social
Workers
7981 Eastern Avenue
Silver Spring, MD 20910
(301) 565-0333

American Psychological Association

The APA has a Student Affiliates category rather than student membership. Journals and subscriptions are extra. Each year in mid-August or late August the APA holds a national convention. For further information write to:

American Psychological Association
1200 17th Street, NW
Washington, DC 20036
(202) 955-7600

In addition to the national organization there are seven regional divisions, each of which has an annual convention. For addresses or information about student membership in any of them contact the main office of the APA or see a copy of the association's monthly journal, *American Psychologist*.

- New England Psychological Association
- Southeastern Psychological Association
- Eastern Psychological Association
- Southwestern Psychological Association
- Western Psychological Association
- Midwestern Psychological Association
- Rocky Mountain Psychological Association

The APA has a number of publications that may be of interest to you. The following can be ordered from:

American Psychological Association
Order Department
P.O. Box 2710
Hyattsville, MD 20784
(703) 247-7705

Specialty Guidelines for Delivery of Services by Psychologists:

- "Delivery of Services by Clinical Psychologists"
- "Delivery of Services by Counseling Psychologists"
- "Delivery of Services by School Psychologists"
- "Delivery of Services by Industrial/-Organizational Psychologists"

Careers in Psychology (pamphlet)
Graduate Study in Psychology and Associated Fields. Information on graduate programs in the United States and Canada, including staff/student statistics, financial aid deadlines, tuition, teaching opportunities, housing, degree requirements, and program goals.
Preparing for Graduate Study: Not for Seniors Only!
Ethical Principles in the Conduct of Research with Human Participants
Standards for Educational and Psychological Testing. Revised standards for evaluating the quality of tests, testing practices, and the effects of test use. There are also chapters on licensure and certification and program evaluation. New in this edition are chapters on testing linguistic minorities and the rights of test takers.

National Organization for Human Service Education

Human-service educators will find the National Organization for Human Service Education of use. Members are drawn from diverse disciplines—mental health, child care, social services, gerontology, recreation, corrections, and developmental disabilities. Membership is open to human-service educators, students, fieldwork supervisors, and direct-care professionals. For further information, write to:

National Organization for Human
Service Education
Executive Offices
National College of Education
2840 North Sheridan Road
Evanston, IL 60201-1796
(312) 256-5150, ext. 2330

Index

To the owner of this book:

We enjoyed writing *Becoming a Helper,* and it is our hope that you have enjoyed reading it. We'd like to know about your experiences with the book; only through your comments and the comments of others can we assess the impact of this book and make it a better book for readers in the future.

School: _____

Instructor's name: _____

1. What did you like *most* about the book? _____

_____

_____

2. What did you like *least* about the book? _____

_____

_____

3. How useful were the *annotated reading lists and activities* at the end of the chapters?

_____

_____

4. What class did you use this book for? _____

5. In the space below or in a separate letter, please tell us what it was like for you to read this book and how you used it; please give your suggestions for revisions and any other comments you'd like to make about the book; include, if you'd like, your own ideas for group techniques.

Optional:

Your name: _____ Date: _____

May Brooks/Cole quote you, either in promotion for *Becoming a Helper* or in future publishing ventures?

Yes _____ No _____

Sincerely,

Marianne Schneider Corey
Gerald Corey